POLITICS
OF
NOVA
SCOTIA

DISCARD

Volume One

Nicholson-Fielding

1710-1896

J. Murray Beck

Acknowledgements

The publisher wishes to express his appreciation for the generous financial support of the **Nova Scotia Department of Culture Recreation and Fitness** and the **Canada Council.**

Richard Rogers, Publisher

FOUR EAST PUBLICATIONS
P.O. Box 29
Tantallon, Nova Scotia B0J 3J0

1st edition November 1985

edited by Goose Lane Editions
layout by Desmond M. Trim
printed by McCurdy Printing & Typesetting Limited
   This book is printed with acid free paper that should neither yellow with age, nor become brittle.

Canadian Cataloguing in Publication Data
Beck, J. Murray (James Murray), 1914-
   Politics of Nova Scotia

Bibliography: p.
Includes index.
Partial contents: v. 1. 1710-1896: Nicholson to Fielding.
ISBN 0-920427-04-9 (v. 1)

1. Nova Scotia — Politics and government.
I. Title.

FC2311.B42 1985   971.6   C85-099843-3
F1038.B42 1985

To
Linda, Heidi,
and Katrina

Preface

This book does not fall within the rubric of political science; it simply attempts to recount 186 years of Nova Scotia's political history. Not intended especially for academics, it aims to provide the generality of Nova Scotians with a knowledge of their political past. It does not try to reach high-flown conclusions, but hopefully it will throw some light upon the appearance of the province's conservative political culture and the playing of the political game within that context.

Those who wish fuller accounts of the period covered by the first two chapters may turn to John Bartlet Brebner's *New England's Outpost* and *The Neutral Yankees of Nova Scotia*, and to the accounts of specific individuals in volumes II, III and IV of the *Dictionary of Canadian Biography*. The remaining chapters are based largely on primary research, including an examination of the personal papers of the leading politicians. The research I did for the two volumes of my biography of Joseph Howe has been put to use in the appropriate chapters of this book. I am grateful to McGill-Queen's University Press, the publisher of those volumes, for permission to use some of this material.

My thanks go to Dr. Phyllis Blakeley, the former Provincial Archivist; Mr. Allan Dunlop, the assistant Provincial Archivist; and the entire staff of the Public Archives of Nova Scotia for continuing to help me cheerfully and efficiently. I have benefited particularly from Mr. Dunlop's wide knowledge of Nova Scotia politics.

Because the book covers a lengthy period, most of it not dealt with in the secondary literature, I hope the reader will excuse any imperfections.

Contents

CHAPTER 1

The Neutral Acadians of Nova Scotia

Government may have been largely absent in early Nova Scotia, but politics was not. All the actors on the stage, old England, new England, old France, Canada, the Acadians, and, to a limited extent, even the Indians played it in one way or another.

Unfortunately for the Acadians, their mode of playing it would have dire results for them. In October 1710 a British force under Colonel Francis Nicholson, assisted by provincial troops from New England under Samuel Vetch, captured Port Royal. This was the fourth time that the British had taken it. What would be new was their decision not to give it up; what was unchanged was the treatment they accorded it. For forty years the French had neglected it; for the next forty Britain would treat it no differently. James Bartlet Brebner, the historian of early Nova Scotia, has used such phrases as "phantom rule," "counterfeit suzerainty," and "mock government" to describe the situation up to 1749.[1]

Those who regarded the Acadians as obstinate, mistrustful, and even stupid, were confessing to a failure to understand them. Expecting little from France before 1710, less from Britain after that time, all they wanted was to be left alone and not to be mere pawns in contests in which they had little interest. By 1700 more than half of them had moved up the Bay of Fundy to Minas and its environs, and hence put themselves in a better position not to be used for the designs of their masters. That was the situation inherited by the British. The articles of capitulation gave them control over Port Royal (renamed Annapolis Royal) and over the inhabitants living within three miles. These people were to have the choice of remaining and taking the oath of allegiance or moving elsewhere.

Vetch, commanding the garrison, faced a steadily deteriorating situation as he contended with desertions, dwindling supplies, and decaying fortifications. Acadia, for all practical purposes, was still Acadian. When Francis Nicholson became governor of Nova Scotia in 1712, neither his commission nor instructions defined his jurisdiction precisely, nor did the Treaty of Utrecht of 1713. Britain returned Louisburg and Cape Breton to France, but otherwise retained "all Nova Scotia or Acadia, with its ancient boundaries," whatever they might be. As for the Acadians, the treaty allowed them a year to move or remain as they saw fit and promised them freedom for their religion if they remained. It was Vetch who, now in England, persuaded the Board of Trade during the winter of 1714-5 to require them to remain. In light of subsequent events it might be regarded as a case of perfidious Albion, but practically it made little difference. For, after examining other lands, the Acadians found them inferior to the ones they held; even if they had determined otherwise nothing could have prevented them from moving. As Brebner puts it, their decision was to "ignore the politics of the European world."[2]

In England Vetch used his influence to effect the removal of Nicholson — a vindictive man with a hot temper — and replace him as governor. The outcome was that Nicholson governed the province only from August to October 1714, Vetch not at all. Although the absentee governor was a common phenomenon of the day, Nova Scotia may have suffered from it more than any other colony. Thomas Caulfeild, lieutenant-governor of the fort at Annapolis Royal, struggled on without clear direction from home or legal instruments to exercise the power he needed. On the accession of King George I in 1714 he sought an unqualified oath of allegiance from the Acadians, but all he could get was a signed paper acknowledging the king as their legitimate sovereign. Forced to use his own money to procure provisions for the garrison, worn out, and debt-ridden, he died in 1717.[3]

Perhaps recognizing its almost total neglect of Nova Scotia at a time when the French were building a fort at Louisburg and claiming the fishery at Canso, the responsible British authority, the Board of Trade, finally took positive action. In 1717 it chose Colonel Richard Philipps as governor and Captain John Doucett as lieutenant-governor of the fort at Annapolis, both shrewd, energetic men. Doucett went at once to Annapolis and kept Philipps informed of the Nova Scotia situation. The latter, wanting to know exactly where he stood, waited for a formal commission and a new set of instructions, fitted, he hoped, to his responsibility. Although colonists were not to be sent out in the immediate future, the Board of Trade had decided that Nova Scotia was to remain a colony of Britain. Because the constitution of Massachusetts placed too much power in the assembly, the board repudiated it for that of Virginia in the hope of securing laws and procedures more agreeable to those of Britain. Even so, the provisions requiring an elective assembly for the making of laws were meaningless at the time and would be an unending source of trouble. As for the Acadians, they were to lose the privilege of emigration, to be required to take the oath of allegiance, and to be made gradually into English settlers. Not surprisingly, the specifics for accomplishing these objectives were not spelled out.

On reaching Nova Scotia in April 1720 Philipps set up a council consisting of himself and eleven officers and townsmen. His time limit for the Acadians to take the oath no more overawed them than those of Nicholson and Caulfeild before him. All he could do was to accept their signed submission promising to be good subjects if they were not required to bear arms, and to ask for instructions from home which, again not surprisingly, were never forthcoming. Nevertheless, he developed a good relationship with the Acadians, especially with those in the Annapolis area. Following a practice begun in 1710, he dealt with them through deputies whom they elected. The latter reported to him for their communities and he transmitted his orders through them; "they were, in effect, the local government bodies of the Acadian population."

Philipps appreciated the threat to the New England fishery at Canso by the French on Cape Breton and their Indian allies, and when the latter plundered it in August 1720 he sent troops to help the fishermen build a small fort. The next year he moved to the site, which was much the largest English settlement in the province. Then in 1722 he left for home, not to be seen again for six years, and Doucett took charge of the neglected colony. And neglected it was, for the Board of Trade had lapsed back into its seemingly uncaring, apathetic attitude. Despite Philipps' part in the framing of his instructions, he had found them of limited use since an elective assembly was out of the question in a colony where almost all the inhabitants were debarred from voting because of their religion. Accordingly his resort, the best available, had been to article 10 of his instructions, which stated that until an assembly was established he might have recourse to the instructions of the governor of Virginia. The outcome, as aptly described by Brebner, was "government by analogy and rule of thumb."[4] In effect, the governor (or his substitute) pieced together bits of authority from various sources: limited powers from his military command; the laws of Virginia as a model to determine what was appropriate in content; dispatches from England which could be treated as special legislation; and proclamations in time of emergencies which had all the force of law. These devices were not an imposing framework, but they at least permitted government to be carried on. In the circumstances Nova Scotia may not have deserved much more.[5]

As for the Acadians, they had no reason to complain; certainly they were permitted to practise their religion without interference. Under these conditions they thrived, their numbers increasing from 1773 in 1714 to about 10,000 in 1749. Yet their position was an anomalous one. Both the French of Canada and of France were content to leave them as they were, since through continued contact with their priests they hoped to use them in the reconquering of Acadia. In May 1725 the Acadians got a new master in Lawrence Armstrong, formerly an officer and member of the council at Annapolis Royal, who had used his four years in England to get himself made lieutenant-governor of the province. Historians assess Armstrong in different ways, but all would agree that he was a brooding, moody man given to violent action. In September 1726 he called upon the Acadians to take an unqualified oath of allegiance and, in a characteristic personal touch, to affirm that "no hopes of Absolution from any in Holy Orders" would cause them to change their minds.[6] When they requested exemption from bearing arms, Armstrong, in what one writer called an ingenious dodge and another a spontaneous reaction in keeping with his character, indicated that it did not matter since British law prevented Roman Catholics from serving in the army. He then agreed to note the exemption on the margin of the document which the Acadians signed, supposedly with the hope of winning them over by degrees.

If that was so, the violent side of his character defeated him. For in September 1727, after again demanding an unqualified oath from the Acadians at Annapolis and receiving in reply requests for additional priests and an exemption from bearing arms, he had four of them arrested and three imprisoned. Later, after displaying the velvet glove to the Acadians beyond Annapolis, he summarily rejected their demands for a qualified oath. Any slim hope of his achieving his objective disappeared completely when, believing that the priest at Annapolis was intervening in secular affairs, he had his house pillaged and forced him to take refuge in the woods. Once again he was seeking to "meet a problem head-on, without much subtlety and with an insistence on complete success that made disappointment inevitable."[7] Meanwhile, exasperated New England merchants with grievances of their own were petitioning against him to the Board of Trade.

Whether there is any connection between Armstrong's difficulties and the board's order for Philipps to return to Nova Scotia cannot be determined with certainty. In any case, in response to another flurry of interest in Nova Scotia by the board, Philipps arrived at Annapolis late in 1729 and, in contrast with Armstrong's heavy-handedness, sought to placate the Acadians before requesting an unqualified oath. By September 1730 he was reporting "the entire submission of all those so long obstinate People." But actually he was guilty of "a spectacular and portentous lie" in not telling his superiors that the Acadians had taken the oath only because of his verbal promise exempting them from the duty to bear arms. Although Armstrong had done much the same thing in 1726, Maxwell Sutherland sees an important difference, for "the Acadians took no particular reassurance from the former and placed their faith in the latter." Philipps' compromise would "haunt the masters of Nova Scotia for 25 years and contribute significantly to the tragic elements of the expulsion of 1755."[8]

A host of problems, including petty personal disputes and tangled treasury accounts, made Philipps' last months in Nova Scotia unhappy ones and led in 1731 to his recall to England, never to return. But he remained governor in name until 1749, a total of thirty years, of which he spent fewer than six in Nova

Scotia. Later in 1731 Armstrong arrived back at Annapolis with a new commission as lieutenant-governor. For the next eight years, while still regarding the Acadians as "a Rebellious crew" and "an ungovernable people," he treated them with unusual patience; once he even suggested that they serve as justices of the peace — a strange aberration since British law forbade it. But although his relations with the Acadians were better, he had never-ending personality clashes with his councillors and officers. Given to "Melancholy Fitts," he stabbed himself to death in December 1739, an act attributed to "Lunacy" by his inquest.[9] All in all the principal significance of the work of Philipps and Armstrong was to convince the Acadians that they were exempt from bearing arms and hence that they were officially neutral.

As senior councillor Paul Mascarene assumed the administration of the province in 1740 and kept it until the founding of Halifax nine years later. Maxwell Sutherland has suggested that "personality is largely irrelevant to an assessment of any resident authority's influence on events in Nova Scotia during this confused period." Philipps used "blandishment and poise" but failed to get an unqualified oath of allegiance from the Acadians; Armstrong's reliance on "imperiousness and the imaginary prestige of the lieutenant-governor's position" proved just as futile; so did Mascarene's efforts even though his greater assets enabled him to establish an excellent rapport with the Acadians. A Huguenot, who could speak to them in their own language, he got to know them exceedingly well. Historians of the mid-nineteenth century extolled him for his "respect for moderation, justice, learning, public service" and found its inspiration in his being educated in the classics in Geneva. But Sutherland wonders if this is the correct explanation of the attributes of a British career officer who had become a thorough New Englander and had brought up his family in Boston.[10] Perhaps the better course is to treat him as a common sense pragmatist.

He started out in difficult circumstances: a fort in disrepair and a badly maintained garrison at Annapolis, and a blockhouse in a state of collapse at Canso, confronted by a strong, well-maintained fortress at Louisburg. Besides, Walpole's peace appeared finally to be coming to an end and open hostilities with France were expected at any time. But Mascarene had two things going for him. When the authorities in England, in typical fashion, did not reply to his dispatches for two years, he appealed to Governor William Shirley of Massachusetts for aid in the event of war and received a sympathetic reply. More importantly, pragmatist that he was, he quickly realized the futility of seeking an unqualified oath and sought instead to keep the Acadians neutral by fair and proper treatment. Knowing the great influence of their priests, he started a correspondence with them, hoping in that way to win the good will of both the priests and their flocks. Apparently his designs were well conceived, for in the hostilities which ensued he generally had the neutrality which he hoped for from the Acadians.

Although the War of the Austrian Succession broke out in 1740, it was not until March 1744 that France declared war on England and in short order captured Canso. But three major attempts to take Annapolis between 1744 and 1746 all failed because of Mascarene's resoluteness, aid from New England, poor French leadership, and, most important of all in Mascarene's view, the neutrality of the Acadians. Unable to affect the result were the Micmacs and their mentor, Abbé Jean-Louis Le Loutre. The factors were already in motion which would play a vital part in determining the outcome of the war and the fate of the Acadians. One was the religious revival which in the previous decade had created an evangelical and militant Protestantism in the northern colonies that was hostile to anything which savoured of popery. Another was the determination of the New Englanders to avenge the loss of Canso and to eliminate the threat to the fisheries. As Brebner pictures it, amateur soldiers from New England went to war, both acquisitive and religious.[11] How much of it was militant business and how much militant Protestantism cannot be calculated.

In any case over the winter of 1744-5 the plans were laid which culminated in the capture of Louisburg in 1745 by a largely New England force assisted by British naval ships. Even when, for reasons of high policy, Britain handed Louisburg back to the French in 1748 by the Treaty of Aix-la-Chapelle, New England ardour was undiminished. Governor Shirley, with the assistance of Mascarene, was crystallizing his plans for the peninsula of Nova Scotia. Convinced by Mascarene of the great difficulty of transporting the Acadians, he concluded that the peninsula might best be secured by building a fort at the Isthmus of Chignecto.

Meanwhile, on the other side, Le Loutre was doing his utmost to induce the Acadians to move to new territory north and west of the peninsula. So, once again, these "luckless people"were to be enmeshed in matters which they abhorred. "Their role was to be that of the football in an international match."[12]

Partly to counter the New Englanders' indignation at the loss of Louisburg, even the Board of Trade awoke from its old apathy and committed itself to a fortress on the Atlantic to balance Louisburg and, among other things, protect New England and its trade. Under Lord Halifax, the new president of the Board of Trade, it perfected its plans with amazing rapidity and the outcome was the arrival at Chebucto Bay in June 1749 of Edward Cornwallis and 2,576 settlers from Britain, attracted by promises of free transportation and free victualling for a year. Within a month Mascarene received orders to come to newly established Halifax for the swearing in of the new council on July 14. Almost its first business was to deal with the Acadians. In an attempt to carry out the instructions to Cornwallis to settle the question the council decided to require them to take an unconditional oath of allegiance within three months. For Mascarene the events which followed were "terribly familiar"; indeed, he must have felt like something of an "anachronism." On going to Boston in 1751 on official business he did not return.[13]

By September 1749 the Acadians had made it clear to Cornwallis that they would rather leave the province than take the unqualified oath. Accordingly he had no choice but to request further instructions from the board; the sequel, as on all previous occasions, was that he did nothing to cause them to move. He did try, however, to cut off their communication with the French on the Saint John and the Isthmus of Chignecto by building small posts in the Minas Basin area and by sending Major Charles Lawrence on several expeditions to confront the French at the isthmus. These culminated, in the fall of 1750, in the building of Fort Lawrence on the south bank of the Missaguash River. Brebner estimates that during this period Le Loutre's influence caused Acadians numbering between 1,500 and 2,000 to move north of the isthmus or to the islands in the Gulf of St. Lawrence. But, partly because of apathy, most remained, clinging to "the policy which had saved them before and in which the temporizing

British policy had fatally confirmed them. It was to continue to do so."[14]

Under Peregrine Thomas Hopson, who succeeded Cornwallis, nothing much happened between August 1752 and October 1753. He dealt fairly with the Acadians and sought to redress their ills as best he could. In contrast, change was the order of the day under his successor, Charles Lawrence, who had undoubted military and administrative abilities. Although not the "sort of malevolent demon consumed by a hatred of the habitants" that some writers have pictured, he was a man of "smaller human sympathies" than his predecessors. In his first major dispatch to the Board of Trade he indicated a determination not to let the Acadian question drift on interminably: the Acadians must take the oath or suffer the consequences. Brebner concludes from the tone of his dispatches in late 1754 that he had begun to "enlarge his own opinion of himself, of his office, and of the role which he felt it incumbent on him to play."[15] By this time, too, he had become aware that war with France was almost inevitable. In Nova Scotia real peace had not come in 1748 and a state, neither of peace nor war, had existed ever since. So when Governor Shirley, now commander of the British forces in North America, approached Lawrence about capturing Fort Beauséjour, the counterpart to Fort Lawrence, and driving the French out of Chignecto, he quickly responded: he sent his deputy, Lt. Col. Robert Monckton, to Boston, where he spent the winter of 1754-5 in recruiting and organizing a New England force. The sequel was the capture of Beauséjour in June 1755.

Undoubtedly Lawrence was not only exasperated but somewhat uneasy when he learned that three hundred Acadians had been under arms at Beauséjour. Yet the expulsion of the Acadians appears to have been almost independent of that fact. Dominick Graham has suggested that "confusion, misunderstanding, and fear" were the chief elements in the forceful actions against them.[16] The decision to expel was not made until July 1755, by which time Lawrence had even greater reasons for uneasiness. Braddock had suffered a disastrous defeat near Fort Duquesne and a French fleet with reinforcements for Quebec, Montreal, and Louisburg had been allowed to escape. The hindsight of time, if nothing else, has demonstrated that the Acadians constituted no

CHAPTER 2

The Pre-Loyalists in Politics

To establish a British presence in Nova Scotia was the primary aim of Edward Cornwallis and from his letters emerges the picture of a stern man with a strong sense of duty and convinced of the importance of his mission. His instructions emphasized the military side but, as noted earlier, he had minimal success in dealing with the Acadians, or for that matter, with the Micmacs. On the government side the Virginian model, supposedly the guide since the time of Nicholson, was to be abandoned. The governor was to appoint twelve councillors according to general North American practice and to call general assemblies as the situation warranted. But for the moment even the Board of Trade recognized that an assembly was impossible in a colony in which Cornwallis could not "trace the least glimpse of an English Government" and did not "believe that the King had one true subject without the Fort of Annapolis."[1]

As a result, the council — largely a continuation of the Annapolis one in spirit, if not in composition — acted with the governor in handling almost all the provincial business. Despite the intentions Virginian precedents tended to survive, especially in the court system where, following the Virginian model, Cornwallis and his council created a general court to deal with major offences and a county court to handle minor ones. The form of government, however, was the least of Cornwallis' worries as he sought to establish a new colony in a hostile environment. Much more serious was his continuing battle with the Board of Trade over frugality in public spending. It came to a climax in March 1751 when he was told he could not retain the good opinion of Parliament unless he refrained from "exceedings" in the future. He replied even more bluntly than usual that to "flatter Your Lordships with hopes of savings" would be "dissimulation of the worst kind." Accused a little later of negligence in not keeping the board fully informed, he listed the numerous difficulties he had brought to the board's attention without receiving a word in reply and asked to be relieved.[2] By October 1752 he had gone.

His successor, Peregrine Hopson, served only fourteen months, a time altogether too short to leave much of a mark, except in one respect. Because of a lack of trained law officers, he appealed to the Board of Trade to appoint a chief justice and in October 1754 — a year after he had left — New England-born Jonathan Belcher, with English training and Irish experience, was installed as chief justice and councillor amidst great pomp and ceremony. Although strong in legal and academic attainments, his "aloofness, pomposity, and learning" were quite "incompatible with the political aspirations instilled by his father."[3] Under him the General Court of governor and council became the Supreme Court in which he invoked the powers of his office with little questioning from anyone. His training and experience led him to oppose the Massachusetts precedents which were dominating Nova Scotian courts and in accordance with the instruction that the province's laws were to be "as near as may be Agreeable to the laws of Britain," he promoted English precedents. But the English law officers did reject one of his most important opinions, that the colonists had taken English statute law to America as part of their heritage.

On Hopson's departure Charles Lawrence became administrator in October 1753, lieutenant-governor in October 1754, and governor in July 1756. Unimaginative and unsympathetic when it was a matter of duty — his expulsion of the Acadians is the major example — he was both a good soldier and a good administrator. Early in 1753 Hopson had made him responsible for settling the foreign Protestants, mostly Germans, at Lunenburg and "little by little this 'inconceivably turbulent' crew was brought to see that they must either 'proceed [as he wished] . . . or have [their] throats cut' " by the Indians.[4] But one battle he could not win, that to stave off the calling of an assembly.

Hopson had been instructed to do so when the townships, presumably at least two in number, had fifty or more families settled in each of them. In effect, Halifax was the only one since the Lunenburgers needed to be in the province seven years before they qualified as voters. Although Lawrence's instructions for the calling of an assembly seemed to be even less compelling than those of Hopson, the Board of Trade had begun to have doubts about the validity of laws enacted by the governor and council. Accordingly, when Belcher went out in October 1754, it asked him to report on the question. After some months he concluded that Nova Scotia being a conquered colony, the King might govern by such laws as he thought expedient or delegate that power to others, in this case, the governor and council. As a secondary argument, he contended that the governor was restrained by his instructions from calling an assembly to represent one township only.

At the same time Lawrence attempted to demonstrate the utter impracticability of an assembly. Noting that most of the Englishmen brought out by Cornwallis had proved to be unsuitable as settlers and that many of them had departed, he concluded that any assembly would be "dominated by the New England mercantile group at Halifax, for whom profit rather than patriotism seemed to be the main motivation."[5] Nevertheless, in April 1755 the law officers of the Crown decided that laws could not be validly passed without an assembly, apparently on the ground that once a conquered colony had been promised one — in this case by the governor's commission and instructions — only Parliament could withdraw that promise.[6] Accordingly Lawrence was instructed to concert with Belcher in devising a scheme for an assembly and meanwhile not to make the opinion of the law officers public until that assembly could confirm the laws already passed.

Belcher, always obedient to higher authority, did the best he could under difficult circumstances by drawing up a plan which called for a small assembly of twelve elected from the province at large. But when Lawrence forwarded it, he again argued strongly that the province was not ready for an elective body. The inconveniences, the inability to give representation to the landed interest, and its certain domination by the Halifax mercantile element were fundamental arguments in his case. And so a three-year trans-Atlantic struggle began between governor and board. In March 1756 the board insisted that, despite all the inconveniences of summoning an assembly, the want of a proper authority to enact laws was "an Inconvenience and Evil still greater than all these." Moreover, some of the difficulties relating to the landed interest might be overcome by attaching a landed property ownership, however small, as a qualification for voting. Nonetheless, Lawrence could still find excuses: this time the general satisfaction with the existing situation and his preoccupation with the war with France.

But his first excuse was negated almost as he made it. For Haligonians had got an inkling of the correspondence between Halifax and London, and had complained to the board against the denial of an elective body. Hence in July 1756 the board could tell Lawrence that so long as the province was without an assembly "malevolent and ill designing men" would misrepresent things. Though still protesting, Lawrence replied that he would consult Belcher on the matter and in January 1757 a new scheme emerged from the council which provided for an assembly of twenty-two members, twelve at large, four for Halifax Township, two for Lunenburg Township, and one each for other townships. Only the governor's order was needed for the writ to be issued. But he was absent most of the summer on military business and when the board sent him a conciliatory letter he decided to continue his inveterate opposition. In November he told it that conversations in New England had convinced him that to call an assembly "in a state of hostilities with so dangerous and near a neighbor" could not be regarded "otherwise than as Chimerical."

The board had had enough of Lawrence's delaying tactics. By this time the complaints from New Englanders in Halifax had become a torrent. They had even appointed a London agent in the person of John Ferdinando Paris and at the beginning of 1758 he presented the case of the petitioners directly to the board. It did not wait long. In February it gave Lawrence a peremptory order to act and at the same time changed his more recent plan to provide that, outside of Halifax, township representation should be two members, but only for those with fifty families or more. Knowing that no further delays would be brooked, Lawrence set up a naturalization court in Lunenburg and issued writs for the election of twenty-two assemblymen, four for Halifax Township, two for Lunenburg Township, and sixteen at large. On October 2, 1758 the first session of the First General Assembly (and the first in what is now Canada) met in Halifax with nineteen members in attendance. Five had come with Cornwallis, one was German Philip Augustus Knaut of Lunenburg, and more than half were New Englanders.

With the election of a representative assembly the council had a rival in the governance of the colony. In its legislative capacity it met under the chairmanship of its president, the senior councillor, and according to the governor's commission and instructions possessed the same rights and powers as the assembly, even in the initiation and amendment of money bills. The inevitable result was a clash which extended over several decades as the lower house insisted more and more on the British practice relating to money bills and eventually succeeded in usurping functions which in Britain belonged to the executive. At the outset, however, the council had several devices at its disposal which it used to keep the assembly largely in its place. In its executive capacity it met under the chairmanship of the governor to pass minutes of council on a wide range of subjects, especially the making of appointments. Its twofold functioning would last for eighty years until 1838, when it was finally separated into distinct executive and legislative bodies.

Governor Lawrence could devote his full attention to the First Assembly, for although he had commanded a brigade in the successful expedition against Louisburg earlier in 1758, he did not get a similar appointment in the expedition against Quebec the following year. On the whole, he had "surprising little trouble" with it although to him it was a body "entertaining idle jealousies of the council about particular rights and privileges." Twice, after the council had rejected a number of its bills and it requested an extended adjournment, he applied salve to its wounds and persuaded it to continue for the sake of the public good. Only once, and then only for a short time, was he indignant in public at one of its actions. That was when it arrested and confined one of his clerks, the excitable Archibald Hinshelwood, for "a profane verbal assault" on member William Pantree. Annoyed that it had acted against someone so near to him without letting him know, he relented when he discovered that it had attempted to contact him only to be told that he could not be disturbed at dinner.

From the beginning the assembly showed no reluctance to take action which it must have known that the council would summarily reject. So it was with a bill which would have excluded any councillor or assemblyman from holding any office of emolument under the government. So it was with its attempt to regulate fees in the Court of Vice-Admiralty, a source of contention for another half century. When its judge refused to make public his table of fees, it called his action "an High Contempt of the Authority of the House and of a Dangerous Nature." Lawrence explained that, since Parliament had not regulated these fees, the General Assembly could not. But he promised, first, to submit any complaints about their exorbitance to the Board of Trade and, later, to ascertain if the fees were excessive when compared with those in other provinces. Broadening its argument, the assembly then declared that it could never have faith in a council, one member of which was a former judge of the Court of Vice-Admiralty, another its present judge, and a third its registrar.

Among the bills upon which the assembly was most insistent was one to provide bounties for the encouragment of agriculture and fishing. It required a meeting with the full council and the levying of impost and excise duties on spirituous liquors sufficient to pay for the bounties before an accommodation could be secured. Until the 1830s the granting of bounties remained a source of contention upon which the council and assembly clashed almost annually, often with nothing to show for it but conflict. Two other matters of far-reaching concern appeared to have been approved without great ado in 1758. Perhaps the statute recognizing the Church of England as the established church in Nova Scotia was accepted as a matter of course because it provided for freedom of worship and exemption from tithes for dissenters.

More puzzling was the adoption of provisions which laid the foundations of local government that were to last until 1879. Before the First General Assembly were two alternatives: the New England practice, which vested the functions of local government in proprietors' town meetings and the officials whom they elected, and the Virginian system, which entrusted these functions jointly to the justices in sessions, who were selected by the governor and council, and the grand juries composed of substantial proprietors chosen by lot. In the first two weeks of its first session the assembly apparently decided upon the former option by passing a bill which established a president and common council to regulate town affairs. But in the end the official clique, which dominated the council and, by various devices, often controlled the assembly, carried the day. As a result, the instrument chosen to regulate the local government was a Virginia-type statute, an "Act for Preventing Trespasses," which authorized the grand jury to appoint the local officials that the situation seemed to require: four overseers of the poor, two clerks of the market, two hogreeves, and four surveyors of highways.[7]

After only two sessions the First General Assembly was dissolved in August 1759. The main purpose of the dissolution was to get rid of representation at large now that the arrival of settlers warranted it. The Nova Scotia which Lawrence inherited had been greatly lacking in people, the expulsion of the Acadians having almost depopulated its rural parts. Although the war would later increase the population of Halifax, it had dwindled, to 1,300, no more than the number of foreign Protestants at Lunenburg. On the repeated urging of the Board of Trade Lawrence was ready to take action to attract settlers on his return from the capture of Louisburg. It took the form of proclamations dated October 12, 1758 and January 11, 1759 — Thomas Chandler Haliburton called the second "The Charter of Nova Scotia" — which were issued for distribution in the other American colonies. They sang the praises of the 100,000 acres of Acadian plowlands, the 100,000 acres of pasture, orchard, and garden, and "the riches of farm and forest and sea which were ready to be taken." Before Lawrence died in October 1760 New England pre-Loyalists, the so-called Yankees, had begun to occupy these lands and he could write: "I perceive already they have but to see the lands and to be in love with them."[8]

He himself would witness the arrival of about 1,800 newcomers, the bulk of whom, according to Brebner, were ambitious, capable fishermen and farmers, "whose scope at home was cramped by the entrenched position of wealthier, more privileged men." Even without getting permission from the Board of Trade Lawrence and his council granted three townships on special terms: Horton and Cornwallis to settlers from Connecticut and Falmouth to those from Rhode Island. After his death the incoming tide continued when all the obstacles that might have stood in the way failed to thwart it. "The British authorities were conscious enough of their own limitations to accept the really basic decisions of the men on the spot. The New England proprietors [fightened of the depopulation of their own areas] failed to do more than hamper and delay the exodus to Nova Scotia. Speculation of several kinds did exist, but its detrimental effects were little felt because land was still plentiful . . . New Englanders were coming into Nova Scotia in sufficient numbers to ensure that at last it would really be a British colony."[9]

Even by August 1759 the newcomers were numerous enough to permit writs to be issued for the counties of Halifax, Lunenburg, Annapolis, Kings, and Cumberland, and for the townships of Halifax, Lunenburg, Annapolis, Horton, and Cumberland. Halifax Township was to elect four members, all the other townships and counties two, for a total membership of twenty-two. Interestingly, the Second General Assembly had fewer New Englanders than the last — no more than eight of them — perhaps because they were too busy getting settled. In fact, the township of Horton returned no members at all.

The two sessions of this assembly did not produce memorable actions, marked as they were particularly by efforts to reach agreement on bounties and the means of paying for them. The assembly came to an end on October 25, 1760 following the death of King George II. Although the practice had no meaning in Nova Scotia, it followed the example of Britain where parliamentary dissolution occurred on the death of the monarch. Much more significant to Nova Scotia had been the unexpected death eight days earlier of Governor Lawrence from pneumonia. None could have done more than he to establish and confirm British authority in the province. During his governorship three men dominated the council: Benjamin Green, New Englander and provincial treasurer, "whose affairs were so complex that he was almost left alone in authority"; Richard Bulkeley, one of Cornwallis's aides-de-camp who had become provincial secretary: "in him the British soldier became the Nova Scotian official first by favour and then by merit and application"; and, of course, Jonathan Belcher, the chief justice. Having outmanoeuvred Green at the Board of Trade, Belcher became administrator of the province in 1760 and lieutenant-governor the following year. Since Henry Ellis, though commissioned as governor, never came to Nova Scotia, the province was Belcher's to run.

On the surface, the Third Assembly, with which he had to deal throughout his governorship, appeared to be more representative than its predecessor. But that was less so than it appeared. The Lunenburg members, for example, held small official positions which brought them within Halifax influence. In addition, at least half a dozen Haligonians, like Charles Morris II, Malachi Salter, and Benjamin Gerrish, were elected for non-Halifax seats. Since, in addition, absenteeism was prevalent among the country members, Halifax interests often controlled the assembly. The council, entirely Halifax in composition, was basically a merchant-official oligarchy. In case its merchant members failed to secure their objectives through the council, they had other avenues of influence. In fact, to a very considerable extent, the Halifax merchant clique dominated the province over two decades, much of it done under cover. Generally they made their interests known to government, helped to frame mercantile policy, and lobbied fiercely to defend their interests. Among their group were Thomas Saul, John Fillis, and Malachi Salter, but the kingpin turned out to be Joshua Mauger, an acquisitive and unscrupulous sea captain and victualler to the navy, who developed a variety of interests in Nova Scotia. Perhaps chief among them was a distillery which he established in 1751 behind the protection of a duty of 3d. a gallon, which would rise to 1s. 3d. over the next dozen years. Leaving John Butler to manage his affairs, he moved to London in 1760. There he bought his way into Parliament and became the assembly's agent and influential consultant to the Board of Trade on Nova Scotian affairs.

That Belcher was a complete failure in his political capacity was not entirely his fault. Even though he evoked little criticism in 1761, the first signs of trouble had appeared. The reduction of Nova Scotia's parliamentary grant from £21,181 in 1750 to £5,684 in 1762 was causing the province to be riddled with debt. Enjoined by the Board of Trade to observe the strictest economy, he regarded the order, said one observer, "as giving him a complete Ascendency in the Govt." But other matters led mainly to his undoing. Starting with Cornwallis a debtors' act had protected Nova Scotians against being prosecuted for debts which they had incurred before coming to the province. The act had been a temporary one, renewed from year to year, and both Belcher and the Board of Trade believed that it constituted a "manifest injustice" to honest creditors. So with the board's agreement he proposed to announce the expiry of the act at the next session of the legislature. But his main purpose in summoning it in November 1761 was to proclaim the royal disallowance of an act that had set up a government-supervised monopoly in the Indian trade under Benjamin Gerrish as commissary. Experience had proved that the fur trade could "not support an elaborate apparatus of warehouses, truck-masters, and assistants," especially when the greedy Gerrish was more than willing to take commissions at every turn.

Hoping to prevent the expiry of the debtors' act, and, to a lesser extent, any action on the Indian fur trade, a group which included Gerrish and his brother Joseph organized a strike of at least seven assemblymen, who prevented a quorum from being obtained until March 1762. Throughout November "the helpless Belcher could only prorogue and prorogue while ten faithful Assemblymen kicked their heels and swore at the others who were walking about the town."[10] Eventually the Board of Trade would order the offending assemblymen and Joseph Gerrish to be dismissed from their offices, but that did not end Belcher's difficulties. During 1762 and 1763 he was continually baulked by his enemies in Nova Scotia and Mauger in London. After he refused his assent to a new debtors' bill, Mauger got the Board of Trade to reverse itself on the matter. When he rejected a new impost and excise tax favouring local distilling interests on the grounds that some of its provisions were contrary to British mercantile law and practice, the Board, probably influenced by Mauger, told him that his interpretation was faulty.

The new procedures which he introduced for the supply of goods to the Indian trade did not reduce the cost of the service as he had anticipated. After offering the same assistance as Lawrence to new settlers, he found himself stymied when the British government withdrew it. Commander-in-chief, but actually a civilian without military experience, he revealed his insecurity and ineptitude in "a small-scale repetition of Lawrence's deportation of the Acadians." Again he was embarrassed when Massachusetts refused to receive them and the Board rebuffed his "fears as unwarranted and the expulsion as inexpedient." What may have concerned the board most, however, was his overspending by forty percent in 1762, much of it necessitated by the reduction in the parliamentary grant.[11]

In 1762 and 1763 Mauger appeared several times before the board, complaining of Belcher's "Impudent Conduct" and charging that he was "so unacquainted and unskilled in the Art of Government, and has behaved in such improper manner, as to have occasioned a General Dislike to him . . . and Disgust to his Measures."[12] The outcome was almost inevitable. Because of his "demonstrated lack of political judgement, the financial chaos of his administration, and his inability to offset Mauger's influence in London,"[13] he was replaced as lieutenant-governor in September 1763. Complaints about too much power being concentrated in one man also led to a provision barring the chief justice from governing the province, a change which would have its repercussions early in the next century.

Belcher's successor, Montague Wilmot, has been treated by historians as "an easy-going, complacent soldier," "a man of weak character . . . poorly fitted for the post of governor," and to a large extent rightly so. Lieutenant-governor at the outset, he became governor in May 1764 on the resignation of Henry Ellis. Although Joshua Mauger was no longer the assembly's agent after December 1763, "he remained the colony's unofficial spokesman with more apparent influence than a succession of governors," including Wilmot. New Englanders continued to arrive in Nova Scotia, partly the result of the royal proclamation of October 1763, which forbade settlement west of the Appalachians. Most notable during Wilmot's governorship, however, was the granting of between 2.5 and 3.5 million acres of public lands to local and foreign speculators. It started in a small way, "but soon everyone was picking up a piece here or there." The greed of Nova Scotians was small compared with that of outsiders. To the credit of Wilmot he did try to resist or delay some of the larger grants, especially that to the Scottish adventurer, Alexander McNutt. The saving grace was that these grants generally had conditions attached to them, which required the holder to bring in a stated number of settlers under penalty of escheatment.

Known particularly for long, stilted speeches which he delivered whenever the occasion presented itself, Wilmot did not survive long in the harsh climate of Nova Scotia. Suffering from gout and rheumatism, he often found it difficult to sign his name and was forced to remain indoors in winter. Seventeen days after he applied for leave to take "the Bath Waters" in Europe he died in May 1766 and was buried beneath St. Paul's Church in Halifax. Because of the province's serious financial situation and its heavy debt, the assembly refused to pay his funeral expenses of £245 11s. 4d.[14] This was the lower house of the Fourth General Assembly which had been elected the previous year to give recognition to the burgeoning population. At its outset the four previous counties had become seven; the eight townships twelve. But since Halifax Township was to have only two members and the others one, the membership increased to only twenty-seven. Later the addition of one county and four townships brought the total to thirty-three.

Both the council and the merchant clique must have dreaded the growing non-Halifax representation. Brebner suggests that the meeting of the legislature during the farmers' busiest season in 1765 was deliberately prolonged so that many of them would leave and let the council get its measures enacted. Even though the bills of that summer might seem to "cancel out in a roughly equitable compromise," he thinks it "more likely that the true township members were outnumbered" and that the council triumphed. Yet the session of 1765 is notable for the assembly's first tentative move towards asserting that it initiate all money votes and that it and the council approve in advance any moneys paid out by the treasurer of the province. Hitherto "this denial of long-established British and American constitutional right clearly indicated the immaturity of Nova Scotia and was excused on the ground that the Executive must have the power to authorize expenditures in emergencies." In 1765 the assembly did not get much further than to demand that the treasurer furnish it an itemized rather than a consolidated account in the hope that it might devise ways to lower the debt. Apparently much of its new assertiveness was due to John Day, a small-time Halifax merchant and member for Newport, whom Brebner describes as "the leading, perhaps the only, independent, public-spirited statesman in Nova Scotia."[15]

In 1766 the assembly could fire its shots directly at the administrator since Benjamin Green was acting in that capacity for a few months following Wilmot's death. Describing his making of unauthorized payments as "a Infringement on the Liberties and Properties of his Majesty's good Subjects in this Province," it insisted in an address that any moneys which it voted not be used for "any other Purposes than those for which they were intended without the Concurrence of the House of Assembly."[16] After bitter recrimination the assembly at least won acceptance of the principle of annual estimates subject to its approval. By the time the legislature met in the fall of 1766 Michael Francklin had taken over as lieutenant-governor, placed in that position by the influence of Mauger. Over the next six years, in the absence of the governor, he would serve four times in that capacity for a total of about two years. Historians have failed to reach a consensus about him. Clearly he participated in graft growing out of land speculation to the advantage of himself and his friends. But it was also he who welcomed back the Acadians to Nova Scotia and established for them the township of Clare on St. Mary's Bay, which become one of their main sites of population. Accordingly L.R. Fischer does not think he ought to be evaluated "in terms of 20th-century morality superimposed on an earlier age . . . He was in many ways a typical colonial merchant-politician, meshing private and public concerns in an age when such intermingling was widely accepted."[17] Certainly he had a significant role to play in "helping to build the foundations for Nova Scotia."

In the autumn session of 1766 Francklin had to face the constitutional question revolving around money matters which had been left unsettled in the spring. As Brebner indicates, both the "Legislature and Province were basking under royal approbation for their dutiful acceptance of the Stamp Act, doubly warmed by the news of its repeal." But that did not prevent the assembly from publishing its earlier address in the *Gazette*. Although Francklin and the council refused either to accept or reject its basic principle in explicit terms, they had no choice but to agree to the assembly's paring down of the recommended expenditures for the next year. In the end the assembly succumbed to paying for previously unauthorized expenditures, but it did refuse some to which it had violent objections.[18]

Lord William Campbell, who succeeded Wilmot as governor in November 1766, was "a relatively honest, ingenuous, and generous ex-officer of the East India Company's service who was at first a babe in the hands of the Haligonians.''[19] A popular young hero at thirty-six, he remained well regarded as a person even when there were doubts about his ability. Compared with that of his successor, his governorship was uneventful, although it could have been more fruitful if his good intentions had not been restrained by circumstances beyond his control. In his initial report to the authorities in Britain he pointed out that the province was £23,000 in debt and contributing little towards its own expenditures. Anxious to secure funds for road building, he was denied permission to use revenue from quit rents or the Cape Breton coal mines. Having secured £500 for roads on a trip to Britain, he returned to discover that Francklin had spent most of it on his own initiative. Like his predecessors, he found the Mauger influence in Britain more powerful than his own; as a result, Francklin escaped relatively unscathed when Campbell reported unfavourably on his activities in Nova Scotia.[20]

Typical of these years, the assembly's behaviour was bewildering and inconsistent throughout the Campbell period, dependent as it was on the presence or absence of the country assemblymen. Towards the end of the summer session of 1767 Campbell actually managed to get the two houses to cooperate on a bill relating to the duty on spirits. Mauger's opponents in the assembly wanted the rum manufactured by the local distilleries to meet price competition from foreign rum; his friends in the council and assembly hoped to keep up the impost on rum while keeping down the duty on molasses and raw sugar and the excise on rum. With Campbell's approval even the council agreed to drop the impost on spirits from 5d. to 3d. and to raise the excise from 10d. to a shilling. But it was a short-lived victory since the merchants' lobby in London soon caused the new act to be repealed.

In contrast the sessions of 1768 and 1769 — Campbell was absent for the first of them — could not reach agreement on anything contentious. Discouraged because of his inability to increase the revenue or reduce the debt, Campbell dissolved the Fourth General Assembly in April 1770. The Fifth would survive fifteen years and seventeen sessions, and become known as the "Long Parliament." The addition of Hants County, and Windsor and Amherst Townships increased its membership by four to thirty-seven. Since three fifths of the members were new Campbell had hopes of a different spirit. But after a promising start the Fifth reverted to the recriminations of the Fourth. Campbell did manage to regularize the procedure for dealing with money votes. Henceforth the governor and council would send to the assembly their estimates for the following year; it would return individually those which it approved to the council in its legislative capacity, which in turn would accept or reject them individually. Although the executive refused to acknowledge these procedures in principle and continued to make what it considered to be emergency expenditures, the assembly had made a step forward which would last until it could alter the system still further in its favour.

In 1773, the year of Campbell's departure, Nova Scotia was in a sorry state. According to Brebner, "poverty and economic depression had bred greed and shamelessness in the officials and had prevented some of the representatives of the general population from going to Halifax to do their duty there."[21] To cope with the absenteeism long characteristic of the assembly, the Third Assembly had used punitive means such as expulsion, but with little success. Starting in 1770 the resort was to more positive devices, such as the ancient English practice of requiring a county to provide pay for any representative who wanted it. It was wishful thinking, however, to expect any of the Nova Scotian counties to respond favourably[22] and absenteeism continued to prevail.

Governor Campbell had not only failed to get the legislature to deal effectively with the province's major problems; he had also succeeded in annoying Mauger and his associates, especially by a second act increasing the excise tax on spirits. Hence, although their possessions and interest in Nova Scotia were declining, they took the usual steps to remove him and, in fact, boasted that they had done so. Actually Campbell, who had serious eye trouble which the harsh Nova Scotian climate worsened, had asked to be transferred to a more southerly climate. Taking advantage of his request, the recently appointed secretary for the American colonies, the Earl of Dartmouth, made him governor of South Carolina. Dartmouth had reasons of his own for moving him. More than a little puzzled by the conflicting information he was getting about Nova Scotia and anxious also to provide for a distant kinsman, Major Francis Legge, he sent him out as governor to get at the truth of the difficulties. Summing up Legge, Brebner calls him "dutiful, loyal, and courageous, . . . but . . . also very stupid."[23] Undoubtedly, because of events in the southern colonies, the British government wanted political quiet, something Legge might have had if he had cooperated with the powerful merchant élite. Instead, he chose to regard it as socially inferior and in his dealings with it "there was always more than a faint aroma of inconsistency and bullying." But this was only one facet of his complete failure to "understand the dynamics of Nova Scotia politics."[24]

As Brebner sees him, he could not make himself agreeable to those whom he sought to influence; could not compromise with human frailty, "which alone can grease the wheels of politics"; and did not understand how influential men behave when they are cornered. Like many military men of those years, he thought that an elected assembly savoured too much of democracy, never realizing it could be a natural ally in his contests with the council and the merchant oligarchy. Since the council would not help him to uncover the province's ills, he had to rely on others, most of them of moderate abilities and poor judgment.[25] Shortly after his arrival the legislature met late in the year for a month, during which it behaved as it did during the Campbell period, struggling much of the time over the estimates and past unauthorized expenditures. The session did Legge no harm, however, and probably gave him some ideas of how he might proceed.

He immediately became active in many directions. As part of "the new broom," he devised proposals to reform the orphan house, the pilot house, and the lighthouse, and in the process made enemies of those who stood to lose by the changes. During these months his right-hand man was James Burrow, comptroller of the customs, loyal and well meaning, but lacking the ability to restrain his more extreme associates. Since Attorney General William Nesbitt was largely inactive and unsuited to the task at hand, Legge made use of two others to ferret out evil-doers and clean up Nova Scotia: the able lawyer Richard Gibbons, Jr., who produced two first-rate memoranda on the provincial debt and the administration of justice, and James Monk, who had been sent out by Dartmouth as solicitor general at Legge's request and who "swept into the task of rooting out the rascals of Nova Scotia with extravagant vindictiveness."

When the legislature met in October 1774, the provincial finances were, if anything, in a worse state than previously. Once again the assembly called for a reform of the treasury and better methods of collecting the revenue, but for the moment without success. In order to reduce the public debt it also proposed a tax on unimproved land, again to be frustrated by the landowners in the council. John Day, back in the assembly as member for Halifax Township, called the council "a Junta of cunning and wicked Men" and accused its members of consistently thwarting the assembly's attempts to improve the province's financial position. Their views, he said, "extend no further than their own private Emolument, and [they] further the Distresses of the Community in order to produce a slavish Dependance on themselves."[26]

During the assembly's three-week adjournment in December the council in its executive capacity took two steps which would have wide-ranging consequences.[27] Although it found that the accounts of Benjamin Green, now deceased and succeeded by his son Benjamin Jr., were "just," it agreed that they could have been kept "in a more clear manner." Accordingly the governor and council chose Morris, Butler, and Burrow from the council, Day and Bridge from the assembly, and the newly appointed provost marshal, John Fenton, to constitute a committee to audit the accounts. Knowing, too, that Legge had been annoyed by the absenteeism of country members and the difficulties of obtaining a quorum, the council suggested that the assembly's quorum be reduced from eleven to nine and that Halifax County elect six members, Halifax Township four, a plan which would have "delivered up Nova Scota bound hand and foot to Halifax rule." Without even consulting the assembly, Legge asked Dartmouth for his opinion. That he could have gone this far with proposals which would have been rejected outright by the great majority of the assembly, his natural allies, indicates his complete lack of understanding of political forces and demonstrates, in fact, that he was stupid.

When the assembly resumed its sittings in December, a good many of its country members were not in attendance. This undoubtedly accounted for the triumph of the distillers' interest in the form of an increase in the impost on spirits from 5d. to 10d. a gallon. After the committee to audit the accounts started its work on December 16, John Butler quickly stepped down, knowing that his associates would be under attack. All its remaining members were on Legge's side, although Day got out at the end of April for unexplained reasons. The committee soon discovered that the records of Benjamin Green, Sr., were so incomplete as to be almost useless, a fact that Legge blamed on Michael Francklin, whom he believed had suppressed or destroyed them. Accordingly the committee sought to reconstruct the missing parts from all sorts of official sources, including the accounts of the collectors of public revenue. In the end they found deficiencies amounting to £6,881 in senior Green's accounts and £4,500 in those of the collectors. Although laxity and corruption had undoubtedly occurred, some of the irregularities had legitimate explanations. Monk used these findings as a basis for prosecutions and despite the absence of a court of exchequer with equity jurisdiction secured judgments in a number of cases. As he proceeded with reckless abandon, someone — Brebner thinks it may have been Michael Francklin — decided that he must be checked and in Jonathan Binney he found a willing martyr. For, when sued for deficiencies of £800, he refused to provide bail for that sum and went to jail instead.

When he and John Newton were tried in the Supreme Court before a "packed" jury, Legge committed an error which would cost him dearly later. At his request the chief justice provided him with a seat in the gallery of the courthouse, where he sat ostentatiously throughout the trial. A judgment having been found against Binney, he could not or would not pay. Instead he went to jail with his family, a martyr to the "tyranny" of Legge. The governor expected the gratitude of the assembly when it met in June 1775. He needed it since by this time he had alienated almost all the Halifax élite. For about two weeks the assembly refused to let itself be used by the council and it enjoyed a happy relationship with Legge. Then he presented it with the council's plans relating to its representation and quorum to which Dartmouth had agreed provided that the legislature approved them in the form of a statute. Dropping everything else, the assembly declared on June 28 that they were "replete with Mischief, subversive of real Representation, and [calculated to] render a Governor of this Province Absolute." At the same time it outdid itself in expressions of loyalty and pleaded for the removal of the long-standing ills.

What was astonishing to Legge, and is not fully understood by modern historians, was the incredible turn-about of the assembly after July 8. Hitherto it had pursued its attack on Binney with as much vigour as Monk; after that date it became an advocate for him "upon the Principles of Justice and Equity." Hitherto it had had nothing but praise for Monk, Fenton, and the other auditors; after that date it declared several of their reports to have been "devoid of any Foundation, either in Justice, Equity, or the Reason of Things." Brebner explores a series of possibilities for the sudden volte face. He does not attribute much of it to the assembly's anger over the quorum proposals and only a little more to the reaction of moderate men against the extravagance of Monk's prosecutions. To him "only one possibility remains open and persuasive — a decisive shift in the balance of the Assembly through departure of the country members." That alone would explain the assembly's growing insolence in the last days of the session and its ill-concealed "elation over having the Governor on the run." Although Legge could not have believed it, "his Nova Scotian course was run." Until the General Assembly prorogued on July 20 both houses seemed to take delight in thwarting and even insulting him. Much to his displeasure, the assembly cleared some defaulters and reduced the amounts which others owed. Following a serious break with him as the session closed, it told him that, because of the dangerous situation in the colonies to the south, it dare not enter into a debate with him for fear "it might tend to lessen your Power, and destroy the confidence of the People in you."

The sequel is soon told. During the last half of 1775 the evidence kept piling up against Legge in London. The governor sent Burrow to counteract it, but he was a flyweight compared with the formidable forces arraigned against him. From the outset Mauger, fortified with all sorts of information from Butler and Francklin, had the ear and goodwill of John Pownall, one of the permanent under secretaries at the Board of Trade. Legge's position suffered further when his kinsman Dartmouth gave way to Lord George Germain. The latter revealed the difficulty of his position: "But what can I do, Mr. Burrow, in my Situation? The

Universal Cry, is against Mr. Legge, that the Province, will be lost, utterly lost." Clearly Legge's enemies had influenced him with their argument that Nova Scotia might go in the direction in which the thirteen colonies were heading. Ordered back to England in February 1776, Legge defended himself in lengthy hearings at the Board of Trade. While taken aback by his personal appearance at the defaulters' trial, it found no evidence of "serious and well grounded matters of misconduct" which would deny him the royal confidence in future. Yet although he remained governor until July 1782, he was not permitted to return to Nova Scotia. It was the obvious fate of one whom the board had found wanting in the qualities that most mattered: "that Gracious and Conciliatory Deportment which the delicacy of the times and the Tempers of Men under agitation and alarm more particularly demanded."[28]

To secure his recall, Legge's enemies had used the loyalty cry. To what extent was Nova Scotia loyal during the American Revolution? A distinction needs to be made between Halifax and the out-settlements. Halifax, "with navy, army, and government, was the capital of the Church of England, and St. Paul's was its basilica in Nova Scotia." Also, London and Halifax were almost one "in a mercantile and financial sense . . . The London merchant overlords and their satellites in Halifax were ultra-loyalists by profession."[29] In contrast, outside of Halifax the great bulk of the inhabitants, the pre-Loyalist Yankees, were Congregational and had a markedly different attitude towards the revolution than that of the Halifax oligarchy. According to Brebner, they might have been tempted to rebel if only to repudiate their debts. But, as he sees it, their settlements were too scattered and insubstantial to permit them to take concerted action. Strewn along the edge of a long narrow peninsula largely without roads, communication was inordinately difficult. "Perhaps, then, the principal clue to Nova Scotian behaviour [at this juncture] lies in her insulation from the rest of North America."[30] The one attempt at insurrection — Jonathan Eddy's raid on Fort Cumberland — was an abject failure. A few of the New Englanders were active supporters of Great Britain; quite as many, and probably more, sided with the rebels, but in each case the numbers were negligible. Certainly the pre-Loyalists showed a distinct distaste for becoming involved in fratricidal strife with their former

neighbours and were quite as prepared to trade with Massachusetts as with the British forces. They were not so much loyal as
neutral — "the neutral Yankees of Nova Scotia."

Academics like Maurice W. Armstrong and S.D. Clark generally
affirm this version of the neutrality thesis. But Gordon Stewart
and George Rawlyk argue that, although it is not "completely
irrelevant," it is "too limited to account for all the forces
operating in Yankee society."[31] Brebner had pictured the Acadians
as being transformed by the forces of geography in Nova Scotia
into neutrals and then sought to impose the same "deterministic
framework" on the Yankees. The implications would be, suggest
Stewart and Rawlyk, that the Yankees had a clear view of their
predicament, carefully calculated the options open to them, and
embarked, like the Acadians, on a deliberate campaign to be
recognized as neutrals. But these academics consider the situation
in the outsettlements to have been much more fluid. They
contend that up to 1775 the Nova Scotia Yankees had retained
their dual loyalty both to Britain and the colonies. But when the
war came "their patterns of allegiance became dislocated as their
familiar loyalties suddenly became incompatible." Social
scientists have shown that in such circumstances a feeling of
instability appears in the society and new ideologies arise to make
the social situation more meaningful. According to Stewart and
Rawlyk, it was the revival, the great awakening reflected in Henry
Alline and the New Light movement which provided meaning
and direction to Nova Scotia outside of Halifax in the period of
disequilibrium after 1775. The revival led to an increased sense of
solidarity among the various outsettlements and in its wake
produced a new sense of regional awareness and an emotional
commitment to the geographical area. Politically the function of
the awakening was to "prepare the Yankees for a basic shift in
loyalty. By questioning first and then undermining their
allegiance to New England, [it] made them receptive to new
commitments . . . [it] made most of the Yankees more content
citizens of the British Empire than they had been in 1775 and
1776." But whoever has the better explanation, Brebner or Stewart
and Rawlyk, the fact remains that most Nova Scotia Yankees
remained neutral during the revolutionary period.

The Board of Trade having accepted the merchant oligarchy's
prescription to keep Nova Scotia loyal, the province carried on

until 1783 with a succession of three naval lieutenant-governors, who concerned themselves primarily with their professional interests and let the merchants have much their own way. Between 1776 and 1778 it was Mariot Arbuthnot, Commissioner of the Navy Yard at Halifax, a "gullible, affable person who never seemed to learn from his mistakes in preferring men's protestations to their actions." Apparently he was also vain. Assemblyman Henry Denny Denson described a sermon preached at the time of prorogation as "the most fulsome praise to the Lt. Gr. that was parhaps [sic] ever heard, which would have made any other Man blush, but he swallowed all."[32] Succeeding him between 1778 and 1781 was Richard Hughes, another Commissioner of the Halifax Navy Yard, a "competent and realistic, if not greatly distinguished," officer. His principal concern was not political, but the protection of the province during the last years of the American Revolution. Succeeding him, but only for a year, was Sir Andrew Snape Hamond, a commodore in the Royal Navy. Hurt to the quick when John Parr and not he succeeded Legge as governor, he resigned forthwith.

Clearly the political and constitutional developments from 1776 on were insignificant, but the same was true to a lesser degree of the entire period. This seems a little surprising since pre-Loyalists used to governing themselves at both the local and state levels constituted a majority in practically all the assemblies, and often a decided one. The lower house succeeded in establishing its privileges, powers, and immunities to the extent of removing many of the obstacles which might have militated against the proper performance of its duties. But in asserting the rights of the British Commons in matters of finance the pre-Loyalists found that the gains of one session often tended to be lost in the next. Their failure to make headway stemmed partly from the obstruction of the council and probably even more from the chronic absenteeism of country members.

One change during the naval lieutenant-governors' time would go a long way to remove the second difficulty and affect markedly the character of the assembly. Although the council declined to allow assemblymen to be paid by statutory enactment, it agreed in 1781 to a resolution which permitted members living outside of Halifax to receive ten shillings a day out of the sum allowed for the contingencies of government. Henceforth the assembly made certain that the contingency fund was large enough to provide compensation at that rate and used every weapon at its disposal to prevent that vote from being eliminated. Apparently it was the major factor in enabling the counties outside of Halifax to have their members in regular attendance. "After 1781, all the former indications of absenteeism on the part of country members — the wholesale vacating of seats, the difficulty of securing a quorum at the beginning and the end of sessions, the excessive number of Halifax residents representing country seats, the bewildering reversals of viewpoints in the closing days of the sessions — are missing."[33] Also contributing to the evolution of a stronger assembly would be a large influx of influential newcomers in the 1780s.

CHAPTER 3

The Loyalists in Politics

The Loyalist era was about to begin when John Parr was sworn in as governor on October 19, 1782. None could have been more delighted than he with his new office and its perquisites. After using much of his means to purchase his military promotions and after surviving many dangers, he was elated that his patrons in England had got him an appointment in which he could slumber away his declining years in comfort.

> the greatest civility and attention from all Ranks of People, a most excellent house and Garden, a small farm close to the Town, another of 70 or 80 Acres at the distance of two Miles . . . with good fishing, plenty of Provisions . . . with a very good French Cook to dress them, a Cellar well stock'd with Port, Claret, Madeira, Rum, Brandy, Bowood Strong Beer etc., a neat income . . . of £2200 Ster[g] p. annum, an income far beyond my expectations.[1]

Slight in stature, with a sharp, metallic voice and quick, jerky walk, he was soon dubbed "Our Cock Robin" and the name stuck.[2] In time he would be referred to even less favourably as "Pontiff" for his unwanted interference in religious matters and "Bashaw of Siberia" by Loyalists who disliked both his imperious manner and the harsh climate.

The governorship of Nova Scotia quickly turned out not to be the bed of roses which Parr had anticipated. Almost immediately he had to cope with settling about 30,000 Loyalist newcomers in a relatively short time. Despite his best efforts he found it difficult to satisfy an articulate people, many of whom had lived in affluent circumstances, and who, having sacrificed much to remain under the British Crown, had great expectations and were not loath to blame the governor and his officials when they were not realized. In the spring of 1784 the Loyalists on the Saint John were highly indignant because Parr sent Chief Justice Brian Finucane and did not go himself to settle doubts about the location of their lands. In turn, he was highly annoyed, after his unending efforts to accommodate them, that some of them could be "possess'd of so much unreasonable Impatience as to Express any discontent." Early in 1785, when disorders occurred for similar reasons in Shelburne, he reported that they were instigated by "a few persons noted for their factious dispositions," who "led a deluded Multitude in Opposition to the best people." Already his patience with some of the Loyalists was wearing thin.

Many of them, particularly on the Saint John, felt the same way about him. Accordingly they hailed with delight the creation of New Brunsick as a separate province in 1784 and were certain that their new governor Thomas Carleton would "check the arrogancy of tyranny, crush the growth of injustice, and establish such wholesome laws as are and ever have been the basis of our glorious constitution."[3] Somewhat dour and brusque, Parr did not treat the Loyalists as solicitously as they would have wished, but it is doubtful if any governor could have satisfied them. Parr may not have regretted the loss of the troublesome newcomers to Carleton, but he was completely taken aback by the downgrading of his status in 1786. Except for Newfoundland, Guy Carleton (Lord Dorchester) became governor-in-chief of all the British North American provinces, and Nova Scotia, New Brunswick, Prince Edward Island, and Cape Breton were placed under lieutenant-governors, who in the normal absence of the governor-in-chief, exercised the functions of his various commissions. To the end of his days Parr would contend that the change served "no one earthly purpose" as it related to Nova Scotia and he had good reason for saying it.[4]

To "quiet the minds" of the Loyalists Parr asked the Secretary of State to approve a scheme which would increase the size of the assembly and at the same time ensure them adequate representation. Told that the legislature must in future participate in all changes of this kind, he had it approve an act in 1784 which separated the new counties of Shelburne and Sydney from Queens and Halifax, each with two members, and which provided a member each for the townships of Shelburne, Barrington, and Digby. The Loyalists were so located that they might have elected one of their own in all seven of the new seats and, in fact, did in all but one. But no other changes designed specifically to serve their interests would be made and the thirty-nine seats provided by the act of 1784 remained unchanged until 1819.[5]

Loyalist representation in the assembly assured, Parr was also instructed to give them favourable consideration in making appointments. The result was that Sampson Salter Blowers, formerly the solicitor general of New York, became the province's attorney general in 1785. A few months later he was elected speaker at the first session of the Sixth General Assembly (1785-93), even though Loyalists held only fourteen of its thirty-nine seats. The members from Annapolis County and its townships illustrate some of the experience and talent that the Loyalists brought to the assembly. Stephen Delancey had been recorder of the city and county of Albany, New York; he would give way to his brother James, who had long been an assemblyman for Westchester County in the New York state legislature. But both were overshadowed by their lawyer brother-in-law, Major Thomas Barclay, the ablest of the Loyalist members and their driving force until he was appointed British consul-general in New York in 1799.

Sometimes the rise of party divisions in the province has been attributed to the clashes in the assembly in the late 1780s between Loyalists and non-Loyalists, but this is more than a little simplistic. By themselves the Loyalists could always have been outvoted since at most they counted for no more than forty per cent of the total membership. Occasionally, on a question involving a purely Loyalist interest, a solid group of Loyalists might be arrayed against an equally solid group of non-Loyalists. But more typical, as time progressed, were the divisions in which Loyalists were joined by other members to advance the privileges and powers of the assembly. Generally the Loyalists had lived under mature assemblies which had established for themselves most of the powers of the British Commons; in contrast the Nova Scotia assembly had remained relatively immature largely because of obstacles beyond its power to control. Undoubtedly the payment of members after 1781 would have permitted it to become more assertive,[6] but in a very real sense the advent of the Loyalist members speeded up materially its constitutional awareness. However, because of the small number of recorded divisions, the incompleteness and even inaccuracy of the *Journals* of the assembly and the council (in its legislative capacity), and the almost complete lack of reports of debates, the legislative history of these years can never be fully told.

In 1786 the assembly split almost entirely along Loyalist, non-Loyalist lines in deciding that, despite a scarcity of live cattle, the Loyalists of Shelburne could not import them from New England. An equally polarized division occurred on an alleged violation of privileges by Major Barclay. Outraged when the assembly voided the election of Loyalist David Seabury for the county of Annapolis, he addressed letters to a number of his friends stating that the "Majority of Members appeared to have come determined right or wrong to vacate the Election" and had entirely disregarded Blowers' convincing arguments.[7] Over the opposition of nine Loyalists and one non-Loyalist, eighteen non-Loyalists forced an apology from him. The increasing demand during the Sixth Assembly that the council not amend revenue bills and return them either assented to or rejected, appears to have been due largely to the Loyalist members since it had seldom been put forward before, and certainly not with the same insistence. Strangely, however, the assembly's major gain in 1786 came, not from the Loyalists, but from the secretary of state. Hitherto the lower house had secured approval individually for its votes without bringing them together into a single appropriation bill. Somehow Lord Sydney got the idea that assembly resolutions, when approved by the council, completed the grant, thus depriving the Crown of a negative. Accordingly, he ordered an appropriation act in future. "This meant that after 1786 the Assembly could refuse to vote any money at all if its wishes were not met on points of sufficient import to justify risking the total loss of supply."[8]

Early in 1787 the old established families of Halifax expressed indignation when Loyalist John Halliburton, who had already received a lucrative appointment as director of the navy's medical department in Halifax, was named to the council. Why, they asked, should preference be shown to these "damned Refugees"? That year also saw another blow dealt at Parr's power and prestige, again by the English authorities. Their decision to create a bishopric in Nova Scotia meant that he had to give up to Bishop Charles Inglis some of the powers which he had previously exercised over the Church of England. But it did not stop him clashing now and then with Inglis on authority still resting in him relating to such matters as the issue of marriage licences and the stationing of missionaries. By far the most significant event of the year, however, was the beginning of the judges' affair, which would bedevil the rest of Parr's governorship. Following complaints by Loyalist Thomas Millidge about the administration of justice, an assembly committee heard evidence from two Loyalist lawyers, Jonathan Sterns and William Taylor, who made serious charges against Isaac Deschamps and James Brenton, both judges of the Supreme Court and non-Loyalists. At this stage much of the public regarded the affair as simply part of the conflict between "old comers and newcomers, loyalists and ancient inhabitants." When the assembly requested Parr for a full investigation so that the public might be convinced of the judges' "Innocence or Criminality," he replied that the charges appeared related to "matters of legal opinion" on which the judges and the legal practitioners had differed; nevertheless he promised to do justice to all the parties.

Even though the legislature failed to meet in 1788, Parr did not escape the judges' affair. He laid the matter before the council which, after considering the evidence and the judges' reply in secret, declared that the charges against them were "groundless and scandalous." It also decided that a memorial presented by Sterns and Taylor was "altogether undeserving" of Parr's attention. Not unnoticed was the conduct of Blowers, who previously as an assemblyman supported Loyalist interests, but who now as a councillor acquiesced in the council's decision on the judges. Outraged by that body's action, Sterns and Taylor published letters in John Howe's *Halifax Journal* reflecting not only on the judges, but on the governor and council as well. In April, as a result, both found themselves struck off the roll of barristers and denied access to the council on matters of business.

By this time the old inhabitants of Halifax had become even more perturbed. To them it would be nothing less than cruel to deprive Deschamps and Brenton of "their bread in the decline of life," especially since their faults at most were errors in judgment on a few trifling matters. The bitterness manifested itself in a raucous by election in Halifax towards the end of February 1788 between Sterns and non-Loyalist Charles Morris II, in which armed men paraded the streets, a shot was fired, two persons had their skulls fractured, and one died.[9] Parr himself must have realized that Deschamps and Brenton, however worthy otherwise, were not highly trained in the law and he undoubtedly breathed a sigh of relief when a truly professional man, Jeremy Pemberton, arrived from Quebec in July to take over the chief justiceship.

The non-Loyalists were victors at the opening of the 1789 session when Richard John Uniacke defeated Barclay for the speakership. On Barclay's motion that Parr be asked to furnish a copy of the council's report on the judges, seven non-Loyalists joined six Loyalists in supporting the motion only to lose by a single vote to fourteen non-Loyalists. Thus the Loyalist members could expect considerable additional support when, as in this instance, they adopted a moderate position. It was different when Loyalist Isaac Wilkins proceeded on more extreme lines by moving that the governor, deceived as he was by his council, should "remove from his Presence those evil and pernicious Councillors until his Majesty's Pleasure shall be known."[10] The debate of remarkably high quality which followed was reported in the *Weekly Chronicle* and reprinted by Beamish Murdoch.[11]

Both Wilkins and Barclay maintained that the council's action was analogous to acquitting a prisoner solely on his own plea of not guilty. Barclay condemned his fellow Loyalist Blowers for his change in stance since he became councillor. Surely, as attorney general, he should have told the council that the simple answer of the judges could not justify the decision it had reached. "If their answer could legally be admitted as an evidence of their innocence, justice was at an end, and every species of villainy might passed unpunished." This time only two non-Loyalists joined the six Loyalists and they were turned down by a phalanx of twenty-one non-Loyalists. The division illustrates as well as anything the attitude of the Nova Scotia assembly towards immoderation, something which has persisted to modern times.

That same year, when the assembly forcefully asserted its rights on money bills, it exhibited no differences along Loyalist, non-Loyalist lines. The council had no quarrel with the ordinary items in the appropriation bill, but sought to amend the provisions which extended the funding of the debt over additional years and put the provincial creditors on different footings. Tenaciously the assembly clung to its "inherent right . . . to originate all Money Bills" and to demand that they be accepted or rejected without amendment. But apparently agreeing with some of the council's objections, it reframed its original bill to meet them in part. By this means it managed, at least technically, to adhere to the principle it was espousing. Although this stronger assertion of principle was that of a united assembly, the Loyalist members may well have been its leading spokesmen.

Upon the establishment of King's College, later to be the source of continuing disagreement, some questions remain difficult to answer. When the preliminary plans for the college were being made in 1787, a committee of the assembly pointed to its necessity as a means of preventing Nova Scotian youth from going to universities in the United States and imbibing principles unfriendly to the British constitution, a view concurred in strongly by Parr. Among the proposals was that it be under the direction of a clergyman of the established church nominated by the Archbishop of Canterbury and Parr foresaw one of its major functions as that of preparing youth for the service of that church.[12] It was along these lines that King's College was established by statute in 1789, perhaps, a little surprisingly, without opposition. This fact might be more readily explainable if the precise religious composition of the assembly were known. Although the leading Loyalists had been largely Church of England, most of the pre-Loyalists were not and hence a considerable number of dissenters must have been sitting in the assembly. Perhaps they did not think the provisions for King's College unusual or objectionable in a province in which the Church of England had been established for three decades. Their attitude might have been different if they had known that the governors of the college would impose religious tests which had the practical effect of barring dissenters from its doors, especially as they had agreed to an annual grant of £444 8s. 10 1/2d. in perpetuity to the institution.

Parr may have thought that he was done with the judges' affair, but his troubles were only beginning. Early in the 1790 session Barclay, apparently urged on by Sterns, presented thirteen articles of impeachment to the assembly charging Deschamps and

Brenton with high crimes and misdemeanours. Nine Loyalists and eight non-Loyalists agreed to hear them over the objections of eleven non-Loyalists. The judges' defendant, John George Pyke, probably regretted using the argument that the council had already acquitted them. When he did, he incurred derision in abundance for the "mock inquiry" in which the council had shut itself in its chamber hearing direct evidence from nobody, not even the judges. For three weeks in March and April the assembly continued its hearings. Parr's perturbation grew when the Commons of Nova Scotia, "as they call themselves," adopted all the forms of a court of judicature, summoning, swearing in, and cross-examining witnesses with all the formality of a trial "in the presence of almost half the Town who were admitted by Tickets."[13]

In the end the assembly accepted the general validity of the charges and later in April it presented the first three articles of impeachment in their final form to the governor with a request that he suspend the judges. On the advice of his council he refused and the assembly responded by sending two of its members to London, partly to get money for King's College, but mostly to press the judges' affair. In dispatches to the secretary and under secretary of state Parr bewailed these proceedings, attributing them to "a cursed factious party spirit which was never known here before the emigration of the loyalists, who brought with them their levelling republican principles." The chief prosecutors, he was certain, were those who wanted to succeed the judges and they were joined by six or seven "most violent dissatisfied spirits," the usual abettors of mischief.[14] None of this might have happened, he thought, if "a steady professional Chief Justice resident in the Province" had arrived earlier. In the final analysis, however, the most noteworthy feature about the judges' affair was that it was not, as is commonly supposed, a clear-cut struggle between Loyalists and non-Loyalists. Typical was the division on the second article of impeachment in which nine non-Loyalists joined eight Loyalists in opposing twelve non-Loyalists. Unlike the councillors, many non-Loyalists believed not only that justice must be done but also that it must appear to be done.

An assembly with a growing consciousness of its position in government caused Parr concern in other matters as well. In 1790 its demands included the incorporation of Halifax, the division of

Halifax and Annapolis Counties, the reduction of the naval officer's fees, and "a fixed and determined period" for the length of assemblies. Though unsuccessful in the first three, it had its wishes met in the fourth through the enactment of a septennial act which eventually won approval in Britain.

As usual, however, and as it would continue to be, the council and the assembly clashed mainly on the revenue and appropriation bills. The position of the council had altered in one important respect in the 1780s. The dominating Mauger influence in London had disappeared and with it the struggle to secure a relationship between impost and excise duties which would cater to the interests of the local distillers. But the council remained a merchant-official oligarchy, almost entirely Halifax in its composition, which at times protected the public interest, but which, more often than not, was self-serving. While its merchant members often sought to better their own interests by lowering impost and excise duties, the officials invariably acted to maintain and, where possible, to expand their vested interests. Naturally both combined to defend the powers and privileges of the council. The assembly, which three decades earlier had sought to adopt the New England practice of having local services paid for through assessments levied by town meetings and been repelled, had veered in the opposite direction. Reflecting its constituents' hostility to direct taxation, it almost invariably resisted local levies of any kind and, reflecting public demands for improved roads and bridges, sought to secure funds for that purpose through increased impost and excise duties. The result was continuing confrontation with the council on the amount that could be appropriately raised from these sources.

Between March 25 and April 3, 1790 these differences erupted in complicated and bewildering procedures on the revenue bill. Following a request by Parr, the assembly framed one which not only renewed the existing laws but also increased the customs and excise duties to help meet an accumulated deficit of more than £20,000, mostly incurred for the settling of the Loyalists. Considering the revenue raised the previous year to be sufficient and all that the province could bear, the council amended the bill to accord with its own views and thereby provoked a controversy on privileges. The council maintained, quite correctly, that the governor's instructions permitted it not only to amend money bills, but even to originate them, while the assembly insisted on the right of the Commons to originate all money bills and have them accepted or rejected without amendment. The council then requested two revenue bills, one to continue the existing laws and one to impose new taxes, only to have its proposal summarily rejected. Finally, after several interventions by Parr, the council agreed to one revenue bill without amendment, "but without prejudice to [its] rights and privileges in future," and with the understanding that in succeeding years the revenue bills would be sent up separately. Elated with its victory, the assembly told Parr that not only had it prevented the system of revenue laws from being "double voluminous and complex," but that it had also vindicated its basic position that, as representatives of the people, it was the best and sole judge of "the Quantum of Taxes and Impositions they are able to bear, and also what may be necessary for the Exigencies of Government for the ensuing Year."[15]

But the council would have its innings. In dealing with appropriations it refused to accept a vote of £650 for the contingent expenses of the assembly, in other words, for indemnities to the assemblymen. In public it stated that these payments should be borne by the towns and counties which the members represented and not be a charge on the moneys voted for the general support of government and the discharge of the public debt. In private it admitted that it acted because "a better time could not offer to Stop a growing Evil."[16] Naturally the assembly could not accept the rejection of a vote which had been granted uninterruptedly since 1781 and refused to pass an appropriation bill in 1790. Finding the assembly's turbulence and assumption of authority extremely troublesome, Parr blamed the difficulties on those assemblymen who "talk and paint well . . . but . . . who swerve confoundedly" from the truth and who "want to have the whole management of the Province in their own hands." In contrast, he said, the councillors had conducted themselves "with Temper and Moderation" and with "a desire to support the authority of the Royal Instructions." As a result they had been subjected to invective and unless new intructions were forwarded from England on impeachment and money bills he feared that some of them might resign.[17]

Mercifully for Parr, the session of 1791 was relatively quiet. Both houses were generally accommodating as they sought to repair the earlier damage. Parr died later in the year. The quiet, comfortable existence he had envisaged for himself a decade earlier had not materialized. Instead, the problems associated with the Loyalists and the new assertiveness of the assembly had made it more like a nightmare. As one biographer has put it, the profound upheaval and dislocation of the day would have taxed the talents and energies of any governor: "a lesser man would have been dilatory and incompetent; an abler man might have shown more dexterity and resourcefulness."[18]

Parr's successor, John Wentworth, did not wish to slumber away the rest of his life, but did want peace and quiet after the troublous times of his earlier years.[19] Born in New Hampshire, where both his grandfather and uncle had been governors, he succeeded them through the influence of his patron, the Whig magnate Charles Watson Wentworth, the second Marquess of Rockingham. Although the most popular of the American governors, he was forced to flee during the American Revolution. Not getting the governorship of Nova Scotia at once, he had to be satisfied with the surveyor generalship of the King's Woods for eastern British North America, "charged with preserving the lofty white pine trees for masts for the Royal Navy." In that capacity he became a resident of Halifax in September 1783. On the death of Parr it was touch and go whether he became governor of Cape Breton or Nova Scotia and it was the Tory Dundas who decided it would be the latter.

Meanwhile several things had been established about the life styles of Wentworth and his wife Frances. Because they insisted on living in the grand style, they would continue to remain poor, no matter what their income. In 1786 Frances became the mistress of George III's third son, Prince William Henry, on his visit to Halifax and in the years that followed she and John maintained a "liberalized relationship . . . which included extramarital affairs for both in a style typical of the most civilized as well as the most debauched of Georgian aristocracy in England."[20] More important for Nova Scotia politics was the fact that Wentworth, haunted by memories of the disloyalty of the officials in New Hampshire, would tend to regard any opposition to his régime as outright disloyalty. To ensure attachment to himself he made sure that the higher offices within his appointment or recommendation always went to Loyalists and so long as John King remained permanent under secretary he was overruled only twice.[21] Brian Cuthbertson is undoubtedly right that he laid the foundations of a predominantly Loyalist official oligarchy, but its significance for Nova Scotia's politics and government must be treated with caution. Many of the major office-holders whom he appointed became councillors in the natural course of events, but it would be difficult, in fact impossible, to find divisions of the council along purely Loyalist, non-Loyalist lines. Certainly in its resistance to the assembly the council almost always acted as one.

It was much the same with the assembly. Although the Seventh and Eighth General Assemblies had marginally larger numbers of Loyalist assemblymen than the Sixth, the non-Loyalist members might easily have outvoted them at any time, but seldom, if ever, did they feel the need. Although they might grumble outside the house that Wentworth invariably gave preference to Loyalists in appointments, contention between the two groups on the floor of the assembly seldom, if ever, occurred. During the last days of Parr the Loyalists had come to realize that they would not be denied patronage and Wentworth more than confirmed it. They had also discovered that the others would not gang up against them in the assembly except on extreme, uniquely Loyalist demands and hence, during Wentworth's time when the concern was largely with the normal business of government, they saw no need to take specifically Loyalist positions.

For about the first half of his sixteen years as governor Wentworth enjoyed almost uninterrupted political peace. By his own conduct he seemed determined not to be forced to go on his travels again. Each session opened with a grandiloquent, rhetorical speech in which he exulted in Nova Scotia's connection with Britain and the natural advantages which rendered it "in many Respects equal, and in none inferior to any other" country. But Brian Cuthbertson's contention that his greatest accomplishment was to "make Nova Scotians conscious of themselves as a distinct people"[22] seems to be going much too far and certainly would not be accepted by many historians.

Although Wentworth's first session of the General Assembly in 1792 was uneventful, by a strange coincidence William Cottnam Tonge, the Naval Officer, who was destined to become the governor's major antagonist, took his seat for Newport Township only two days after it opened. Four months earlier he had been appointed provisionally to his office, in succession to his father, by Richard Bulkeley, then administering the province. While still in England prior to assuming the governorship, Wentworth fought against the confirmation of the appointment and when he lost he promised to give Tonge his full support. Instead he pursued him with unparalleled vindictiveness throughout his entire governorship, mostly behind the scenes in the early years.[23] Perhaps he disliked being stymied in the appointment; perhaps he thought that Tonge played too active a role in his first session in upholding the interests of the country districts against the town of Halifax. Before the legislature met again, an election necessitated by the septennial act occurred in which members of the pre-Loyalist establishment like Richard John Uniacke and Charles Hill chose not to run, apparently feeling that their influence would disappear under the new régime. Uniacke even went so far as to declare that he would never enter the assembly again. But although three of the four Halifax County seats in the Seventh Assembly went to Loyalists Jonathan Sterns, Lawrence Hartshorne, and Michael Wallace, their numbers increased only from thirteen to fifteen or sixteen in a house of thirty-nine members.

As the 1790s advanced and the revolution in France led almost inevitably to conflict with Britain, Wentworth expressed in even more high-flown language his pride in "our Attachment to his Majesty's Person and Government, under which we enjoy the best fruits of a Free Constitution, Peace and Security, undisturbed by Animosities, or differences, whatever." On the whole, the assembly responded to his overtures, partly because his major requests were reasonable, partly because it seemed proper to do so in a time of insecurity. Frequently Cottnam Tonge introduced motions which might have annoyed Wentworth, but he was almost always in a small minority. In 1792, when Wentworth urged action to reduce the provincial debt of about £23,000, the assembly agreed forthwith to increased duties. It was equally responsive in 1795 when, because of the reduction in the debt, he invited it to encourage agriculture; and in 1796 when, because of the near extinguishment of the debt, he advised a reduction in taxation. As usual in time of war and rumours of war, Halifax and hence Nova Scotia were prosperous following an increase in the military establishment and trade.

In the absence of confrontation within the legislature, it occasionally appeared outside at the personal level. Relations between Solicitor General Uniacke and Attorney General Blowers had never been good and when Uniacke said "rude things" to Blowers in 1791, the latter challenged him to a duel. As a result, the province was treated to the spectacle of the chief justice binding the two law officers over to keep the peace. When the chief justiceship became vacant in 1797, both were claimants for the office. As was to be expected, Wentworth recommended Loyalist Blowers and, to succeed him as attorney general, Loyalist Jonathan Sterns. This time the governor was, in effect, reprimanded for presuming to think that the claims of Uniacke could be overlooked. The outcome was that, although Blowers got the chief justiceship, Uniacke became attorney general and Sterns solicitor general. A little later Uniacke gave the weak and sickly Sterns such a beating in a street fight that he may have contributed to his death. Again Blowers challenged him to a duel and again Haligonians witnessed the unseemly spectacle of the magistrates binding the chief justice and the attorney general over to keep the peace.[24]

Despite the period of political peace the storm warnings were out. Although the *Journals* are unclear, the assembly appears not to have been forceful in dealing with amendments to money bills in 1792 and 1793. But from 1794 to 1797 it unceremoniously turned them down, sometimes ordering the amended bill to be thrown under the table. Each time, however, it apparently tried to reach an accommodation with the council by framing new bills which met at least some of the council's objections and hence, technically at least, maintained its basic position on these bills.

The session of 1799 provided a foretaste of what was to come. Although Wentworth exulted, as usual, that prosperity continued to prevail and that British forces had "frustrated the daring and wicked Designs of His Majesty's Enemies," the assembly was not to be put aside even "when all the Priviledges of civilized society are in the utmost danger." The difficulties began when the council amended a revenue bill and then refused to accept a temporary bill of a few days' duration which would have continued the existing law until a new one could be enacted; the outcome was a loss in public revenue. Tonge took the lead in conferring with the council on the privileges of both houses as they related to money bills. The council declared that, although the royal instructions gave it the right to frame money bills equally with the assembly, it was not disposed to act on that right. In addition, it would henceforth either agree or disagree to tax and spending bills without amendment provided that they did not contain foreign matters or matters of regulation unconnected with the duty to be levied.

In its indignant reply the assembly did not object to these conditions. Instead it pointed out the uneasiness caused by the council's statement and unanimously declared "that it is the sole inherent and inalienable Right of the Representatives of the People . . . to frame and originate Money Bills, . . . that such Right is one of the main pillars of the British Constitution, and is a Right which British Subjects will never surrender, but with their Lives." Accordingly it asked the council to withdraw its declaration and "in unequivocal Terms relinquish a Claim, Which can do his Majesty's Council no kind of service."[25] Not only did the council not respond, but by refusing to increase the £5,650 already voted for roads and bridges to £10,000, it thoroughly annoyed the assembly and especially R.J. Uniacke, who had been elected speaker at the opening of the session following the departure of Thomas Barclay.

Sensing trouble with the Eighth General Assembly at its first meeting following an election late in 1799, Wentworth hoped that harmony would be continued and "rendered further conducive to the Public Welfare." He was quickly to be disappointed. For by 1800 it had become clear that issues would continue to arise which would produce confrontation between the two houses. Three times in 1800 the council rejected a revenue bill which proposed to continue a number of expiring bills. It took the position that any laws to be continued must be proceeded with as separate bills so that it would not be deprived of its right to agree or disagree with each bill singly. When Michael Wallace, the province's treasurer, who would soon be translated to the body in which he could practice his highly conservative, authoritarian views with abandon, proposed that the assembly give way, only one fellow Loyalist and six non-Loyalists supported him. After almost interminable wrangling the assembly appealed to Wentworth, who replied that in conforming to the council's wish to consider each bill separately, "there would be no Concession of any Rights or Privileges on the part of the Lower House."[26] This year the council was clearly the victor.

After a year of relative quiet, contention came back in 1802, although not on revenue bills.[27] The first major controversy developed when the commission entrusted with building Government House, the residence of the governor, reported that it could not complete the building for £10,500, the amount which the assembly had said was not to be exceeded. Its committee declared the principal commissioner Michael Wallace to be reprehensible for proceeding without the advice and concurrence of his fellow commissioners and for exceeding the limits set by the law. But when the assembly requested Wentworth to name a new commission, he replied that he was satisfied with its members, and when a dozen assemblymen wanted to delete an additional vote for Government House, eighteen opposed it, fearing that the money already spent would be wasted.

This division has significance in shedding light on the so-called "country party," which made its appearance during the later Wentworth years. Espousing country interests and generally unsympathetic to Halifax concerns, it was even better known for practising economy and defending the constitutional rights of the assembly. Its composition was, to say the least, nebulous. In its extreme stances it might number fewer than a dozen; in its more moderate positions a majority of the assembly. If its leader was William Cottnam Tonge, as he reportedly was, it was because he was its most outspoken member and could be counted upon either to propose or to support forcefully anti-council, anti-Wentworth motions. In every division, as on the Government House vote, it included a goodly mixture of Loyalist members, and almost always Loyalists Simon Bradstreet Robie and Lewis Morris Wilkins, who later, after becoming members of the establishment, manifested a much more conservative stance.

The country party might not have assumed even the nebulous form that it did had it not been for the challenge to the system of road and bridge grants, the second major object of disagreement in the 1802 session. First, there were difficulties on the amount to be spent — £5,000, said the assembly; £3,500, replied the council. Although Wentworth had generally supported higher expenditures for the road service before 1800, he later tended to side with the merchants, who were continually opposed by the country assemblymen in their attempts to reduce excise and impost duties, and incidentally the funds available for roads.

A second difficulty arose in 1802 from efforts to limit the assembly's participation in the spending of road moneys. Shortly before 1800 it had succeeded in having clauses introduced into the appropriation act providing for the regulation of these expenditures by the governor and council, and their very existence implied that the assembly had some voice in the disposition of these moneys. In 1801 Wentworth had rejected the assemblymen's claim to any share in appointing road commissioners on the ground that, as servants of the Crown, they had to be nominated and commissioned by the governor. Practice, however, appears to have been much more favourable to them since even in Wentworth's time many of their nominees were confirmed. Under his successors it tended to become the general practice. The assemblymen had also taken it upon themselves to review the road commissioners' accounts, to pronounce on the quality of their work, and to fix the rate of compensation within limits. When, in 1802, the council proposed to place the road expenditures under the courts of sessions, each of which would supervise a commissioner appointed by the governor, the assembly resolved, on motion of Tonge, not to receive directions of this kind from the council on money votes.[28] The outcome was to leave unsettled the problems relating to the size and mode of dispensing the road grants. The proceedings of the session, however, did permit Wentworth to escalate further the vendetta which he had been conducting in secret for a decade. Tonge, he told Secretary of State Hobart, had led a "party to oppose, embarrass and obstruct the measures and the Officers of Government . . . with speeches of invective and virulence tending to excite dissention between the Council and representatives, and discontent among the people at large."[29]

Perhaps reflecting the crotchety and less agreeable Wentworth of the later years, he opened the session of 1803 with a shorter and less exultant speech than usual. The revenue bills having been assented to by both houses, the assembly sent to the council a vote of £5,710 for the road service. Receiving no response it sought to examine the council's *Journals* but was denied access. Discovering that searches of the *Journals* of the House of Lords were treated as a matter of course, it called on the council to admit the error of its ways and, on the motion of Tonge, instructed its speaker not to sign the revenue bills. It hoped by retaining them in its possession to secure favourable action on its money votes, but the device failed, as it would in the future, because the council insisted on an adequate revenue before it voted supply. Eventually some assemblymen who usually supported the country party joined the consistent supporters of the governor and council to order the revenue bills to be signed, but only on the deciding vote of the speaker. Even then the council objected to being sent two appropriation bills and when the assemblymen appealed to Wentworth he, as usual, took sides against them. Agreeing that a second bill was unprecedented and unnecessary, he told the assembly that it was in its power to expedite proceedings, "which is seriously recommended."

Until now Wentworth had intervened directly in the affairs of the General Assembly only when requested. But in 1804, perhaps encouraged by a council of which Michael Wallace had become a member, he determined at all costs to institute the proceedings which he considered proper for the voting of the road moneys. To that end he recommended that £3,200 be spent by commissioners appointed by him, acting under his instructions, and accountable, as the law directed, to the executive branch only. Through Robie the assembly replied that it would consider an amount for roads and bridges, to be "expended and accounted for in the mode heretofore adopted." Wentworth was quick to assure the assembly that he had no intention of depriving it of its "constitutional right of enquiring into the conduct of all Public Accountants" and that he was simply reclaiming the normal prerogative rights of the executive to superintend and direct the appropriation of all moneys granted to the Crown. Some of them, he conceded, might recently have been left to the management of the assembly, but the governor could constitutionally resume them whenever the general interest required it.[30]

To the assembly this would have made sense only if it possessed some control over the executive. Fully realizing the threat to its position, it passed the revenue bills but again retained them to provide leverage in the proceedings to follow. When, as usual, it asked the council's approval of individual votes for roads and bridges, it soon discovered that the upper house was in collusion with the governor to turn the clock back. For the council declared that it was not in a position to judge the propriety of each vote and that the particular distribution of the road moneys should be left to the executive branch which had the means to investigate where they might appropriately be spent. It also insisted, as before, that the revenue bills be signed and forwarded before it voted money for any purpose. Eventually, over the opposition of the more determined members of the country party led by Tonge, Robie, and Wilkins, the same sort of grouping was mustered as in 1803 to instruct the speaker to sign the bills.

On matters of appropriation, however, the assembly would not budge an inch. It remained unconvinced when presented with a proposed schedule of road expenditures which differed little from its own; it refused outright the council's proposals to change the method of compensating road commissioners and to eliminate the clauses in the appropriation act which had regulated the mode of contracting and paying for road work; it found distasteful the idea that a person in the high estate of governor should become a public accountant. Above all, it resented "the frequent attempts which His Majesty's Council make every session to infringe the privileges of the House." Only the critical state of affairs had induced it to remain silent; otherwise it would have made His Majesty aware by petition of the difficulties it had in securing the rights and privileges of his Nova Scotian subjects. No way out of the impasse being acceptable to all parties, Wentworth prorogued the legislature without an appropriation act. But he foresaw no great inconvenience. The votes agreed to by both houses, he said, would be honoured, just as they were before appropriation acts were passed; the usual salaries to the public officers would be paid out of revenues not otherwise appropriated; and, perhaps to forestall the loudest criticism, the assemblymen would get their usual ten shillings a day.

Delaying the next session as long as he could, Wentworth did not summon the legislature until late November 1805. Although he called on both houses to "avoid every thing which may occasion irritation between them," the auspices were not favourable. For one thing, because of Uniacke's absence in England, the assembly chose Tonge as its speaker. For another, even though the assembly's reply to Wentworth was the least truculent of several proposed messages, it told him that when it extended the revenue bills to a later date than usual it had expected to meet earlier to appropriate the moneys derived from them. As in 1804, the proceedings relating to appropriations were long drawn out, but this year the emphasis was different. The assembly missed no opportunity to point out the injurious effects resulting from the absence of an appropriation act the previous year: the failure to pay some public servants and to meet the debts of the province; the operation of duties which constantly drew out of circulation the current specie and put nothing back; and the "illegal and unconstitutional applications of the publick Money" for Government House.

Almost interminable wrangling occurred on the desirability of two appropriation acts and, if two, what the content of the act for 1804 should be. In the end only one was passed. Not wishing to risk its loss for two years in a row, the assembly conformed almost entirely to, the governor's estimates, even to that for completing Government House. So it was a victory for the governor and council, although the assembly won a small concession. Unable to get regulatory clauses inserted in the appropriation act, it secured a second act regulating the road expenditures and fixing the commissioners' compensation at five per cent instead of leaving it variable at the discretion of the determining authority. Actually most of the recrimination this year was on the revenue bills. Because of the difficulty in getting a statement of the funds remaining from the previous year's receipts, some assemblymen deliberately detained the revenue bills long after the lapse of the ones which they were to replace. As a result, Wentworth complained bitterly of the loss of nearly one third of the revenue and contended that it operated to "the detriment of the many in favour of a few."

In two long reports to Secretary of State Castlereagh and his successor Windham[31] he set about preparing the way to rid himself of Tonge, in his mind the author of all his troubles. On the one hand, his picture of provincial politics was that of councillors disinterestedly devoting much of their time to maintaining the constitution and promoting the prosperity of the province. On the other, he found those whose views were more republican than were congenial to the British constitution and who, as his recollections of the years preceding the American Revolution affirmed, always attempted to gain control over the treasury. In Nova Scotia their leading spirit was Tonge, who had long been engaged in spreading "calumnious reports and discontents . . . diligently [and] artfully" throughout the province. This session, by promising to act impartially and not to obstruct business, he had been elected speaker. Yet from the first day to the last he had acted against His Majesty's interests and had goaded and encouraged other members to invent measures of delay and obstruction which protracted the session five weeks longer than was necessary. Worst of all, sometimes almost single-handedly, he had delayed the revenue bills until large cargoes were landed free of duty and sold, the loss to the treasury being more than £1500. If he persisted in this conduct, Wentworth should consider it his duty to suspend him from the Naval Office.

Continuing on the offensive, Wentworth had some success in the short run, but in the process likely shortened his governorship. In May 1806 he dissolved the General Assembly a year early, expecting it would be "attended with usefulness." But it resulted in his losing two of his strongest supporters, the aging Thomas Millidge of Annapolis County, an assemblyman since 1785, and John McMonagle, who had been foremost in resisting Tonge and whom Tonge kept out of the assembly this time by contesting his seat in Hants County. When the Ninth General Assembly met in November, almost the first act of Wentworth was to refuse the choice of Tonge as speaker, a course unprecedented in Nova Scotia and not resorted to in Britain for many years. Wentworth had calculated correctly that he could get away with it, for the assembly's lament at an exercise of the "prerogative long unused in Great Britain" was decidedly feeble. Perhaps Tonge's unbecoming private conduct may have begun to weaken his influence. In an assembly containing twenty-one new members out of thirty-nine he had been chosen speaker by a majority of only one and he would find it somewhat more difficult than before to have his way. Unfortunately for Wentworth, however, Tonge the private member would remain and continue to be the bane of his official life. Unfortunately for him, too, he would still have to rely on a council whose regular attendants were Chief Justice Blowers, Dr. John Halliburton, Andrew Belcher, and Michael Wallace, joined

occasionally by Judge of Vice-Admiralty Alexander Croke. No
Nova Scotia governor has ever had a more reactionary group of
advisers.

The major disagreements in the 1806-7 session were not
constitutional *per se*. They began when the assembly, on the
initiative of S.G.W. Archibald, later to be among the most
celebrated of the province's first commoners, expressed displeasure that it had to adjourn because its new speaker, L.M. Wilkins,
had been summoned on short notice to attend a meeting of the
governors of King's College. Later the assembly, perturbed by the
mounting costs of Government House, made numerous efforts to
embarrass Michael Wallace, but according to Wentworth, even his
enemies were "compelled to acknowledge his merit." Wallace
himself, anticipating correctly the judgment of posterity, boasted
of "a Building erected in this comparatively infant province,
equall'd by few, perhaps exceeded by none in the Western
Hemisphere and worthy of the Capital of this Important and
highly favour'd British Colony."[32] But when Wentworth sought
an increase in salary for the treasurer, now one of his chief
confidants, the assembly refused to consider it because of the
lateness of the session.

On one aspect of money votes, the granting of bounties, the
council had its way, as it usually would for many years to come.
The two houses agreed on the bounty to be paid for the importation of salt used in the fishery. But instead of the agricultural
bounty being granted for the clearing of lands, as the assembly
wanted, the council insisted that it be paid for the production of
wheat and other grains, and instead of the fishery bounty being
paid on the tonnage of vessels engaged in fishing, the council
required that it be paid on the actual export of fish to the West
Indies. Generally in the voting of money, however, the assembly
had much the better of it. Largely ignoring the governor's
estimate, it first explored with the council the total expenditure
that would be accepted as well as the amount for each major
service. Then it decided on the specific allocations much as it
pleased.

The session over, Wentworth persisted in his vendetta against
Tonge. Late in February 1807 he suspended him from the Naval
Office for "still persisting in very disrespectful and pernicious
opposition to His Majesty's Government." When, in April, some

of Tonge's constituents in Hants County asked the sheriff to convene a meeting intended to petition the king on their member's behalf, Wentworth enjoined him to prevent meetings designed to disturb the public peace. Later he took similar action in Annapolis County. Meanwhile he had sought to ensure that the council would remain the institution he conceived it should be by naming Brenton Halliburton, son of Dr. John and an assistant justice of the Supreme Court, to its membership and by persuading Lawrence Hartshorne, who had left on a question of precedence, to resume his seat.

Except for economic matters, Wentworth's last year as governor was a trying one. After an economic downturn recovery was on its way and until the end of the Napoleonic Wars the province would enjoy unparalleled prosperity. Personally, however, his finances were in their usual bad shape, his wife was in poor health, and he would probably have resigned gladly, as some have suggested,[33] had he been assured of financial security. It did not help him when in May 1807 Castlereagh again became secretary of state since for the first time he was without influential patrons in high places. Perhaps it was only fitting that Tonge should play a leading part in his final undoing.

Because three regiments of regular troops were stationed in Halifax, Wentworth had done little to put the militia in an efficient condition. So when the regulars were ordered to Canada, the province's defences left much to be desired. This was the situation found by Major General Sir John Skerrett when he took over as commanding officer and, encouraged by Tonge, laid much of the blame on Wentworth. The governor's credibility was hurt, too, by the Berkeley affair. Because of excessive belligerency in a naval incident, Vice-Admiral Berkeley was recalled to Britain in the fall of 1807. Apparently his friend Tonge persuaded Robie to propose that he be presented with an address and £100 for the purchase of a sword or piece of plate. With some difficulty the vote passed the assembly and, more surprisingly, the council by five to three. After lengthy deliberation Wentworth rejected it on the ground that it was "objectionable in so many respects" and added to his unpopularity.

Other proceedings of the 1807-8 session were equally distasteful to Wentworth. To his request that his favourite Michael Wallace be granted an increase in salary because of the increased burdens of his office, the assembly replied that any person of integrity who had a knowledge of accounts could perform the duties of provincial treasurer and that Wallace's additional work resulted from functions not connected with his office. Once again the assembly chose largely to ignore the governor's estimates; once again it got the council to agree on the total amount to be voted for each service and then determined the specific amounts by itself. Only on the question of bounties did serious disagreement occur, the council refusing to alter its previous position on either the agricultural or fishery bounties. As usual, Wentworth supported the upper house, especially in its insistence that the bounty be paid only on fish exported to the West Indies. Otherwise, he said, the fish would be sent to the United States and there used to purchase East Indian and continental European goods for smuggling into Nova Scotia. Almost pleadingly he asked the secretary of state not to listen to the assembly's complaint as presented by the provincial agent in London and hence give comfort to those "who seek to subvert the influence and independence of the Council."

Wentworth would suffer another serious loss of face before relinquishing the governorship. In 1806 the assembly had vacated the return of Thomas Walker for the township of Annapolis and following normal procedures requested a writ for a new election. Much to its surprise, Wentworth referred the question to the council, which in turn requested the opinions of the law officers. Both R.J. Uniacke and James Stewart declared it the undoubted right of the assembly to vacate seats, Uniacke even going so far as to base his judgment on the premise that the *lex et consuetudo parliamenti* belonged to a colonial legislature. Nonetheless, the council, on this occasion consisting of three ultra conservatives, Blowers, Hartshorne, and Wallace, held that the law of parliament was peculiar to the Parliament of England and that the Nova Scotia election law did not permit the removal of Walker until he was proved guilty of bribery or corruption in a court of law. When Wentworth accepted the council's advice to get a final decision in England, the assembly characterized the entire proceedings as an "unconstitutional attack upon the most undoubted rights of the people of Nova Scotia." Not until after prorogation in the spring of 1808 did it become known that the English law officers, while not agreeing that a colonial assembly possessed all the rights and privileges included in the law of Parliament, found that it was competent to "decide exclusively and without appeal on the validity of the Election of one of the members."[34]

The decision reached Halifax only shortly before the new governor, Sir George Prevost, who arrived unexpectedly because of a failure in communications. To the very end Wentworth warned Castlereagh that only a steady support of the council would ensure "the peace, prosperity and proper attachment to Great Britain of this, and all the other Colonies on this Continent."[35] Yet, almost since the turn of the century, he and a council no less conservative had attempted to check a popular assembly and even to turn the clock back with but short-lived success. The end results were that the executive branch lost much of its power to propose expenditures successfully, and the assembly divided the road money almost as it wished and named some of the commissioners to spend it, privileges which the country assembly-men came to consider their main *raison d'être*.

The foregoing account, concentrating as it necessarily does on the politics of Wentworth's relations with the assembly, presents only one side of him, although the most important one. Brian Cuthbertson demonstrates that, outside the purely political realm, he made contributions of great advantage to Nova Scotia. Somewhat less favourable to him, Judith Fingard concedes none the less that by all accounts he was "a well-beloved governor, a kind, charming, earthy little man, devoted to the service of his monarch and hospitable to citizen and stranger alike."[36] In a very real sense it was his misfortune to serve the period of at least two normal governorships. If he had retired at the turn of the century, historians would have called him a highly successful governor. But an aging man, confronted with dangerous times and possessed of an exalted view of the prerogative, developed the obsession that those who opposed him were disloyal and threatening to destroy the established order. He fought the battle, lost, and, after surrendering a significant part of the prerogative to the elective assembly, relinquished his office to a series of military governors.

CHAPTER 4

Four Military Governors and Political Quiet

For two decades under four military governors constitutional agitation was almost a forgotten thing in Nova Scotia. Except for the question of bounties, the most prolonged controversy occurred within the council, and between council and assembly, on the status and financing of Pictou Academy. The assembly, generally satisfied with the gains it had made, especially in the voting and disposition of road moneys, had little interest in disturbing the status quo. The closely-knit relationship between the governor and the council of the Wentworth period loosened and the persistent attempt to check the assembly ceased. Some of the governors may have felt much like Wentworth about the elective house and provincial politics, but if they did, they concealed it in private communications. So well did they maintain harmonious relations with their assemblies that sharp words occurred in only one instance and then in the case of an oversensitive governor who believed that the dignity of himself and his office had been impugned.

After considering the recent troublous events in Nova Scotia Secretary of State Castlereagh became convinced that Wentworth had outlived his usefulness and would have to go. He could replace him less painfully since the accelerating pace of the Napoleonic Wars and deteriorating relations with the United States made it desirable that the governor in Halifax be also the military commander. When Wentworth's successor, Lieutenant

General Sir George Prevost, first addressed the General Assembly in May 1808, he almost apologized for his "want of knowledge and experience in discharging the duties of the civil authority." Yet, as military governor of St. Lucia, he had dealt with the French population so successfully that he was appointed civil governor and both in Nova Scotia and later in Canada he performed the civil function with competence. Towards the end of his career, strangely enough, it was in his military capacity that he had to accept responsibility for two humiliating episodes of the War of 1812-14 and he escaped court martial only by dying a week before the proceedings were to begin.

The session of 1808 saw the closing stages of the Wentworth-Tonge imbroglio. Castlereagh had requested the legislature to supplement the British government's retiring allowance to Wentworth with an annuity of £500, but Tonge managed at first to have that payment limited to a single year. Only when the council pointed out that the assembly was not meeting the secretary of state's request did it relent and grant the full annuity. In the unending dispute over the fisheries bounty Prevost supported, though not in public, the council's position that a bounty, not restricted to the export of fish to the West Indies, would be harmful to Nova Scotia. Most of all Prevost asked for changes in the militia law which would put the province in a better state of defence. Both houses were quick to respond although they differed on the specifics of the changes and Prevost did not get precisely what he wanted. The assembly did agree to provide funds at the next session for the arms and accoutrements issued to the militia out of British stores, but in private Prevost still found the militia law defective and attributed the failure to put it right to "the jealousy manifested against measures emanating from Government and to tendency of democracy imbibed from our neighbours."[1]

To strengthen his council, or so he thought, Prevost received permission to add Bishop Inglis with precedence next to the chief justice. Also appointed, in accordance with an arrangement made earlier, was Richard John Uniacke, who had remained outside because of his disagreement with Wentworth on many matters. Even at this late date he was still lamenting that Wentworth had consistently appointed to office men with a lack of ability, namely Loyalists, the result being a "lamentable tendency to reduce and weaken the government." Governors, he said, should not be allowed to remain long in a colony since it inevitably led to "a low venal system of corruption and favour."[2] In September 1808, as Prevost was preparing to leave Halifax to fight the French in the West Indies, he told his superiors in England that the civil administration would "devolve on an able tho' rather unpopular character," Alexander Croke, judge of the Court of Vice-Admiralty. He also noted that Chief Justice Blowers, debarred from taking over the administration by the prohibition which had existed since Belcher's time, was likely to withdraw from the council rather than serve under an officer of lesser rank. In the absence of Prevost the session continued, marked primarily by disagreement between the council and the assembly on whether the proceeds of the revenue bills would be sufficient to meet the appropriations. In the end the assembly declared that it was the constitutional judge of the articles on which duties might be laid and the amount of those duties, and that in case of a dispute with the council its opinion "in a Money Bill, should prevail."[3] The council gave way.

Little in evidence during the session, Croke ended it by agreeing to all the other bills and then, to the surprise of everyone but himself, refusing assent to the appropriation bill. When the speaker of the assembly tried to address him, he was "prevented in a turbulent and violent manner" by Michael Wallace, the acting president of the council. Supposedly at this juncture the assembly's sergeant at arms, the comedian Charles Stewart Powell, "sprang into an attitude, (as if performing the part of one of the witches in MacBeth), and declaimed aloud — 'When shall we three meet again: in fire, thunder, or in rain.' — in allusion to the three branches of the legislature, about to separate."[4] Typical of the timidity of the newspapers, none of them, even at the assembly's request, ventured to print its resolutions condemning Croke's action.

In justifying his behaviour to Castlereagh, Croke declared that the bill encroached upon the king's prerogative and would involve the province heavily in debt. He had objected, for one thing, to the provision for a second provincial agent in London without his being given a chance to say yea or nay. But, more importantly, he had acted to restrain "the inconsiderate profusion" of the General Assembly which had provided revenues of

£17,080 to meet probable expenditures of about £25,649. From this starting point he developed his view of provincial politics. To him the assemblymen had always tried to appropriate as much money as possible for roads and bridges, and then divided it among themselves as "Commissioners, Contractors, and in a variety of other capacities." Despite every effort by the council to restrain them, these votes had increased year by year even though substantial sums were also being spent on bounties. In his view, the process accorded with "the avowed object of the Democratic party to involve the country in debt" and hence make the assembly absolutely necessary to government for the payment of the interest. Unfortunately, he said, some newer councillors were showing "a disposition to court popularity by supporting the Assembly in their favorite views." Demonstrating his extreme reactionary attitudes, he proposed as possible remedies to make the whole civil establishment independent of the assembly by placing all the officers of government on the parliamentary grant; to direct the governor not to assent to the pay of assemblymen now totalling £800 a year; and, perhaps, even to direct the governor not to agree to any appropriation bill.[5]

By April 1809 Croke was writing again to Castlereagh, this time with indignation and no little embarrassment. For, contrary to his expectations, he found himself largely restricted in the spending of money in the absence of an appropriation act. Michael Wallace would have let him spend as he pleased, as apparently Chief Justice Blowers would have, but he refused to attend the council even when admonished to do so. The remaining councillors including the law officers saw things differently. Croke dismissed Attorney General Uniacke's interpretation of clauses in the governor's instructions and the revenue acts as "an artful argument in favour of the claims of the Assembly"; perhaps, he added, Uniacke was reverting to his habit of defending the assembly while he was its speaker, or perhaps he remembered he was dependent upon it for £200 annually. This time Croke saw his main problems as stemming from the province's nearness to the United States. Through family relationships and commercial connections many Nova Scotians were attached to American ways and democratic modes of thinking and their loyalty to Britain was therefore superficial. To prevent further encroachment upon the prerogative action was necessary while the province remained weak, poor, and thinly settled. Certainly the governor should not surrender the right to dispose of unappropriated revenue; otherwise the assembly might add objectionable clauses to the appropriation bill and he would have either to accept them or reject the bill, knowing that he would be without money to provide the normal services.[6]

To remedy the ills left by Croke, Prevost decided to call the General Assembly on his return to Halifax and to leave "untouched the nice and difficult constructions on Colonial Legislation" relating to the appropriation bill. It was a veritable love feast. The assembly began by voting him 200 guineas for a sword or piece of plate for his part in the capture of Martinique from the French. Not a cloud crossed the horizon and the governor could say that business was conducted without "reference to the events which had marked Dr. Croke's administration" and that "a more favorable and expeditious Session has not been witnessed in the Province". But he was not yet done with Croke's annoyances. For his failure to handle the assembly as Croke advised, the latter absented himself from the council for several months and refused, for a time, to sit on the special court trying Edward and Margaret Jordan for piracy. Worse still, even though he had received the governor's fees during Prevost's absence, he also claimed half his salary, pursuant to a special instruction, explicitly operative in some colonies but not in Nova Scotia, that this was a perquisite of the administrator. With some heat Prevost told Castlereagh and his successor Lord Liverpool that, if they recognized the claim, his only recompense for his services at Martinique would be a diminution of salary. He need not have worried for not only did they reject the demand, but Prevost had his salary increased to £1,000. He fired his own shot at Croke by suggesting that either the provision which prevented the chief justice from administering the province be removed or that it also apply to the judge of vice-admiralty's position "as it equally deserves it." By this time Croke had few friends in Nova Scotia; perhaps even ordinary Haligonians were showing their dislike, for in the *Royal Gazette* of March 6, 1810, he offered five guineas for help in discovering the person who had killed his dog Brutus.

"The greatest cordiality" also marked the session of November-December 1809. Buoyant economic conditions permitted Prevost to recommend the unprecedentedly large sum of £9,000 to improve the roads from all parts of the province to the capital. Uniacke, a conservative, but above all a constitutionalist, apparently hoped to restore what he considered to be proper procedures in the voting of money. But when he called upon his fellow councillors to ask the governor how far the assembly had departed from his estimates and whether he approved of the deviations, he had no support. Since the General Assembly had provided funds for an extended period, it did not meet in 1810, making it and 1788 the only two years in which it has not assembled since its establishment in 1758.

When it convened again in February 1811, it was under almost euphoric conditions and with but a single cloud on the horizon, the fear that the United States would join in the war against Britain. A flourishing treasury led Prevost to recommend not only generous road votes, but also better accommodation for the legislature, courts of justice, and public offices. The assembly responded quickly. It proposed £15,000 for roads and bridges, considerably above the governor's estimate, and came close to getting what it wanted. It also arranged to construct Province House, another imposing edifice which would not be completed until 1819. Once again Uniacke raised the constitutional issue relating to the voting of money by opposing the appropriation bill and entering his protest on the council's *Journals*. To him it was deplorable that Nova Scotia was departing from British practice and that the assembly was considering motions for granting public money without their first being recommended by the executive. As a result, the governor often had to deal with money votes which he had not previously seen, but which he could not reject without risking the total loss of supply.[7] Strangely, none of the authoritarians on the council supported Uniacke. Apparently their functioning in both executive and legislative capacities forced them to make a choice and they had decided that their independence in their legislative capacity would be violated if they were unable to consider any vote of money presented to them, whether recommended by the executive or not.

An assembly growing more confident of its position spread its net wider this session. Through S.G.W. Archibald it sought a suspension in the collection of quit rents; through a committee headed by S.B. Robie it demanded that customs officers institute their cases, not in the Court of Vice-Admiralty where the costs ranged from £60 to £100, but in the common law courts, where they were of the order of £15. Expanding revenues led it to approve the setting up of grammar schools in seven counties and three districts, and make another attempt to encourage education in general. Because an act of 1808 which made grants to schools supported only through assessment had become the "forgotten school act," it sought to get wider acceptance through more palatable provisions, including payments to schools maintained through subscription and bequests as well as assessment. But despite continued tinkering the act had only limited success.

Shortly after the session Prevost made his final commentary on Nova Scotia when he sought instructions from Lord Liverpool on two matters. One related to the question twice raised by Uniacke, the other to the contingent vote, now £800 and likely to rise, which was left to be "divided among the members of the House of Assembly *ad libitum.*" Unless a wholesome and moderate corrective was applied to the second evil, he thought that in time it might constitute a danger to the prerogatives of the Crown. Actually he differed little from Wentworth and Croke in attributing the assembly's disposition to encroach upon the prerogative to the "spirit and democratic forms of the Government of our immediate neighbours." Moreover, since the ties to Britain were more ones of necessity than of gratitude and affection, he expected that, as the province became "sensible of [its] adolescence," its efforts to throw off the restraints of the Mother Country would become more frequent.[8] Late in July 1811 Prevost learned that he was to succeed Sir James Craig as governor general and by August 25 he had left for Quebec. His advice to put the senior officer commanding the forces in Halifax in charge of the province had not come in time and so, undoubtedly to the fears of many, Alexander Croke again took over the administration.

This time he could do no harm. The legislature was not in session and in less than two months Sir John Coape Sherbrooke had arrived to succeed Prevost. The situation obviously demanded a military man and Sherbrooke, "a short, square, hardy, little man, of a very determined character," had been stationed in Halifax as early as 1784 and later in India and Europe, notably as second in command to Sir Arthur Wellesley in Spain in 1809. The grasping Croke annoyed him in the same way as he had Prevost.

Not only did he get more than £500 as the commander in chief's share from the seizure of a cargo of flour during his short administration, but he also wanted half of Sherbrooke's salary. Apparently he fared no better than in 1809.

Twenty-four members of the Tenth General Assembly, which met for the first time in February 1812, had sat in the last house. Tonge was not among them; lacking employment, he had gone to Demerara late in 1808, never to return. None of the newcomers would make a great mark and old members like Simon Bradstreet Robie and Samuel George William Archibald assumed a leading role. Archibald was particularly forceful in devising a reply to the secretary of state, who had agreed to suspend the collection of quit rents, but only if the legislature made some suitable provision for the established church, a course suggested privately by Prevost. The assembly first ascertained that the amount due yearly from quit rents was £3,500 stg., the amount in arrears £40,000, and then accepted Archibald's motion that, because the great majority of Nova Scotians did not belong to the Church of England, it could not, without producing disharmony, provide money for the clergy of that church out of the public treasury, or "in any way raise money by taxes on other classes of Christians" for its support.[9]

The first session of the Tenth General Assembly witnessed a further move in the evolution of a peculiarly Nova Scotian mode of voting money. More and more the governor's estimates were becoming merely a rough guide. By trial and error the assembly would continue to determine how far the council was prepared to go, first, in total expenditures and, then, in each of the principal services. From that point on it was almost complete master of the appropriations and especially of road moneys, the greatest concern to most of its members. In 1812 a committee consisting of one member from every county and some townships divided the total moneys into more than a hundred votes ranging as low as £15 and the council gave its approval in almost every case.

Following the outbreak of war with the United States Sherbrooke again convened the legislature for a few weeks in July and August 1812. As usual in such circumstances, the assembly needed no urging to place the province in "a respectable state of defence." In short order it had provided £22,000 for the militia and £8,000 for such things as erecting blockhouses and arming boats. After conferences with the council it agreed to meet these outlays in the time-honoured way by imposing additional duties of sixpence a gallon on wines, fourpence a gallon on rum, and sixpence on all other spirits. It also approved the issue of £12,000 of treasury notes and the borrowing of up to £20,000 as the governor required it. Amity and harmony disappeared for a time, however, when the assembly refused to consider an amendment to the appropriation bill. In high dudgeon, the council declared that the lower house's conduct was "subversive of the principles of Constitutional Legislation" and that in rejecting an amendment which it considered its duty to make, the assembly was adopting a position which, if accepted, would "totally annihilate the legislature of the Province."[10] The kind of game which it was playing is unclear, for it could hardly have acted as it did out of ignorance; perhaps it thought that in troubled times it might get away with resuming a right which it had surrendered earlier. Only once again, in 1830, would it adopt a somewhat similar course and then with much worse consequences both for itself and the province.

Except for minor differences on bounties and the payment of a provincial agent in London, 1813 was another year of harmony. Responding willingly to Sherbrooke's request, the General Assembly voted an additional £50,000 for defence. Surprisingly, the council agreed, apparently without much ado, to increase the assemblymen's allowances from ten shillings to eleven shillings eightpence a day, provided that the total did not exceed £900. In its turn the assembly accepted, even if only to a limited degree, the governor's suggestions relating to roads. He had pointed out correctly that the existing method of dividing the road moneys into excessively small amounts could never "produce a lasting and beneficial effect" since it led to "the labour of one year . . . [being] scarcely perceptible on the return of another."[11] The outcome was that the assembly agreed to regulate the expenditures on the great roads to conform with his wishes. But it allocated only £2,500 of a total of £8,000 to those roads, leaving the rest to be distributed in the normal way among 144 cross roads. Clearly the country assemblymen were determined not to lose their most prized prerogative.

When the legislature met early in 1814 Sherbrooke could exult that the British flag flew over Niagara and that the revenue resulting from the booming trade through Halifax would soon permit all the treasury notes to be cancelled. Under these circumstances the assembly was the most unrestrained it had ever been in voting money: £15,000 for roads and bridges, the largest sum to date for that service; £1,500 towards a residence for the naval commander in chief in Halifax; £2,500 for the relief of Upper Canadians whose properties had been destroyed by the Americans; and increases of £100 in the salaries of the judges and even Provincial Treasurer Michael Wallace, the implacable foe of the assembly.

Before the legislature met again Sherbrooke had participated personally in military action. Without opposition, an expedition headed by him and Rear Admiral Griffith captured Castine, a fort on the east side of the Penobscot River in Maine. Awaiting the British government's pleasure, he arranged for the government of the captured territory and authorized a limited trade with a customs officer to collect duties, an action which would have significance for Dalhousie College. Altogether exuberant when the legislature opened in 1815, he hailed the arrival of peace in Europe and "a succession of events so wonderful, that we cannot but acknowledge in them the manifest interference of a Superintending Providence."[12] Revenues having increased beyond all expectations, he again stressed the need to improve the province's major roads. The assembly met his wishes in part by allocating to those roads £5000 of the record sum of £24,950 voted for the road service. But, as usual, the country members kept control over the expenditure of most of the money under commissioners more and more nominated by themselves.

The war had brought difficulties along with benefits. It had led to a shortage of labour and a slowing down in the building of Province House which had already cost £14,000. It had brought scores of transients to Halifax who, together with the multitude of soldiers and sailors, made policing the town difficult. The legislature sought a way out by establishing a bridewell or house of correction for vagrants and disorderly persons. The war was also responsible for the coming from Maryland and Virginia of blacks who had taken refuge aboard the British warships in Chesapeake Bay. When Sherbrooke requested the assembly to help these "people of colour," he met a decidedly cool response. After noting the frequent arrival of negroes and mulattoes, many of whom had become burdensome to the public, it expressed fear that the introduction of more would discourage white labourers and servants, and establish "a separate and marked class of people, unfitted by nature to this climate, or to an association with the rest of His Majesty's Colonists."[13] Accordingly it voted only £400 to assist the newcomers, a niggardly amount at a time of abundant revenues. Worse still, the continued settlement of blacks on stony, inarable lands made it certain, as Joseph Howe would point out later, that they would be unable to sustain themselves and would lay the foundation of the black problem in Nova Scotia.

The end of the war would usher in a new wave of immigration which by mid-century had led to the entry of about 55,000 newcomers. Many of them were Scots, whose forerunners had come in 1773, and who continued to go to the northeastern part of the peninsula and Cape Breton Island. The large number of Irish who arrived remained largely in Halifax. In anticipation of provincial development, the legislature concerned itself in 1815 with such things as the opening of coal mines and establishing a steam ferry service between Halifax and Dartmouth.

The session of 1816 was much of the same. Because the post-war recession had not yet begun, optimism continued to prevail. Again £5000 went to the great roads and £20,000 to the cross roads, divided into 280 separate votes. Liberality continued to be the order of the day: £1,500 towards a bridge over the Cornwallis River; £1,200 towards paving Water Street in Halifax; £400 for an associate judge to travel the circuits of the Supreme Court; £1,500 for seed grain to indigent persons. Much more important was the incorporation of Pictou Academy.[14] Thomas McCulloch's school at Pictou had qualified for a grant under the Grammar School Act of 1811, but that left him far short of what he now wanted: a non-denominational liberal arts institution possessing degree-granting powers. Bishop Inglis had just died, but his son, Rev. John Inglis, opposed the attempts to incorporate the academy in 1816 on the ground that it would constitute a threat to the established church. The bill easily passed the assembly although seven members, all Church of England, opposed it on third reading. Many of the councillors, however, had the same suspicions as Inglis and one action of theirs — the insistence that the academy's trustees be either Presbyterians or members of the established church — would contribute to its undoing. It meant that many dissenters would regard it as a denominational college and be reluctant to support it. It also suffered because its charter, unlike that of King's College, provided neither a permanent annual grant nor the right to confer degrees.

This was Sherbrooke's last session. Not a single note of disharmony had ever marked his relations with the assembly. Nor did his dispatches to the secretary of state picture that body in the same disapproving manner that Prevost had portrayed it. War, of course, had let him govern a province moved by forces not operative under his predecessor's term. Little of the personal Sherbrooke emerged during his governorship. But high society in Halifax must have been amused by his treatment of the grim, foreboding figure, Michael Wallace. When, on rainy days, Government House developed a leak, he would demand his presence and say, "Wallace, here's this bantling of yours making water again." On Sherbrooke's departure late in June to succeed Prevost, Major General George Stracey Smyth, the senior officer in Halifax, became administrator. Actually the change in instructions was not needed since Alexander Croke had left the province.

Sherbrooke's successor, George Ramsay, Lord Dalhousie, would be more successful in other areas than as governor. Under Sir Arthur Wellesley in Spain he won great distinction as a division commander. In pursuing farming on his Scottish estate between 1805 and 1808, he reportedly became one of "the foremost scientific and successful agriculturists of his time."[15] But his personal make up did not let him take kindly to having his well-conceived plans ignored by a colonial assembly and he might change overnight his opinion of someone who, he believed, had thwarted his good intentions. Incidents of this kind, however, were few and only disturbed the even tenor of Nova Scotia politics in the closing days of his governorship.

At the end of his first session in 1817 he could report that both houses had performed their duties with "assiduity and undisturbed tranquillity," and that Simon Bradstreet Robie, the newly elected speaker, had presided over the assembly "with great satisfaction." To him it was only natural that "a little self interest and private friendship" had a place in the distribution of road moneys. Although the first signs of recession were at hand the appropriation act provided for expenditures of £62,000 including

£25,000 for the road service. The treasurer Michael Wallace thought the amount "improvidently large," but Dalhousie did not agree. To him it was entirely proper in a province which had not a shilling of debt and in which the only tax was for the support of the poor; besides, an increased circulation of money would provide relief to "the lower orders" in times of growing distress.[16]

Dalhousie attributed the assembly's much more assertive role in 1818 to its members "working for popularity . . . under the apprehension of the approaching dissolution."[17] Twice they strongly upheld the privileges of a fellow member, once by exacting an apology from Anthony Holland of the *Acadian Recorder* for his jocose critique of Edward Mortimer of Pictou, and again by securing the release of Jacob Van Buskirk of Shelburne, kept in custody in a civil case. Asserting the usage of the Commons, they held that, except for serious criminal charges, no member should be arrested during a session or within forty days before and after a session. This year the assembly refused to yield to the council in any instance. It insisted that Nathaniel Atcheson succeed Scrope Bernard as the province's agent in Britain and summarily rejected the council's proposal to have him serve jointly with Edward Belcher, a former Halifax merchant now resident in London. It received delightedly Dalhousie's recommendation to provide encouragement to the fisheries and agriculture, and it sent to the council a bill incorporating the three bounties which it had been proposing for years. When the upper house demanded three separate bills, it replied that its bill had one object in view as recommended by the governor and refused to consider the matter further that session.[18]

This year it also indicated that it was going to become more assertive in religious matters. By now more than four-fifths of the population were dissenters, a fact reflected in the religious composition of the assembly. In contrast, the council was solidly Church of England. Some dissenting church leaders had complained by petition that they had not the right to have marriage licences addressed to them. The problem dated back to an act of 1758 which required either the publication of bans or the possession of a licence issued by the governor before a marriage could be performed. In his capacity as ordinary the governor issued licences to a Church of England clergyman, who might pass them on to a dissenting minister for a small fee; even then the marriage was to be celebrated according to the rites of the established church. This year the petition did not receive full attention although the assembly did ask Dalhousie if he considered himself authorized to grant licences to dissenting clergymen allowing them to perform marriages according to their own rites.

The session also brought out clearly the differences on Pictou Academy which would last another decade and a half. Its trustees having petitioned Dalhousie for assistance in erecting a building, he recommended it to the assembly. John George Marshall thought it unbecoming that trustees who, at the time of incorporation, declared that subscriptions would meet all their needs should already be soliciting funds. To him it was sufficient that the lower orders be taught to read the Bible; only those destined for the professions needed a higher education and King's College could provide it satisfactorily if it removed its religious restrictions. In reply Edward Mortimer of Pictou pointed out that the coming of hard times had seriously reduced the academy's expected subscriptions; S.G.W. Archibald recounted that an assembly containing a majority of non-churchmen had agreed to the permanent endowment of King' College in the belief that it would be open to all denominations without religious tests; S.B. Robie contended that at a time when Nova Scotia was building a "palace" like Province House, it could surely provide money for the propagation of knowledge. These arguments prevailed in the assembly, which by twenty-one to four voted £500 to Pictou Academy. But the council turned it down as it did an attempt to repeal the provision requiring the academy's trustees to be Church of England or Presbyterian.

Because of declining revenues, the assembly got only £20,000 for roads, not the £25,000 which it wanted. Strangely, the greatest rebuff on grounds of economy was to Dalhousie himself. When he presented a request from the secretary of state, Lord Bathurst, for a complete reorganization of the militia, an assembly committee declared it was "not expedient to make any alteration in the militia system now in force." Surprisingly, Dalhousie's reaction was mild and he prorogued the legislature with praise of the "uninterrupted unanimity between the several branches of the Legislature." Clearly he believed that "a great proportion of the members were . . . afraid to touch a law already unpopular" just before an election. He had no doubt, however, that the new assembly would deal properly with a matter that touched security.

When Dalhousie convened the first session of the Eleventh General Assembly in 1819, he had to deal with a lower house which contained slightly more newcomers than old. It is dubious, however, if the changes meant, as he hoped, the replacement of "illiterate working farmers, tho' sensible men" by members more "fit . . . for public affairs." By this time he had got to know the province much better through extensive travel and his opening speech indicated that he proposed to play the part of a vigorous chief executive. He had plans for agricultural improvement, for a college in Halifax, for changes in the militia which would make it smaller but more efficient, and for alterations in the system of road making which he found extremely faulty. Should the revenues be insufficient to meet the needs he suggested an increase in duties, something which would do no harm. Before the General Assembly considered his proposals, however, it turned to something which it considered of even greater importance and adopted an address condemning the convention which Britain had concluded with the United States in 1818. Dalhousie concurred in its complaints against opening the province's fisheries to the Americans and letting them "come freely into all our harbours to wood and water when they please." The effect, he said, was to "license . . . a free smuggling trade into the Province which nothing can effectively check."

In his specific proposals Dalhousie demonstrated that he had a great deal to learn about the basics of Nova Scotia politics. His suggestions that the number of road commissioners be reduced and that the great roads be placed under the council, the cross roads under the courts of sessions and grand juries, constituted another attack upon the country members' cherished prerogatives. Not unexpectedly, they argued that the council already had sufficient control over the commissioners and that dissension and mischief would occur if the sessions and grand juries took charge of the by roads. In the end the assembly accepted some of the proposals to a limited degree only to have its bill rejected by the council. Almost delightedly and quite unfairly it told Dahousie that it had been forestalled in meeting his wishes.

In essence the governor hoped to improve the militia by training more suitable men over a longer period of seven years.

W.H.O. Haliburton, father of Thomas Chandler, who should be known more for his common sense views than for the Tory label sometimes attached to him, thought it strange that a militia law which had served well in time of war should be found faulty in time of peace. He was all for telling Dalhousie respectfully that the assembly disagreed with him. Some assemblymen sided fully with the governor, others only in part, and because of the welter of opinions he did not get what he wanted. On finances generally Dalhousie's suggestions also fell by the wayside. The year 1818 had produced revenue of only £53,275 to meet expenditures of £58,681. The council, regarding itself as a check upon an improvident assembly, was interested, not in providing additional services, but in keeping the provincial accounts in balance. Consequently the assembly secured only $15,000 for the road service, not the £20,000 which it had requested.

The outcome was that Dalhousie had only two of his proposals accepted, both admittedly with enthusiasm: the granting of £2,000 for a college in Halifax and £1,500 for the encouragement of agriculture. The assembly was more fortunate in having two highly controversial measures approved, at least for the moment. Almost unanimously it voted £500 to Pictou Academy and the Council accepted it by six to three, with only extremists Michael Wallace, R.J. Uniacke, and T.N. Jeffery, the collector of customs, in dissent. It had more determined opposition on its marriage licence bill, especially from Rev. John Inglis, who acted for the absent Bishop Stanser. Eventually it won acceptance of a measure permitting the governor to authorize ministers of dissenting churches to solemnize marriages by licence, Wallace, Uniacke, and Jeffery again dissenting. Dalhousie, however, reserved the bill for the consideration of the secretary of state. Most surprising of all, the council acquiesced in an increase in the assemblymen's indemnities to twenty shillings a day for no more than thirty-five days. Overall, it was the assembly's session.

Dalhousie was moderation itself at prorogation, simply expressing mild regret that he had been "entirely misunderstood" on the road and militia questions and that an increase in indemnities had been voted at a time when the revenue was "inadequate to the wants of the Public Service."[19] His diary records that, despite this light censure, "we parted . . . very good friends, many of the opulent and independent members and all the Council publicly approving the reprimand." Later he indicated privately his total opposition to the marriage licence bill. In his opinion only the clergy of the Church of England and the Church of Scotland or Kirk could legally perform marriages by licence, but since the latter did not possess the right in Scotland, the best course was to restrict, not expand it. "The object I aim at, is to oblige all parties to be called in Church." One step in that direction would be to charge such heavy fees for licences that only the rich could afford them. The proceeds might supplement the bishop's income, "very inadequate" as it was to "his high station amongst us."[20]

After the session Dalhousie continued his encouragement of agriculture with enthusiasm. For months someone calling himself "Agricola" had been publishing essays in the *Acadian Recorder* which had stirred up interest in farming. At Dalhousie's bidding he revealed himself to be John Young. Joseph Howe would write later that "the great unknown" was "a stout Scotchman, who kept a small grocer's shop in Water Street and whom nobody knew or met in 'good society'," but who, under the patronage of Dalhousie and through fraternization with judges, merchants, and lawyers, was "soon discovered to speak with as much ease and fluency as he wrote. All this was marvellous in the eyes of that generation."[21] In December 1819 the provincial agricultural society received its charter and appointed Young as its secretary and treasurer. Dalhousie reported elatedly at the time that twenty district societies were in operation and that eighteen mills for grinding oatmeal had been erected since the last summer — "now the whole East half of the Province uses oatmeal cake and porridge instead of fine American flour bread."[22]

Late in 1819 Dalhousie learned that he was to become governor general. Two years earlier he had lost the promotion through a blatant case of favouritism. Then he had told Lord Bathurst that he would not remain silent lest it be "construed into a sullen discontent, a total want of feeling, or a silly imbecillity in not daring to speak out." Accordingly he made it known in no uncertain terms that his superiors had not treated him with "candour or justice."[23] Now having got the office, he was in no hurry to move to Quebec, partly because of the lateness of the season, partly because objects of "great interest" remained to be dealt with: the question of marriage licences; the annexation of

Cape Breton, a recent British decision; the subdivision of Halifax and Annapolis Counties; and the "further confirmation" of agricultural societies. He may have been sorry he delayed, for his diary displays a growing sense of impatience with all ranks of Nova Scotians in his last months in the province. In February, after the trustees of the Halifax grammar school declined to restrict it to older children and decided that it was better to let it alone, he wrote: "such is the stupid aversion that I find everywhere, even among the most respectable and most sensible men of this Province against any innovation for improvements." When, two years in a row, "a very indecent mob" misbehaved at the opening of the session, he doubted if either house would apply a remedy: "I . . . dread their natural aversion to all innovation may let even this pass."[24]

Still, his opening speech in 1820 was optimistic and marked by proposals for an accurate survey of the province and for determining the practicality of a canal from Halifax to Minas Basin, in other words, the Shubenacadie Canal. But he must have disliked exceedingly the discussion on the marriage licence bill. Told of its rejection in Britain, the assembly resolved unanimously on the motion of S.G.W. Archibald that the existing situation created an "invidious distinction," not only injurious to the Church of England, but grating to the majority of the inhabitants; and that any extension of the authority of the Church of England violated the understanding which led Christians of other denominations to settle in Nova Scotia. But Archibald could get only eleven of twenty-nine members to accept his second resolution that the influence which prevented assent in Britain "arose from interested individuals within this Province."[25]

Despite a marked decline in the West India trade, generally deteriorating economic conditions, and a balance against the province of £17,953, it was relatively easy for the two houses to reach an accommodation on money matters. The assembly managed to get £500 for Pictou Academy, £1,000 to encourage agriculture, £1,700 as the second stage of a bounty to encourage the fishery, but only £10,000 for roads instead of the £12,000 it wanted. After a close look at the operation of the customs house it rejected the explanation of the collector T.N. Jeffery and accused him of knowingly exacting fees contrary to law, the orders of the Board of Customs, and in violation of his oath. It concluded that unless some relief was forthcoming for the coasting trade, it would "finally sink under the burthen of a ruinous and destructive regulation."[26]

The session ended in haste. On March 27 news came unofficially through the United States of the death of King George III. Because of the belief that proceedings would end when official word arrived, "business was taken up and pushed thro' in great hurry." Although Dalhousie closed the session "in the most amiable manner," the opinion he recorded in his diary that day belied his pretended good humour. The assemblymen, he said, were "petulant and grasping at more than their privileges; they do not abide by the rules of Parliament, . . . they throw aside all regularity and order of proceeding . . . Incredibly ignorant, and too much self-interested, they have . . . wasted a whole session." As for Speaker Robie, he was "an ill-tempered crab, deeply-tinctured in Yankee principles .. not only an unfit person to be the Speaker, but equally unworthy to be His Majesty's Solicitor General." Several other assemblymen whom he had previously praised he now described as "very slippery gentlemen."[27] To all appearances he had abandoned reason and accuracy for emotion and petulance.

This was only the beginning. Though the General Assembly had voted him a thousand guineas for a star and a sword, he became highly perturbed when he examined the *Journals* of the lower house, something he had not done earlier because of the haste in concluding the session. To him it was highly mortifying that the assembly had passed over the survey of the province which he had recommended, had not continued the allowance for the inspection of the militia, and had cast aside long established forms and not accorded the respect due to the first branch of the legislature by failing to return answers to his special messages. Accordingly he turned down the star and sword which he had previously accepted. A shocked Robie accepted responsibility for the failure to respond to the messages and attributed it in part to the confusion surrounding the king's death. But after consulting other assemblymen, he felt better; one of them wondered what "evil genie" had been at work to produce Dalhousie's "inconsistent and absurd" action.[28] Basically the "evil genie" was the loss of dignity which he believed that he had suffered. "I am . . . vexed," he said, "that a very few cunning Yankees in the House of

Assembly . . . should have outwitted and defeated me" in the attempt to "maintain a proper spirit and system in the Militia."[29] But could a governor whose temperament had led him into difficulties with the relatively easy-going assembly of Nova Scotia possibly establish a *modus vivendi* with the tempestuous assembly of Lower Canada? Time would demonstrate that he could not.

Sir James Kempt took over the governorship bolstered with all sorts of advice from Dalhousie for dealing with the assembly, but, a natural harmonizer, he needed none of it. Indeed, he and MacCallum Grant, a hundred years later, may have been the most popular of all the province's governors. He made certain that he was not ensnared by his councillors collectively or individually; he spelled out carefully for his superiors in Britain any proposals which would be altogether unacceptable and those which he might effect if he took precautions in advance. Under him the ethos of the governorship changed markedly. As Joseph Howe would put it, "the agricultural mania died away" to be succeeded by a "passion for road making and pretty women . . . Agricola was voted a bore — a fat Scotchman — and his family decidedly vulgar, and the Heifers about Government House attracted more attention than the Durham cows." Halifax was rife with stories about the gay parties in Government House at which a voluptuous Mrs. Logan could operate freely because her husband, the captain of an Indiaman, was usually gone on long voyages. Perhaps because Kempt was a bachelor much was forgiven.[30]

Kempt's first major action, taken in October 1820, was to issue a proclamation re-annexing Cape Breton. His own fact-finding tour having convinced him that the laws of Nova Scotia could be extended to the island, the legislature quickly implemented his request. The session of 1820-1 was the first of the Twelfth General Assembly following the election necessitated by the death of King George III. The new assembly included most of the members elected two years earlier. Robie, though a reluctant politician after his *contretemps* with Dalhousie, again became speaker. Difficult, indeed almost insoluble, problems quickly came to the fore. Although Pictou Academy got a grant of £400, it was touch and go in the council where Binney and Black joined Wallace, Uniacke, and Jeffery in opposition, and it passed only on the vote of Blowers. The legislature also agreed to give the new college in Halifax an additional £1,000 and with Bathurst's sanction granted it a charter by statute; in their turn the trustees named it Dalhousie. But even with the earlier grant of £2,000 and about £7,000 in Castine funds, the resources to launch a college were meagre and when Kempt sought to give it revenues from the province's coal mines, Bathurst, a stout churchman, refused. Kempt blamed it partly on the intrigues of Bishop Stanser, still in England "living in a state of idleness as concerns the duties of his sacred office" and John Inglis, "one of the most cunning and persevering of men."

The governor showed his diplomatic skill in dealing with customs fees, the most exciting question of the day. Almost five hundred persons had crowded the assembly's galleries to hear speaker after speaker denounce the intolerable burden under which the coastal trade was labouring. The outcome was a resolution stating that a British statute of 1778 prevented any tax, duty, or assessment from being levied in a colony without its representatives' consent. Following his normal style of proceeding, Kempt persuaded the assembly not to pass a declaratory act to that effect and sought instead, through the secretary of state, to have the fees revised. The next session he could report that the British government was taking steps to "substitute a reduced scale of fees, instead of the present exorbitant charges." A second suggestion of Kempt failed through no fault of his. When the assembly decided to consider the badly needed division of Halifax and Annapolis Counties, he intimated that it would be well to examine all the county boundaries. But deep-seated differences between the two houses resulted in stalemate. In a time of declining revenues it delighted Kempt to get funds for the survey of the province and £500 for two inspecting officers for the militia, a sufficient amount if he used half-pay field officers from Britain.

Revenues were still declining when the legislature met in February 1822 and this year the road vote was only £6,250. Pictou Academy got £400, again on the deciding vote of Blowers. Dominating the debate was the status of Roman Catholic Laurence Kavanagh, who had been elected for Cape Breton County and who was willing to take the state oaths swearing loyalty to the Crown, but not those against popery and transubstantiation. The two houses agreed that Catholics might act as

members "without any evil consequences," but on nothing else.
After the assembly passed a bill with a suspending clause
allowing Catholics to sit in the assembly on taking the state oaths,
the council objected on the ground that a general bill so directly
opposed to the governor's instructions would be "indecorous." In
its turn the assembly refused to join the council in an address
requesting the governor to seek a change in his instructions
allowing Catholics to be admitted to the legislature, other public
offices, and the bar without taking the oaths against popery and
transubstantiation. In private Kempt sided with the council and
although he could not solve the general question, his intervention
led Bathurst to agree to Kavanagh's admission after taking only
the state oaths.[31]

In the depressed conditions of 1822 the assembly made a more
determined effort than usual to encourage the fisheries. Because
not a single provincial merchant regularly imported salt, it
proposed bounties to relieve the shortage. It also sought to
promote the growth of bread corn by increasing the duty upon
wheat and wheaten flour imported from the United States. But, as
usual, it could not devise bills free from the council's objections,
and acceptable to itself.

In 1823, when the economic tide appeared at last to be turning,
Kempt himself hoped for "some unobjectionable plan" which
would stimulate the fishery, "that valuable and most important
branch of our industry." When the chamber of commerce in
Halifax re-echoed his feelings, it was almost a command to both
houses to take action and manoeuvrings surrounding the
question dominated the legislative process. In the end the council
turned down a bounty on the importation of salt in favour of one,
eventually accepted, on merchantable fish caught in vessels
outfitted in the province and exported to Europe, Africa, and
South America north of the Amazon in Nova Scotia-owned
vessels. Clearly it intended its bounty to aid both the fishery and
commerce. As such, it brought out in full the differences between
the country assemblymen and the merchants in the council.
Second in interest to bounties in 1823 were matters relating to
education. Following Kempt's pleas to relieve Dalhousie College
from the debt incurred in erecting its building and getting into
operation, both houses agreed to lend it £5,000. But they were not
as harmonious on the method of providing grants to common

schools and the council rejected outright the assembly's attempt to raise Pictou Academy to the status of a degree-granting institution; indeed, it was fortunate to get £300 for one year. Still, none of the differences produced bitter feelings and Kempt could speak glowingly of another harmonious session.

By 1824 economic conditions and the state of the treasury had so improved that the legislature could increase the road grant to £12,000. Also indicative of the new optimism was an act for the incorporation of the Shubenacadie Canal Company. But a highly controversial bill relating to the judiciary attracted the most interest. The previous year, in order to have a resident judge in Cape Breton, Kempt had secured the appointment of a professional man to be chief justice of the Inferior Court of Common Pleas on the island. In 1824 Richard Blair of Cumberland proposed the extension of the system to the entire province. With the active support of S.G.W. Archibald, he introduced a bill dividing peninsular Nova Scotia outside of Halifax into the Western, Middle, and Eastern Divisions, in each of which a professional man would act as first justice of the Court of Inferior Pleas and president of the Court of Sessions, and receive a salary of £400 and travel expenses. Those who favoured the act for the better administration of justice argued that the decisions of the existing inferior courts rested on no fixed principles; that the judges were ignorant of the law; and that dissatisfaction was evident in the large number of appeals to the Supreme Court. Although the assembly was not fully polarized along any lines, the opponents, with the exception of merchant William Lawson, were country members, many of whom, like Lott Church and W.H. Roach, regarded themselves as protectors of the public purse. They contended that the decisions of the incumbent judges, based as they were on justice and common sense, were more acceptable than ones based on pure legality; that no complaints had come by way of petition or otherwise; that the country was too young for expensive innovations costing about £1,500 annually; and that the proposals were simply a pretext to give offices to the "hungry profession." The last argument gained credence when eight of the nine lawyer-assemblymen — all but Charles Rufus Fairbanks — provided the votes which carried the bill in an almost evenly divided house, and when three of them became the first appointees under the act. "Perhaps," wrote

Beamish Murdoch, "there had not been so much in the nature of political excitement aroused in the province since the days of Cottnam Tonge, as was excited by this measure."[32] Kempt himself lost no credibility since, when asked for an opinion, he replied that the council and assembly were the best judges of the benefits which might accrue from the bill.

This session the council again turned down the assembly's bill to enlarge the powers of Pictou Academy and grant it permanent financial assistance although it did agree to provide £400 for one year. After the session Kempt forwarded Chief Justice Blowers' opinion that colonial constitutions should rest on statute rather than on the governors' instructions which the assemblies considered to be binding on the governors only and not on themselves. But Kempt strongly disagreed. Many colonists, he said, believed the instructions to be the more secure foundation of a constitution. Although the British Parliament could always change a statute, it would be difficult for His Majesty to repeal any rights which he had granted by his instructions. Late in April 1824 Kempt left for Britain on private business. While there, he sought to promote a union of financially troubled King's and Dalhousie Colleges. The latter's building had cost much more than expected, while those at King's were "unfit for repair" and even the bishop recognized that the college should be in Halifax. If the union came about "with as much regard as possible to the primary objects of both," Kempt prophesied that the British government would be relieved of conflicting demands for support, the legislature could "direct [its] bounty in one channel," and the resulting bond of harmony would "raise the College to a degree of Eminence and usefulness."[33] He was bitterly disappointed when the Archbishop of Canterbury turned thumbs down on his proposal.

The instruction that the senior military officer should become administrator in the governor's absence being no longer in effect, senior councillor Michael Wallace assumed that role. Laughingly, Mr. Justice Stewart wrote that "King Michael is seated on the throne — There is every prospect of his having a tranquil reign." Perhaps remembering Alexander Croke, Wallace refrained from any action which might cause turmoil. When the legislature opened in 1825, other changes were also in evidence. John Inglis having become bishop, J.T. Twining succeeded him as the assembly's chaplain. Following Robie's appointment to the new office of Master of the Rolls, S.G.W. Archibald succeeded him as speaker, a position he would hold for sixteen years. Murdoch is right that, "moderate in his passions . . . [he] was excellent in calming the ruffled feelings of his audience, and enforcing the prudent, practical, yet honorable course of action." Although sometimes "too prone to be governed by expediency . . . no man could more quickly discern the salient points and true bearings of argument, and by passing the minor questions give force to the greater."[34]

The session of 1825 shed even more light than usual on the political culture of the province and the differences between the Halifax councillors and the country assemblymen. As in previous years, the latter indicated their suspicions of the Halifax merchants by refusing their petition for the incorporation of a bank. As a result, eight of them gave public notice on September 3 of the establishment of such an institution without act of incorporation or charter; so began the Halifax Banking Company. An examination of the common schools by a joint committee of the council and assembly found that, although 5,514 children were in attendance, at least 4,377 were not; accordingly it recommended compulsory assessment as a means of support. The outcome was not surprising. Lott Church called it the most evil proposal presented to the assembly in twenty years; R.J. Uniacke, Jr., described it as oppressive and speculative; and only twelve of thirty-six members favoured it. Once again the two houses displayed their usual differences on fishery bounties: the assembly wanted the bounty paid directly to fishermen on the landing of their catch; the council on merchantable fish shipped to specified destinations. Again the assembly demanded without success an enhanced status and permanent grant for Pictou Academy, this time on the ground that the class of persons attending it would not carry on their studies at King's College or "in the institution of doubtful and uncertain stability now forming in Halifax."

On February 21 the speaker and clerk of the assembly appeared for the first time in wigs and silk gowns.[35] The same day the lower house took steps to use for the first time the Nova Scotia version of the Grenville Act, enacted in 1821 for the trial of controverted elections. The return of John Young (Agricola) for Sydney County having been petitioned against, the assembly struck a committee to try the case. This year something more exciting to Nova Scotians occurred in the British Parliament than in their own legislature. On March 21 William Huskisson introduced in the House of Commons a series of resolutions designed to remove most of the restrictions on colonial trade. When the news reached Halifax on St. George's Day, all classes of people "joined in the exultation . . . Such a day of cheerfulness had not been witnessed in the place for ten years."[36]

In opening the General Assembly in February 1826, Kempt expressed elation at the thriving economic conditions and hoped that increased revenues would permit great public improvements and the province's assumption of some expenses of the civil establishment still on the parliamentary grant. The second suggestion resulted from pressure being applied by Bathurst. Although Kempt did not object in principle, he knew that the time, method, and manner of making the request were crucial. To him a pre-election session was altogether inappropriate and success would be more likely when the removal of restrictions on trade increased the provincial revenue. He also warned that the legislature would on no account support the established church as the secretary of state had proposed. Apparently Bathurst accepted the views on timing and Kempt intended his reference to the matter to be simply a forewarning. In one matter Kempt might have endangered his rapport with the assembly. While in Britain he had pointed out the difficulty of a layman like himself acting as chancellor especially because of the large increase in the business of the Court of Chancery, and had got Bathurst to approve the appointment of Robie as master of the rolls. In presenting the assembly with a *fait accompli* which would cost £600 a year, he was clearly taking a chance. But although members like Roach and Church objected, they numbered only eight, none of whom was critical of the governor.

As usual, the assembly was meticulous in dealing with Kempt's proposals and, whenever necessary, indicated its reasons for not meeting them in full. On the Shubenacadie Canal it shared the enthusiasm of a public meeting which, on being told that an eight-foot deep canal might be built for £56,934, subscribed £13,000, including £500 by Kempt himself. In its turn the assembly voted £15,000, portions of which were to be paid after completion of various stages of the canal. On the governor's suggestion it again took up the question of common schools. Charles Rufus Fairbanks pointed out forcefully that, while the United States was making great strides in reducing illiteracy, more than two thirds of Nova Scotians were growing up in ignorance. In the end the legislature agreed to impose compulsory assessment whenever two thirds of the rateable inhabitants in any district supported it, an almost meaningless gesture. In the council the addition of Bishop Inglis and Charles Ramage Prescott strengthened the anti-Pictou Academy forces, although Robie helped to counter them. When a majority voted against permanent financial provision and enlarged powers for the academy, Brenton Halliburton, supported by Robie, Charles Morris, and James Stewart, entered a contrary opinion on the council's *Journals*, contending that dissenters who composed four fifths of the population deserved favourable consideration, the more so because the province was paying £444 annually to a college which had tests that only a fifth of the population could meet. "Upwards of thirty years' experience has convinced all of us . . . that every attempt to give or retain exclusive privileges to the Church of England has invariably operated to its disadvantage."[37]

Even while expressing gratitude for the removal of the restrictions upon colonial trade, the assembly had one last complaint against the customs house. Its officers continued to deduct their salaries from the revenues derived from the British statutes still remaining for the regulation of trade before paying the proceeds into the provincial treasury. The lower house objected to this infringement of its constitutional rights and to its being treated the same as colonies having no legislatures. Its position was that all the duties should be under its control and that it should provide for the salaries of the customs officials as it thought appropriate. Otherwise, it had been a session marked by optimism and great expectations, too much so for the judges behind the scenes. Chief Justice Blowers, a quiet spectator of the excited activity, could not rejoice because of "the impropriety of involving the province in a heavy debt for posterity to suffer under." Mr. Justice Stewart thought that Nova Scotia was likely to come out well if "our Statesmen would let well enough alone." The recent "explosion" in Europe had brought speculators to their senses, "but here the Child does not dread the fire . . . Canals, Steam Boats, and all sorts of projects and companies are beginning to show their heads among us, and will continue to rise, in spite of the warnings of a few *cool old men*, till the day of reckoning comes."[38]

When the legislature met in 1827 twenty of the forty-one members were new following the elections for the Thirteenth General Assembly. George Renny Young, editor of the *Novascotian*, attributed the large turnover to dissatisfaction with the previous assembly's failure to promote commercial undertakings. Among the new members Alexander Stewart, Thomas Chandler Haliburton, John Homer, and Beamish Murdoch became well known, although only Stewart remained a member for long. This year Kempt was almost ecstatic as he detailed the progress in almost every branch of industry. If Nova Scotians took advantage of the province's situation and resources, he said, it could not "fail to attain a high state of commercial and agricultural prosperity."

It was a session of exceptional oratory. Fairbanks launched out at the absurdity of letting the customs officers pay their salaries out of the imperial duties. Of the £20,000 they had collected the previous year they had retained about £10,000. Was it not extravagant to give £100 to collect £100? Opposing him, Haliburton described as ungrateful the attempt to wring a further concession from Britain when it was conferring a favour. To make his point, he presented an allegorical picture of the family of John Bull. There was "his eldest son — our brother Jonathan, who, when he came of age, struck his father," and there was Nova Scotia, the youngest, favourite child who, Haliburton hoped, would be "the dutiful one."[39] Although he convulsed the house with laughter, he lost the vote by nineteen to fifteen. Haliburton led the assembly in demanding the complete removal of the oaths against popery and transubstantiation. "Who," he asked, "created magna charta? Who established judges, trial by jury, magistrates, sheriffs, etc.? Catholics! To that calumniated people we were indebted for all that we most boasted of." Beamish Murdoch called it "the most splendid piece of declamation that it has ever been my fortune to listen to."[40]

Three continuing questions involving differences between the council and assembly remained unresolved. When the council turned down the assembly's common school bill, Haliburton again put his talents for allegory to use, calling the councillors "twelve dignified, deep read, pensioned, old ladies, . . . filled with prejudices and whims like all other antiquated spinsters . . . Two-thirds of them have never been beyond Sackville Bridge, and think all the world is contained within the narrow precincts of Halifax."[41] An assembly which was generally satisfied with its relations with the council and did not wish to disturb the status quo responded to that body's dire threats by censuring Haliburton. On the perennial question of fishery bounties the assembly was back to its old proposal of payments based on the tonnage of fishing vessels, something which was anathema to the council and which it rejected out of hand.

Pictou Academy lost another round in 1827. Exasperated by their setbacks, Principal Thomas McCulloch and his supporters presented a strongly worded petition which contrasted the position of King's College with their own, "fettered with restraints and embarrassed with difficulties injurious to its success." Over the single dissent of Robie, the council dismissed the petition with some indignation. Had not the founders of the academy stated that they had no desire to set up an opposition to King's College? Were they not adopting a course which would "excite a spirit of hostility to the Established Church among all classes of Dissenters" at a time when the governors of King's were seeking to remove the tests which excluded dissenters? Indicating its attitude towards McCulloch personally, the council expressed a willingness to endow the academy permanently provided that the governor appointed its trustees. Only three councillors of eleven voted to give the academy £400 for even one year. This session the judges behind the scenes thought that Kempt had managed the legislature with no little tact. Mr. Justice Stewart had only one fault to find with his politics, his indulgence to his "spoiled child" Cape Breton, which never ceased to whine and cry.

In opening his last session in February 1828, Kempt expressed satisfaction that the revenues had been sufficient to pay off a quarter of the provincial debt. He had only one regret, that the fishery was not supplying adequate quantities for export. Once again the assembly ran up against the council which elaborated its usual argument with added detail: that bounties be granted to merchantable fish sent to South America in Nova Scotia ships, from which they could easily secure cargoes for European ports, from which in turn they could bring needed exports to Halifax.

Eventually the two houses compromised on a bounty of £5,000 for each of three years, which met some of the stipulations of both houses.

The governor asked for a change in the education act of 1826 which had been generally unsuccessful in increasing the number of schools and students. Again the two houses reached an accommodation which left intact the clauses relating to compulsory assessment and added provisions only slightly more effectual than the old. This year the Pictou Academy question took a turn which would prove to be the institution's death knell. Hitherto the differences within the Presbyterians of Pictou between McCulloch's Secessionists and Church of Scotland Kirkmen had not manifested themselves strongly in petitions to the council, but in 1828 the Kirkmen expressed in bitter terms their dissatisfaction with the academy's management. With obvious pleasure the majority of council declared that it would not provide funds as long as the academy remained under the incumbent trustees.

The previous session Kempt had expressed dissatisfaction with the disposition of the road moneys and in 1828 he outlined his recommendations in detail. None was in a better position to do it since he had travelled almost continually in fine weather and knew the province's roads better than anyone. His proposals were that commissioners chosen for their ability and intelligence assume the responsibility for expenditures on the great roads, and that the surveyors of highways have control over the minute sums for the cross roads and combine them with the statute labour which they administered. The assembly went along with the first proposal, but it was too much to expect it to surrender what it prized most by accepting the second. Perhaps disguising his true feelings, but entirely characteristic of his *modus operandi*, Kempt approved the assembly's "caution and prudence in not adopting the other part of the Plan while you entertain doubts either as to the practicability or expediency of carrying it into effect."[42]

By August Kempt was off to Quebec to succeed Dalhousie, who had been having difficulties with Papineau and the assembly of Lower Canada. In dedicating his *Historical and Statistical Account of Nova Scotia* to him, Thomas Chandler Haliburton pointed out that in eight years he had never had "the slightest misunderstanding with either of the Branches of the Legislature." Mr. Justice Stewart agreed that "we cannot have a better

Governor." Michael Wallace, he thought, could carry on for a while as administrator, but he was "very old, and very unwieldy. Neither his mind nor his body will last much longer."

In maintaining harmony in Nova Scotia two factors helped Kempt greatly. One was the *modus vivendi* in the voting of supplies, arrived at two decades earlier, which was especially pleasing to the country assemblymen. The other was the nature of the assemblies with which he had to deal. The leading members of the Thirteenth General Assembly, Archibald, Fairbanks, Stewart, Murdoch, and Haliburton — all articulate lawyers — conducted stirring debates on Catholic disabilities, quit rents, customs house salaries, and Pictou Academy, but none of them questioned the ethos of the governmental system. Even before Kempt left, however, Jotham Blanchard and the "Pictou Scribblers" had begun to publish the *Colonial Patriot* and it would shortly challenge the system at its foundation. A few weeks later Joseph Howe took over the *Novascotian* and, influenced in part by the Scribblers, he would in time embark on a similar course. Nova Scotia was in for two decades of political ferment.

CHAPTER 5

"Not a Pane of Glass Broken"

Since the second decade of the nineteenth century Nova Scotia had been undergoing what Dr. D.C. Harvey has called an "intellectual awakening." His picture is that of Nova Scotians rubbing the sleep out of their eyes after 1812 until by 1835 they were thoroughly awake. Once aroused to the strength and weakness of their birthright, they were "eager to overhaul the entire ship of state, from the keel of commerce to the captain on the bridge." The new attitudes manifested themselves first in trade and industry, then in literary forms, and only lastly in politics.[1] Late in 1828, at the beginning of the awakening in politics to which he would contribute nothing, Sir Peregrine Maitland took over the governorship. Lord Dalhousie described him as "tall, thin, and silent; very well bred & gentlemanlike"; his wife Lady Sarah as "a thin delicate little person, with a most sweet & engaging cast of countenance."

The contrast between Maitland and Kempt could not have been more striking. A "gloomy Methodist in religious points," Maitland put "an end to . . . unseemly orgies" and, according to one admirer, he and his wife "produced a change in the tone of the community, and the perfume of their sweet lives permeated all classes of the people."[2] In activity, too, Maitland stood at the opposite pole from Kempt. Before he arrived Andrew Belcher reported that he would not be "so active and decided as his predecessors"; after the session in 1829 Mr. Justice Stewart agreed that he was unlikely to "make himself as uneasy about the machine, as Sir James." Retiring and reserved, he seemed uninterested in becoming highly knowledgeable about Nova

Scotia and things appeared to go on much the same as if he were not there. Mostly he was content with acting as a channel of communication between the colonial secretary and the provincial legislature. Perhaps it was just as well, for as governor of Upper Canada he had established a reputation for being hostile to political reform.

With one exception the session of 1829 was largely a repetition of previous ones. The usual differences arose on the spending of road moneys. The council again demanded the removal of the incumbent trustees before it considered a permanent grant to Pictou Academy and refused to vote any money to enable it to pay off its debts. The two houses disagreed as usual on the practicality of requiring fish eligible for bounties to be shipped in British vessels to South American and European ports. Some assembly-men wanted Britain to give up quit rents without compensation, others sought a compromise. The assembly agreed to provide £6,430 9s. annually to defray the salaries of the customs officers, but insisted, despite the council, on clauses which declared that it had the sole right to appropriate all duties, taxes, and impositions levied on Nova Scotians.

The one exceptional, indeed spectacular, event of the session had to do with John Alexander Barry. When he intimated that a fellow assemblyman had consorted with smugglers and refused to apologize, he was excluded from the house. Thereupon he followed a course so defiant and unyielding that eventually he was expelled as a member and imprisoned for the rest of the session. In the earlier stages, when the Assembly reprimanded the editors of the *Acadian Recorder* and *Free Press* for cautioning it about going too far, Joseph Howe warned that "if Editors are brought for offences to the Bar of the House, Legislators may depend upon this — that they will be brought, individually and collectively, to a bitter expiation before the bar of the public." Later some assemblymen were confronted by an excited group of people — Howe called it a Tory mob — and were "hooted and hissed along the streets, pelted with snow, mud, stones and other missiles, and assailed by every opprobrious expression that could be vented by a heedless and unthinking rabble." The assembly quickly reasserted its authority and the "Barry riots" passed into the folklore of the province.[3] But the incident again demonstrated that the lower house would not be slow in asserting its privileges.

The General Assembly met in 1830 without sign of contention or crisis. In the absence of Maitland for reasons of health, Michael Wallace took over as administrator. Wanting the legislature to run well, he showed nothing but his best side. Aged eighty-two and unwell, he hoped, in accordance with the normal hereditary transmission of office, to have his son Charles Hill Wallace succeed him as treasurer of the province. Treating him better than he had ever treated it, the assembly joined in a joint address that his wishes be met and eventually they were. An indication of general prosperity was the voting of £25,000 for roads and bridges. The assembly declined, however, to cancel the loan of £5,000 to Dalhousie College although it did extend it for three years. It also refused the British government's offer to commute the quit rents for an annual contribution of £2,000 towards specific colonial expenses still borne by the parliamentary grant. On education, the council again denied a grant to Pictou Academy and the assembly learned that although the number of schools had increased under the act of 1828, it had been largely through subscription, not assessment. Following Catholic emancipation in Britain the Nova Scotia legislature took similar action and removed all Catholic disabilities. Generally the session was harmonious until the Brandy Dispute convulsed it.

To understand the significance of the dispute (or lack of it) in the movement for responsible government it is necessary to put it in context. Nothing remotely resembling radical politics made an appearance in Nova Scotia until the *Colonial Patriot* of Pictou saw the light of day on December 7, 1827. Although it was rarely extreme and "certainly not violent . . . it was a fresh new breeze, alien to anything in the provincial experience." In a matter of weeks the *Patriot* and its "Scribblers," especially Jotham Blanchard, were clashing with Joseph Howe, who had taken over the *Novascotian* at the beginning of 1828 while still a pronounced conservative. In the light of subsequent events it seems clear that as a result of these exchanges Howe began to peer more deeply into the innermost processes of Nova Scotian politics. "Over the next few years the interplay between Blanchard and .. Howe did as much as anything to bring substantial change in Howe's political stance," and did, in fact, help to "turn him from the error of his ways." In April 1829 Blanchard began to publish in weekly instalments the first detailed examination of the working of the province's institutions. By July, when Howe started his legislative reviews, he had undoubtedly read Blanchard's denunciation of the "system of grandeeism and grasping" which had grown up around the council and which had enabled it to extend its influence over every segment of society. The two sets of writings were quite different in style. Blanchard was partisan and argumentative; Howe was moderate and judicious, and he weakened his case with reservations and qualifications. Yet many of his arguments were much like those of Blanchard. Clearly his open-mindedness had permitted a marked transformation in his views.[4]

On the Brandy Dispute he and Blanchard were as one. It began innocently enough when in 1830 the assembly sought to correct an error in a revenue law. Four years earlier it thought that it had imposed a duty of 2s. 4d. a gallon on brandy, but through a technicality the amount collected was only 2s. a gallon. On the ground of affording relief to commerce the council twice rejected a bill designed to implement the assembly's original intention. Why it chose this particular time to disturb a long-standing accommodation is something of a mystery, but John Young believed that it fitted in with the council's plans to assert a more forceful role in money matters and especially with its aim to reduce expenditures from £60,000 to £45,000, mostly through a reduction in the road vote. In the assembly Speaker Archibald descended from the rostrum to argue that by the law and constitution of Britain and by practice in Nova Scotia the people's representatives had the sole, inherent, and inalienable right to originate all revenue bills, free from amendment. The council argued that it had never abandoned its right to reject money bills, although the manner in which this dispute developed made it appear as if it were seeking to amend a money bill. In any case the council found itself decidedly on the defensive.

In the assembly only R.J. Uniacke, Jr., Lawrence Hartshorne, and John Barry supported the council; the others would not budge even though it meant the loss of the appropriation bill. Cruel blow for him though it was, Michael Wallace had no choice but to prorogue the legislature. Maitland returned undecided what to do, summon the General Assembly or dissolve it. He had not made up his mind when the death of King George IV forced a dissolution. To the youthful Joseph Howe making the third of his rambles two things were apparent. The loss of at least £25,000 in road money was having a devastating effect upon the provincial economy. Some of the newer settlers, in the absence of road work, were even reduced to eating their seed grains and potatoes. Howe also reported that he could discover no one who defended the council, a finding borne out by the election results. Only one assemblyman who had defied the council failed to win. That was in Halifax Township, where Beamish Murdoch lost to pro-council Stephen Deblois. In part, Murdoch's defeat was due to his own "unguarded utterances." Irritated by an opponent of Loyalist parentage, he had commented acerbically on the Loyalist "scum" who monopolized the public offices. But the victory of Deblois was due mostly to the behind-the-scenes influence exercised by the merchant-official oligarchy of Halifax.

One of the most memorable contests in provincial history occurred in the sprawling county of Halifax, which included the districts of Halifax, Colchester, and Pictou. There the council's candidates, Hartshorne, Barry, Starr, and Blackadar, faced three former assemblymen, S.G.W. Archibald, George Smith, and William Lawson, and the newcomer Jotham Blanchard. Because of merchant influence, the council candidates started off well in Halifax, only to be overwhelmed in Colchester, the bailiwick of Speaker Archibald. Until then the election had been peaceful, but it would not remain so in Pictou, where Blanchard had been a main opponent of the Kirkmen and where their clergymen actually mounted the hustings to harangue the electorate. A party of sailors, armed with sticks and carrying the council's banners, precipitated a riot which led to one death. Although the council's candidates polled well in Pictou, they could not overcome the majorities built up in Colchester.[5]

Some have suggested that the Brandy Dispute marked the beginning of the struggle for responsible government. At first Howe himself attributed more significance to it than it deserved. Actually, however, scores of people who later came to be Tories had joined in a general reaction against the council's heavy-handed action. Hence the movement for responsible government which developed over the next half-dozen years had at most only a tenuous connection with the Brandy Dispute. Likely it had much more effect on the disposition of public offices. Some who watched Brenton Halliburton lead the council and S.G.W.

Archibald the assembly on this question treated it as part of their contention for the chief justiceship. R.J. Uniacke, Sr., had been a third contender to succeed aged and ailing Sampson Salter Blowers, but he had died early in 1830. When Halliburton eventually won out, some attributed it to his performing Blowers' work over a long period; others were certain that Archibald's support of the popular cause destroyed his chances. But the colonial secretary insisted, despite Maitland, that Archibald succeed Uniacke as attorney general.

When the General Assembly met later in 1830, the council accepted the additional duty of fourpence a gallon on brandy with an appropriate face-saving explanation. But on Pictou Academy, fishery bounties, and marriage licences, it showed itself to be no more accommodating than before. Once again it demanded that the academy have new trustees and drew a negative response from the assembly. Early in 1831 Jotham Blanchard carried the trustees' case to London only to be countered by Maitland behind the scenes. In 1829, on a visit to Pictou, he had expressed great enthusiasm for McCulloch's conduct of the academy; in August 1831, won over to the council's views, he told Lord Goderich that the Kirk deserved well of the government for its attachment to king, country, and British institutions. The outcome was that Goderich instructed Maitland in the vaguest of language to give "equal consideration" to both parties in reaching a reconciliation.

Under pressure from London to resolve the question, the General Assembly dealt with it for the final time in 1832. On the crucial question of trustees the assembly may have thought that it had won the victory, for seven of the thirteen were to be incumbents, five were to be appointed by the governor, and the thirteenth was to be the Catholic bishop. But when the governor nominated Rev. Kenneth McKenzie, Rev. Donald Fraser, and two other equally violent Kirk men, he doomed the academy. Henceforth the trustees' meetings became verbal battlegrounds in which the Kirkmen's main interest seemed to be that of getting rid of McCulloch. Enrollment went down and tuition revenue decreased. McCulloch left shortly to become president of Dalhousie College and his academy would never achieve the status he had wanted.[6] Any suggestion that the long conflict surrounding Pictou Academy had much to do with the start of the movement for responsible government is misleading for in this case, too, the connection between the two is very tenuous. Although the assembly failed on other matters in 1832, it at least settled the long drawn-out question of marriage licences much as the dissenters wanted it.

The session of 1832 was to be Maitland's last. Earlier Joseph Howe had wondered why Providence had sometimes seen fit to send us "a Governor too indolent or too reserved to mix with and understand the people — too fond of domestic retirement and of the pleasures of art, to busy himself more than he can help with the cares of government — and too much disposed to the opinion that a man's loyalty depends a good deal on the forms of religion he adopts, and the order of parsons he pays." A little later Howe even suggested that if His Majesty removed Maitland, "it would rank among the popular acts of the new reign."[7] For him to treat the king's representative with such disrespect at this stage of his career was extraordinary. After Maitland had left, one public servant declared that he seemed less anxious for the cares of the province than "for a safe passage to a better world." Undeniably he left with few laments.

The year 1832 was the first in which Joseph Howe put on the general trappings of a reformer. Some believe that his part in the winning of responsible government has been exaggerated. Yet more than in any other province the accomplishment was that of one man. Blanchard and the Scribblers had forced him to peer into the motive forces of Nova Scotia society and the more deeply he peered the less he liked what he saw. Between 1832 and 1834 two matters in particular — the interrelated bank and currency issues and the civil list and quit rent questions — let him see the weaknesses of the council and assembly in their utter nakedness as he reported the debates. In 1832 he was hoping, as an entrepreneur and borrower, to have the Bank of Nova Scotia incorporated by legislative charter so as to provide competition to the Halifax Banking Company, which had "flourished like the green bay tree." It appalled him to find that a self-serving council, which included five directors of that company, had inserted highly stringent precautions with the result that the new bank started up with "more safeguards against disaster than any bank of its time in British North America." Over the next two years he became more outraged as the difficulty of coping with a serious recession worsened because of an inundation of paper money resulting from the manipulations of bankers, councillors, and assemblymen. The experience taught him that "even in idyllic Nova Scotia the machinations of individuals in their own interest took the same form and manifested the same subtlety as in more complex societies, and that the assemblymen themselves became part and parcel of the process."[8]

Before 1833 the British government had sought to eliminate or reduce the parliamentary grant which still supported the salaries of the governor, provincial secretary, and some of the judiciary. In September that year the colonial secretary offered to give up quit rents and the casual and territorial revenues of the Crown in return for appropriate salaries for the public officers still paid by Parliament. Some assemblymen were willing to provide salaries of such dimensions that they prompted Howe and others into angry denunciation. By the next session the new governor, Sir Colin Campbell, had arrived with instructions to withdraw the offer to surrender the casual revenues for a civil list and to begin the collection of quit rents unless the legislature, at an early session, agreed to commute them for an annual payment of £2,000. Late in 1834 Howe and John Young begged the assembly not to let Nova Scotia be the first colony to accept commutation for an alleged equivalent. But even members like Herbert Huntington of Yarmouth, destined to be the most resolute of reformers, hearkened to the pleas of their constituents not to let the tax-gatherer loose among them and the assembly agreed to commutation, the money to be made applicable to the governor's salary. The debate led to bitter exchanges between Howe and Alexander Stewart, who took another step in his odyssey from a liberal to the most reactionary of Tories.

Howe's peep below the surface into local government eventually precipitated his direct entry into politics. As a grand juror in 1832, he quickly discovered that "much was not well in this supposedly best of all possible worlds." Typical was the hopeless state of the accounts of the Halifax county treasurer William Cleaveland, but try as it might the grand jury could not have him removed. It did refuse to levy an assessment for 1833 on the ground that, if economies were effected and back taxes collected, the funds available would be more than sufficient to meet the county's needs. In 1834 the grand jurors were of the same mould as in 1832 and middle-class frustration during a period of economic recession spurred them on. Publisher Howe had determined that this time the sessions would not escape even though his father and half-brother were magistrates. On November 6 he warned that unless someone dealt with the ills in local government, "a large part of our people are nearly prepared . . to resist." Throughout December he printed memorials and presentments of the grand jury which were sweeping in their indictment of the sessions. Then, on January 1, 1835, he published a letter which alleged that "from the pockets of the poor and distressed at least £1,000 is drawn annually, and pocketed by men whose services the country might well spare" and that during the last thirty years "the Magistracy and Police have, by one stratagem or other, taken from the pockets of the people, in over exactions, fines, etc. etc., a sum that would exceed in the gross amount of £30,000."

As a result, on March 2 and 3 he faced a Supreme Court jury charged with criminal libel in what was to be the most celebrated of all Nova Scotian trials. The law was completely against him. As it then stood, it was libellous to publish any matter calculated to degrade a person or disturb the public peace and the truth of the charge could not be a defence. But he had things going for him too. He suspected that middle-class Haligonians, some of whom had recently served on grand juries, would be unlikely to convict him. Also, as a layman pleading his own case, he anticipated that he would be allowed to present an unorthodox defence denied to a practising attorney. So repeatedly, as he addressed the jury, he asked if he would not have failed in his duty of keeping the peace had he not acquainted the public with the ills in local government. Under this guise he could bring in the case of Richard Tremain, a commissioner of the Poor Asylum, who had furnished inferior goods at an exorbitant price to an institution he helped to regulate; also, that of assemblyman and magistrate W.H. Roach, the acting commissioner of Bridewell, who had used that institution, its employees, and its inmates as his own property. "He was in truth like the ruler in Scripture, who said to one 'go, and he goeth; and to another do this, and he doeth it'." Concluding with the promise that "while I live, Nova Scotia shall have the blessing of an open and unshackled press,"

Howe, who previously had spoken only occasionally in public, "emerged, almost overnight, as a full-blown orator."[9]

Disregarding the law as stated by Chief Justice Halliburton and principal prosecutor, S.G.W. Archibald, the jury took only ten minutes to acquit Howe. Always a conservative reformer, he still saw no need to effect fundamental changes in local government provided that the governor and council used care in appointing magistrates. But when Sir Colin Campbell chose Halifax lawyer William Q. Sawers as *custos rotulorum* or ranking magistrate and the supervisor of the police establishment, he altered his stance. To Howe Sawers was notoriously deficient in order and regularity, wont to mingle in street affrays, and had no redeeming virtues. To him it was equally apparent that Campbell, like Maitland before him, had become ensnared by his council. Even a conservative reformer had finally come to accept the need for far-reaching change.

For the next while Howe repeated without let up that the first step towards reform was to elect the right kind of assembly. That meant getting rid of the existing "vile system of deception and chicane, backed by a profuse outpouring of bad rum and porter." The proper course, he insisted, was to have the freeholders assemble well in advance of the elections, choose suitable candidates, and make it clear that they were selected because of their principles and would be replaced for failure to follow them. He was elated when the inhabitants of the three Musquodoboit settlements followed that course in choosing him. How much better it was than to have candidates ride over the county for a month, "thrusting themselves into every man's house . . . and telling as many lies as would . . . overwhelm a man of spirit with shame." Sir Colin Campbell dissolved the General Assembly in mid-October 1836, a year early, for fear that a seventh session might prove intractable. But he had waited until the colonial secretary had confirmed the long-sought division of Halifax and Annapolis Counties, and Howe would therefore be running in the new and smaller county of Halifax.

It was an election the likes of which Nova Scotia had never before seen. This time candidates were judged in public meetings. In Annapolis one such meeting refused even to consider the claims of sitting member W.H. Roach. The election cards exhibited a marked difference in tone. Instead of merely promising to behave well if elected, the candidates spelled out their principles. In Annapolis Samuel B. Chipman stood for "a General Reform"; in Kings Augustus Tupper presented himself as "the Working Men's Representative"; in Colchester Isaac Logan advocated the ballot, triennial parliaments, a reformed council, and provincial control of the casual and territorial revenues. Howe himself wanted Nova Scotians to enjoy the same rights as "our brethren across the water." In England one vote in the Commons turned out a ministry; in Nova Scotia it might be defeated five hundred times and yet remain unmoved, "like an ancient Egyptian mummy . . . dead and inanimate — but yet, likely to last forever." All he asked for was "what exists at home — a system of responsibility to the people, extending through all the Departments supported at the public expense."

In Halifax Howe easily outdistanced all the other candidates and elsewhere the results were to his liking. In Cumberland Alexander Stewart had come close to defeat; in Annapolis Roach, who was injudicious enough to run, quickly withdrew. Howe could not tell if the cause of reform had a majority, but if not, "a pretty strong fighting minority . . . [would] see that the Officials and their defenders [did] not have things all their own way." The reformers of pre-election days had become a full-blown Reform party and Reformers almost overnight. It had been largely Howe's doing. Because of Jotham Blanchard's illness, the *Colonial Patriot* had exercised little or no influence since the early 1830s. Although the *Acadian Recorder* had made a useful contribution editorially, the *Novascotian* had altogether outdistanced it in circulation and influence. Through his newspaper Howe had devised both the strategy and tactics which had contributed most to the successes of the popular cause in 1836.[10]

The time of testing arrived when the Fifteenth General Assembly met early in 1837. The reforming assemblymen, almost all of them inexperienced, needed leadership. The found it, in the early stages, in Howe and Lawrence O'Connor Doyle, who turned to good advantage the expertise he had developed in pressing Irish causes. The battle did not become joined until the council spurned an assembly resolution which condemned it for failing to open its doors to the public. John Young, always wanting to be perceived as a reformer but not a radical, proposed conciliatory resolutions in reply. Then "the conviction flashed on [Howe's] mind that the time was come" to act boldly. Accordingly he moved to replace Young's resolutions with his own Twelve Resolutions. Basically they contended that the council's composition and mode of operation led to gross injustices and that nothing would change so long as it contained eight members of the established church including its bishop; a chief justice who was regarded as the head of a political party; five members with a close family connection; and five who were partners in the same bank.

The divisions on the resolutions indicated that the Reformers outnumbered their opponents by twenty-six to twenty. But Howe could not always rely on their votes. Sometimes he was "at the mercy of . . . the men of no decided leaning — no fixed principles — the lovers of peace at all hazards — the timid or the indifferent," those whom he would later dub "loose fish."[11] Nonetheless, the assembly accepted the tenth resolution, which referred to "the disposition evinced by some of [the councillors] to protect their interests and emoluments at the expense of the public." Three days later the blow struck: an ultimatum from the council to break off relations unless the assembly disavowed it. To the dismay of some Reformers and the taunts of the Tories Howe had all the resolutions rescinded. Again it was the action of a conservative reformer. Having witnessed the serious harm done to the rural communities by the loss of the appropriation act in 1830, he did not want a repetition. But it would be a temporary defeat. "Do Gentlemen suppose for a moment that I would consent to rescind these Resolutions, if they were not to rise again in another shape?"

Once the appropriations were secure, the Reformers had the assembly approve an address to the Crown which was a carbon copy of the Twelve Resolutions except in two respects. One was the deletion of the words which the council found most offensive. More significantly, Howe added a second alternative for remedying the main defect in the constitution. Previously he had suggested an elective legislative council in the hope that two popular houses would exercise a salutary effect upon the executive. Now he proposed as an alternative the separation of the executive from the legislative council, hoping by introducing some assemblymen into the former and by making the latter more representative to secure many of the benefits of the British constitution. Apparently he was unaware that in Upper Canada Robert Baldwin was advocating the full British system of responsibility. As for Howe, he rejected outright any idea of turning the executive council into an English-type ministry holding office only while it retained the confidence of the assembly. "I am afraid that . . . this Province . . . is scarcely prepared for the erection of such machinery — I doubt whether it would work well here."

In 1837 Doyle's oratorical talents were highly useful, but he would always be lacking in balance, moderation, and prudence; Herbert Huntington, never much of an orator, had not yet reached the position where his consistency and integrity would let him exercise a kind of moral leadership; William Young, like his father John and his brother George Renny, would never overcome a common belief that he put self-interest before the public good. So, from the outset, the reform cause was largely identified with Howe by friend and foe alike. Writers in the Tory *Times* of Halifax called him the Papineau of Nova Scotia and even said that his radicalism was only "a few removes from thát which provoked the attempts of Fieschi, Alibaud and others" to overthrow the French state.

Somewhat naively Howe believed that things remained as they were because the British authorities did not appreciate the situation in Nova Scotia. He thought that they were learning when in 1838, on orders from Britain, Sir Colin Campbell constituted two distinct councils and put four assemblymen, including the Reformer Huntington, in the executive council. Lord Glenelg, the colonial secretary, also ordered Campbell to avoid even the appearance of favouritism towards the Church of England in appointing councillors, to exclude all judges from the executive council, and to appoint not more than one member of any commercial concern to that council. The Reformers had only one fault to find with the dispatches: the large salaries demanded for the surrender of the casual revenues. Nevertheless, the *Acadian Recorder* described them as *"no mean Charters of the Rights and Privileges of Nova Scotia."*

Later, when the reality differed markedly from the appearance, disillusionment crept in, especially after the Reformers discovered that the new executive council recognized no degree of responsibility other than to act as a channel of communication between the government and the assembly. They also perceived that the old influences had been at work behind the scenes in Campbell's choice of councillors. The final blow struck when it became necessary, because of a difference in the instructions to Campbell and those to Charles Poulett Thomson, the new governor general, to reduce the size of the council and Huntington, the only genuine Reformer in the executive council, lost his seat. Howe still remained confident because of his sympathetic hearing at the hands of Glenelg in London during the summer of 1838. Hence the latter's dispatch which became public knowledge in mid-January 1839 was as crushing as it was unexpected. One year Glenelg's reply had spoken "the language of freedom . . . the next the dictatorial style of a master to his slave."

Among other things he defended Campbell's appointees to the legislative council and made a much more limited offer for the surrender of the casual revenues. To the Reformers he left not even a glimmer of hope for the acceptance of their basic position. But Howe did not place the blame on Glenelg or the British government. He attributed it partly to colonials who used their direct access to the Colonial Office to promote their personal interest by defending the established system. But he also saw the fine hand of Campbell at work. He was right, for behind the scenes the governor called it tragic that in a province without real grievances "two or three designing men" were determined to "excite discontent and make the people believe they are oppressed by their rulers." Had not the time come, he wondered, for "arresting their onward course towards Democracy"? As the assembly debated its next course, the main clash was between Howe, who had been self-taught and exposed to the crudities and vulgarities of the less genteel, and James Boyle Uniacke, who had enjoyed the best in education and lived life under the most refined circumstances. Their exchanges "rank high among the oratorical spectaculars of the Nova Scotia House of Assembly." The outcome was a decision to send Huntington and William Young to present the assembly's case in London.

The year 1839 was most significant, however, in having the Reformers finally decide on the form of government they wanted. Late in March the Durham Report arrived in Nova Scotia and a single reading made Howe a convert to its ideas. His open mind

James Boyle Uniacke   1848-54

Courtesy of N.S. Museum

let Durham persuade him that a British-type executive was entirely appropriate to Nova Scotia. Week after week he published excerpts indicating his agreement with the basic principles of the *Report*. But his major summer work was determined for him when the new colonial secretary, Lord John Russell, rejected

Durham's recommendations while introducing his bill for the union of the Canadas. In four lengthy letters to Russell Howe argued that English rule was being reversed in the colonies by the omission of a principle which was the cornerstone of the British constitution. Did it really matter to the people of England "whether half-a-dozen persons, in whom the majority have confidence, . . . manage our local affairs; or the same number selected from the minority and whose policy the bulk of the population distrust? . . . Would England be weaker, less prosperous or less respected, because the people of Nova Scotia were satisfied and happy?" What had Nova Scotians done to justify the alienation of their birthright? "We seek for nothing more than British subjects are entitled to; but we will be contented with nothing else."[12]

For the Reformers the delegation to Britain had been a last resort. When Huntington and Young returned almost empty-handed, they were in a dilemma about what to do next. Fate presented an opportunity which they did not miss. In a dispatch of October 16, 1839 to Charles Poulett Thomson (soon to be Lord Sydenham) Lord John Russell had stated that the tenure of colonial officers was one during good behaviour and that they might be required to retire whenever public policy suggested its desirability. To Howe it meant that colonial governors were intended to follow the basic Durham proposal and statements by Thomson and New Brunswick's lieutenant-governor, Sir John Harvey, appeared to confirm it. So in February 1840, when Sir Colin Campbell took no action, the assembly passed an address pointing out that the executive council did not possess its confidence. The result was unexpected, even dramatic. J.B. Uniacke agreed with Sir John Harvey's interpretation of Russell's dispatch and declared his willingness to "try the experiment" because the British government had ordered it. Thus in one fell swoop the Tories had lost their brightest ornament. The Reformers might have suffered a similar loss as a result of one of Howe's statements during the debate. He had said that the boys in his printing shop, "with [their] black faces, but brains above them," were no less gifted than the John Halliburtons, the Tom Jefferys, and Master Inglises. For those words he fought a duel near the old tower in Point Pleasant Park on March 14 with John Halliburton, the son of the chief justice. Halliburton fired first and missed; Howe fired into the air and it was all over. Howe had what he wanted: "the perfect independence . . . to explain or apologize — to fight or refuse, in future."

When Campbell replied — correctly it turned out — that he could find no fundamental constitutional change in Russell's dispatch, the Reformers bided their time to save the province from injury through the loss of supply. Then in the closing days of the session, March 24 and 25, came a flurry of resolutions ascribing the failure to implement Russell's dispatch to Campbell himself and an address drafted by Howe himself demanding his recall. For a son of Loyalist John Howe to treat the queen's representative in this way was astounding and Howe admitted that he did it "with a heavy heart." Still, even a conservative reformer may have to resort to extreme action when all else fails.

The sequel was a "government agitation" in which Tory writers became positively apoplectic about the treatment of the governor. The Reformers' response, an open meeting on March 30, saw the direct entrance into the political arena of executive and legislative councillor James W. Johnston. An Anglican turned Baptist, he had influence among a body which had hitherto generally supported the Reformers. More significantly, he gave the Tories the articulate, respected spokesman whom they were lacking. Generally he has been treated as a moderate conservative and certainly he was that in tone and manner. But on key issues such as the preservation of the vested rights of incumbent officials he appeared no less determined than the most reactionary of Tories. His clashes with Howe at the public meeting set the tone of their confrontation over the next seven years. When he stated that radical changes were uncalled for in a colony that was as free as air in the exercise of religious and political opinions, Howe accused him of preferring "the tranquil reign of irresponsibility" to a government based on public confidence. When Johnston prophesied that, because of the absence of great questions in Nova Scotia, the party struggle would become one merely for power and patronage, Howe referred to a dozen questions of internal policy as important to Nova Scotians as those which had brought down British governments since 1688.

Towards the end of April general consternation followed the arrival at the Colonial Office of the address for Campbell's removal. /What was well-ordered Nova Scotia up to? Russell decided that the easiest course was to have Thomson come to Halifax and "with his 'wand' and his 'star' and his magic touch" arrange a settlement on the spot. Even before reaching Halifax Thomson, with his usual certitude, was convinced that petty, personal ambition and imprudent management of public affairs, not real grievances, were at the source of the province's troubles. Seemingly Howe fell "insensibly . . . beneath [Thomson's] spell"; certainly he accepted the argument that as a good Briton it was his duty to promote tranquillity and set an example for the unruly Canadians. But to suggest as Thomson did that he had "made the amende honorable" and publicly "eschewed his heresies" on responsible government was simply not so. He did agree, at least for the moment, to the type of ministry which was Thomson's peculiar contribution to colonial politics — one in which "the governor was to govern, and the Executive Councillors were to be the governor's 'placemen' . . . diverting men's minds from awkward abstractions." He did not, however, interpret Thomson's scheme that way. As he saw it, the council would have to defend the governor's acts or resign; accordingly any governor would be an idiot who did not give due weight to his councillors' views.

Yet Howe had undoubtedly accepted Thomson's proposals with little consideration of their implications. Would future governors possess the initiative and innovativeness of Thomson? Could any Reformers work in the same team as Alexander Stewart and the extreme Tories? Would he and James McNab be the only genuine Reformers in a newly constituted executive council? In August, he wrote to Thomson in obvious perturbation, only to receive the usual bland assurances. He felt better when he discovered that the governor to effect the specific changes would be Viscount Falkland, "a thorough Whig," apparently in the Thomson mould. But because the executive council which he entered on October 6 contained only two Reformers, he sought to justify his conduct to Huntington. The latter, he said, would be admitted once he had demonstrated that he was "an animal that will run in harness, without upsetting the Council and kicking up [his] heels at the rest of the team."[13] At this stage, however, he would have found it difficult to find any Reformer other than himself who was enthusiastic about the new council. Naturally the Tory *Times* was outraged that men like Jeffery, Collins, Cogswell, and Tobin were being superseded as councillors because they were supposed to constitute an official faction or family compact.

The election which began late in October 1840 was unique. To the extent that a coalition existed it was one of political leaders, not of political forces in the constituencies, where few, if any, candidates presented themselves as coalition candidates. "Thus there was the strange spectacle of Tory opposing Reformer, although both professed to support Lord Falkland's government and neither had more than a hazy idea of the principles on which it was based." Both Huntington and William Young expressed serious doubts about the new régime. Only Howe gave it unequivocal support. "Great changes," he said, had been "wrought, and invaluable principles established . . . by the peaceful agitation of four years, [during] which . . . there has not been a blow struck or a pane of glass broken." When the election was over, the returns were not meaningful. Four years earlier, according to their later voting habits, it had been twenty-eight Reformers to twenty Tories; this time in a larger house it was thirty Reformers to twenty Tories. But nobody could have foretold how they would line up on the executive's proposals.[14]

The testing time of the coalition came in the session of 1841.[15] Because J.B. Uniacke, now an executive councillor, had still not decided which direction to take, Howe became the chief defendant of the new order. But when he boasted that the popular party had won the right to determine who was to carry on the government, Huntington and Young wondered why the majority party in the assembly should be a small minority in the council. Two Tory executive councillors also embarrassed Howe, J.W. Johnston by saying that Nova Scotians "stood as far from direct responsibility as they did four years ago" and Alexander Stewart by declaring that "responsible government, in a Colony, was responsible nonsense." Yet, ebullience itself, Howe boasted of the seven government bills enacted into law. The executive council, however, had not initiated most of them, and the one for the incorporation of Halifax was not everything he wanted since the franchise was limited to eight hundred persons and the right to be elected mayor, alderman, or common councillor to a fraction of that number. Left-wing Reformers, critical of Howe's anti-democratic stance, attributed it to "the company which [he] was now in." On several occasions he had sharp exchanges with Huntington and he must have realized that any successes would be Pyrrhic if they led to his losing his party.

By the time the legislature met in 1842 William Young had become a councillor, but Falkland's ministry continued to deteriorate. Over the opposition of five executive councillors Huntington had the council's bankruptcy bill deferred until the next session. Then Alexander Stewart, whose propensity for mischief-making was unbounded, declared that the only kinds of responsibility in a colony were those of the governor to the colonial secretary and the executive council to the governor. That almost broke up the council, but E.M. Dodd kept it intact by propounding the "Doddean Confession of Faith." If the assembly, after full deliberation on a matter that required responsibility, voted non-confidence in the executive council, either a change in administration or a dissolution would occur; if after an election the assembly had the same opinion, the governor would have to secure other councillors.

To relieve his frustration Howe tried another tack. While his own friends had been silent, the relatives and friends of the Tory councillors had condemned the government in public at every opportunity. Their venom increased when Falkland gave the Reformers a fair share of appointments, even defying the hereditary transmission of offices to do so. They appeared to become even more violent after Sir Robert Peel's Tory government took office in Britain. Apparently Falkland suggested more than once in council that someone should teach the "Obstructives" a lesson. Although Howe's friend John Sparrow Thompson warned him that, "as a person of family, Colonial rank, and of fixed official expectation," he should pursue a "more moderate course," he decided, nonetheless, to "give a dressing" to the Tory worthies. So, between June 22 and August 10 all of Halifax waited, almost with bated breath, as Howe lambasted the Obstructives anonymously in eight "Letters of a Constitutionalist," using his unrivalled knowledge of the specifics of Halifax society and its families to do so. It became savage warfare when Howe's enemies replied in kind against "this issue of a cock's egg — who has so long imposed himself upon the people of Nova Scotia as a *patriot*."

William Young   1854-7, 1860

Courtesy of N.S. Museum

By mid-1842 any idealism in the movement for responsible government had vanished. To the Tories it had become nothing more than a struggle for offices of power and emolument, and to confirm it they pointed to Falkland's appointment of an impecunious Howe as collector of excise in Halifax in order to keep him in politics. Meanwhile Howe's relations with the Baptists were developing on two levels in a way that would markedly affect his own career, the life of the coalition, and the subsequent course of Nova Scotia politics. Personally he favoured a single, non-denominational college and had only reluctantly supported the grant of a charter to Queen's (later Acadia) College in 1839. Two years later he incurred Baptist dislike for his part in reducing a grant to Acadia on the ground that 40,000 Baptists should not receive more than 70,000 Catholics. Much more acrimonious was his dispute with the Baptist Missionary Board over money it owed him for printing its newspaper, the *Christian Messenger*. Richard Nugent, the *enfant terrible* of the Reformers and Howe's successor as proprietor of the *Novascotian*, eventually convinced him that he was being made the victim of an informal Baptist-Tory alliance and that withholding the payment of his account was part of its conspiracy to cripple its chief opponent financially.

Howe went through the session of 1843 unenthusiastically. The day before prorogation Tory J.J. Marshall indicated that at the next session he would move to exclude collectors of customs and excise from the legislature. Howe's retort was to call for "the formation of a Provincial Cabinet, united in sentiment . . . calculated to obtain and secure the confidence of the people." Worried that Howe's statement would be regarded as an attack on his colleagues, Falkland demanded an explanation. Howe replied that, when challenged, he had simply expressed himself in favour of the government by heads of departments which he understood that Falkland would introduce when circumstances permitted. Something more was needed to make a strong administration, he said, than "nine men, treating each other courteously at a round table." Relations between him and Falkland were never the same again. The governor complained to the colonial secretary, Lord Stanley, that the Reformers rejected his dictum that party government was undesirable in "this comparatively petty province." To support his position he sent him Johnston's memorandum on the unwisdom of party government. "Clearly a new star had risen in [his] political firmament."

The session of 1843 witnessed a further escalation in the conflict between the leading Reformers, most of whom favoured a single non-denominational college, and the Baptists, who found themselves spurned in their request for a capital grant for Acadia. This led the *Christian Messenger* to propagate the veiled threat that those who sought to wrest from 40,000 Baptists the education of their off-spring might suffer serious political consequences. In turn Huntington warned against the danger of allowing religious fanaticism to usurp the place of representative government. "The thumbscrew — the scourge — and the rack — have been too recently in operation for mankind to desire such a consummation." While Howe was in the country in October presenting his side of the politico-religious conflict, Falkland dissolved the General Assembly without consulting the Reformers. To Lord Stanley he defended his action as the only means of avoiding the adoption of the party government which the Reformers were certain to force upon him. Henceforth his dispatches pictured Johnston as his hero and Howe as something of a villain. Obviously he was viewing politics and politicians through differently coloured spectacles than previously and there is more than a suspicion that he was trying to curry the favour of a Tory government in Britain.

The election saw J.W. Johnston abandon the legislative council to contest a seat in Annapolis County. This meant that for two decades the province's political battles would be directly joined between him and Howe. Any suggestion that the voters saw the election of 1843 in terms of coalition versus party government, or of acceptance or rejection of the principles of Sydenham and Falkland, would be wrong. In the non-Baptist counties most of the voters appeared to have followed their old partisan attachments and the changes were few: gains for the Reformers of one seat in Richmond and two in Pictou. But in the Baptist belt stretching from Annapolis over into Colchester the Reformers lost eight seats while gaining one. They also lost a seat to Andrew Uniacke in the Township of Halifax because of a temporary split with the Catholics. That loss was crucial since the Tories, by gaining nine seats to the Reformers' four, had converted a minority of nine in the last house to a majority of one.

Howe thought of resigning at once, but was persuaded to remain. In December Falkand made the decision easy for him. Supposedly to demonstrate the principles on which the government would be conducted in the future, he appointed a new councillor opposed to party government, M.B. Almon, brother-in-law of J.W. Johnston. Howe, McNab, and J.B. Uniacke resigned as councillors forthwith. Thus Uniacke had thrown in his lot irrevocably with the Reformers. An indignant Falkland accused the three of trying to wrest the prerogative from him. The voters having rejected the idea of party government, he said, and Johnston having requested that a council vacancy be filled by someone having the same views, he had made the appointment to indicate his confidence in "the leader of my government." That Falkland would accord Johnston such recognition in a letter to his retiring ministers was nothing short of astounding.

Within weeks the relations between Falkland and the Reformers, especially Howe, had deteriorated beyond any hope of reconciliation. For, when Howe made what he considered to be a serious overture towards peace, the governor reportedly replied that there would be "war to the knife." When the assembly met, the administration carried the address by two votes with Liberal William Young in the chair. Later its majority was increased to four through the defection of John Ryder of Argyle. But questions of confidence aside, it could carry little of importance in the assembly. Unlike the late 1830s the "loose fish" were Tories and on matters related to economy and retrenchment some Tories from the country districts invariably sided with the Reformers. Because the casual revenues were far from meeting the salaries of the office holders whom those revenues supported, the administration introduced a civil list bill, not with any hope of having the arrearages paid, but of getting future salaries guaranteed at an appropriate level. It was so much a skeleton bill that Howe asked: "Have we an Administration or not?" The result was that the civil bill of 1844, eventually rejected in Britain, was mostly that of Howe and Huntington.

In May 1844 Howe assumed major editorial reponsibility for the *Novascotian* and its accompanying tri-weekly, the *Morning Chronicle*, both now the property of his long-time political associate William Annand. The two of them writhed as John H. Crosskill, the Queen's printer, allowed his own paper, the *Morning Post*, to be used by "every . . . dirty scribbler . . . to besmear gentlemen of the Liberal party, with their filth." About the same time an army surgeon, "long . . . a sort of upper servant about Government House," started a war against the Reformers in the New York *Albion* under the name "Scrutator." Both Howe and Annand took the position that Falkland must share the responsibility for what his close associates wrote and for what Crosskill printed in the *Post* as well as the *Royal Gazette*. This

James W. Johnston   1857-60, 1963-4

Courtesy of N.S. Museum

was their justification for the "torrents of pasquinades and lampoons" directed against Falkland in the *Novascotian* and *Morning Chronicle* starting on May 20 with "The Lord of the Bed-Chamber." For the rest of the year, whenever Howe and his friends found their treatment objectionable, they applied other doses of retaliative medicine. According to Chester Martin, it may not only have cost Howe "the first premiership under responsible government overseas" but also fastened "upon him the cardinal sin of indiscretion that barred him from the career he coveted beyond his native province."[16]

With this background 1845 could be nothing but a year of acrimony and frustration. Typical was the thirteen-day debate on Falkland's dispatch to Stanley in which he suggested that the leading Reformers would agree to enter the executive council even if Howe was excluded. One result was to bring Uniacke even more wholeheartedly into the Reform camp. Because Falkland had sought to denigrate the Reformers further by stating that they had "no acknowledged leader," Howe made it clear that Uniacke held that position. Apparently he was admitting that he had forfeited his own claims by his treatment of Falkland. To the Tories he himself had become a major issue. To them he was the man of indelicate language; the man who, if he came to power, would decide the affairs of Nova Scotia in "Joe Jenning's Grocery, or Sam Carten's shoeshop"; the man who, as collector of excise, had manipulated the accounts to his own advantage.

In 1846 Howe provided further ammunition for his enemies. Falkland, who had lost all objectivity, let a dispatch be published in which he accused William and George Young of associating with English speculators of dubious reputation and being guilty of "reckless conduct" in the publication of prospectuses. Should he persist in such conduct, said Howe, there would be "no course but for some Colonist to hire a black man, to horsewhip a Lieutenant Governor in the Streets." Later when the *Post* called Howe a "mendicant place hunter," he compared his conduct with that of the Falklands to their disadvantage. Falkland had had enough of it. By mid-August 1846 he was gone at his own request, his governorship a disaster.

His successor was the soldier Sir John Harvey, who had previously shown tact and good sense as governor of Prince Edward Island, New Brunswick, and Newfoundland. An appointee of Sir Robert Peel's Tory government, he might have gone the way of Campbell and Falkland had the Whig Lord John Russell not replaced Peel shortly after he took office. Having worked coalition government successfully in New Brunswick and Newfoundland, he hoped to do the same in Nova Scotia. Johnston was willing, but he had no success with Doyle, George Young, and especially Howe, who told him that "political principles and the rights of vast bodies of people" were involved in the struggle. Howe went back to Musquodoboit where he was working the Annand farm and there addressed two further letters to Lord John Russell. One proposed to continue the movement towards self-government, not through act of Parliament, but through precedent based on English conventions and customs. The other asked that the colonies be "indissolubly incorporated" as integrated portions of the British Empire through such devices as the election of colonials to the British Parliament and their employment at the colonial office: "we must be Britons in every inspiring sense of the word."[17]

These letters crossed in the mails a dispatch of Colonial Secretary Earl Grey to Harvey dated November 3 which, in effect, conceded self-government by stating that it was "neither possible nor desirable to carry on the Government of any of the British Provinces in North America in opposition to the opinions of the inhabitants."[18] Howe would not know the specific contents for months, but his correspondent Charles Buller told him that Grey had "impressed on Sir John Harvey the fullest adoption of the principle of Responsible Govt." Yet Harvey, nothing if not persistent, still tried to renew the coalition. By mid-December he presented specific proposals only to have the Reformers turn him down. Privately Howe declared that "the time for seduction, intrigue, and splitting of parties after the French fashion, has gone by." All that Harvey could get from the Reformers was a promise to avoid factious opposition during the session of 1847 and to abide by the results of the election to follow. Accordingly the session was relatively quiet. The Reformers acquiesced in the most important measure, Johnston's simultaneous voting bill, which divided the constituencies into polling districts and required the elections to be held the same day throughout the province. Hopefully, it would prevent large assemblages of voters and hence disturbances, but Howe feared it might result in "a Grog Shop and a Fiddler for every place in which the Poll would be opened." In their turn the Tories sent to Britain two memoranda in defence of the old order, only to have Grey's dispatch of March 3 confirm the principle he had laid down the previous November.

The session over, both parties prepared for the election of August 5.[19] Actually Howe had been testing public opinion since late in 1844 and liked what he saw: "The waters have risen and there will be corn in Egypt yet." Frequently he reminded his audiences that his party embraced "the sturdy independence and agricultural wealth of the country . . . The traders and attorneys and officials, or a majority of them, may be against us, but the sturdy yeomanry, the real aristocracy are with us." His strategy was to concentrate on counties close to Halifax: Lunenburg, Queens, and the four counties of the Baptist belt, which had returned nineteen of the twenty-six Tory members in 1843. Lunenburg and Hants Counties were his special targets.

Irrelevancy seemed to dominate the campaign even though Howe stuck to the great issues. Because these issues had so long agitated the province and were so well known, they were likely the crucial factor in the outcome. The stakes being so high, it was an unedifying campaign with no holds barred. The Reform candidate in Onslow had been consigned a puncheon of rum to defeat the Tories, his counterpart in Truro twenty-five gallons. But these outlays were meagre at a time when Tory wealth was being showered in profusion to prevent the destruction of the old order. Along the eastern shore the Tories used a boat to distribute all sorts of goods to secure votes. They paid special attention to the blacks at Hammonds Plains, seldom noticed other than at election time.

This time the religious differences in Halifax favoured the Reformers since their opponents had alienated the Catholics prior to the election. Because only a handful of Catholics supported the Tories, they lost all four seats. In all other counties but two the changes in party were few and generally cancelled each other out. Hence the Reformers' victory was forged in Hants and Lunenburg, in each of which they gained three seats. In attributing these successes to his own exertions, Howe did not exaggerate unduly. Almost alone, he had wooed both counties assiduously for three years, and "into [Lunenburg] none of our Leaders would venture but myself." He was also right that the Tories were dependent on the local "compacts" in the built-up areas, for although the Reformers won only ten of the twenty-four townships, they took twelve of the twenty-one counties.

Because the overall result was twenty-nine Reformers to twenty-two Tories, the election might appear not to have been decisive. Indeed, if Lunenburg had gone the other way, the parties would have been tied with a Liberal speaker in the chair. But this time

Joseph Howe   1860-3

Courtesy of P.A.N.S.

there were no "loose fish." Hence the precise party standing was known the day after the election. Before long the Reformers would be in a position to put into practical operation the system for which they had been contending since 1837. It had not required the breaking of a single pane of glass, but it might not have come about either as easily or as quickly if the Reformers in the Canadas had not broken something more than panes of glass.

CHAPTER 6

Nova Scotia a Normal School: 1848-63?

The Reformers did not regard the winning of responsible government as an end in itself. In Pictou Rev. George Patterson thought that it would lead to "practical measures for developing the resources and improving the institutions" of the province. Some like Joseph Howe even hoped to make Nova Scotia "a 'Normal School' for the rest of the Colonies."[1] Over the next fifteen years they would often fall far short of realizing that objective. In the immediate future they had to meet all sorts of obstacles. They found it exasperating to be inactive for five months, but by long-standing practice the Tories would remain in office until the spring meeting of the General Assembly. Within four days after it met the Reformers had voted non-confidence in the Johnston government and on February 2, 1848 Nova Scotia became the first of the British colonies to usher in responsible government.

The Reformers expected opposition to the institutionalization of the new order, but none could have foreseen its persistence or ferocity. As a condition to assuming office, they had demanded control over the legal and financial departments as well as the provincial secretary's office. They had no trouble with the legal offices since Johnston and E.M. Dodd resigned as attorney general and solicitor general without ado. But Sir Rupert George, the provincial secretary, declined to give way and, to get rid of him, it took a resolution of the assembly vacating the office and providing a retiring allowance of £400 stg. Leaving the financial departments to be dealt with later, the new administration announced on February 9 that J.B. Uniacke had become attorney general (and leader of the government), W.F. DesBarres solicitor general, and Joseph Howe provincial secretary. Resorting to every roadblock, the Tories contested their ministerial by elections only to be drubbed badly in all three. When Howe got back to the assembly in March, he boasted, a little too patronizingly, that Nova Scotia had completely overthrown an ancient system more quickly than any country he knew and without the shedding of blood.

In the absence of the ministers with office, the assembly had passed a judges' bill as the first step designed to introduce the new order. Remembering how Tory judges had made the wheels of justice revolve to the Tories' advantage, the Reformers wanted the judges to know that they too operated under checks. Accordingly their bill allowed a Supreme Court judge to be removed by a joint address of the legislature, but gave him six months to appeal to the Privy Council in Britain. This was only a prelude to the Reformers' chief measures, the civil list and departmental bills. In 1844 the colonial secretary had insisted that the salaries of the incumbent major officers not be reduced and the arrearages in their salaries be paid before he surrendered the casual and territorial revenues. Nevertheless, the civil list bill of 1848 put the public officers upon the reduced scale of 1844 and paid the arrearages in full only up to that date. Despite the usual appeals to protect vested rights and the honour of the Crown, the government had considerable support for the bills from Tory country members who, like their constituents, had an abiding concern with economical government.

The departmental bill, the very cornerstone of the new system, abolished the office of provincial treasurer and in its place created two political offices with membership in the executive council, a receiver general who did no more than receive and dispense public funds, and a financial secretary, whose responsibility it was to make financial policy. To the Tories it violated the honour of the Crown to remove the incumbent treasurer S.P. Fairbanks without compensation; to the Reformers it was meet reward for one who had connived to obtain the office during good behaviour, knowing full well that its tenure would be altered on a change of government. To the Tories it was absurd that the mere handler of public money should sit in the assembly as an executive council-lor; could not one person maintain the principle of responsiblity as well as half a dozen? To the Reformers it seemed impracticable to expect an executive council composed largely of unpaid members without office to meet regularly throughout the year on policy matters; experience had taught them that few were in a position to serve without being paid.

The hurdles in the assembly overcome, the Reformers looked with foreboding on the legislative council. There, even after filling the vacancies with strong, articulate, party men, they were outnumbered by 12 to 9. Moreover, John Inglis, the Lord Bishop of Nova Scotia, an irregular attendant, had been induced to be present on every division to protect the honour of the Crown. But everything else went against the Tories. One missed the entire session because of illness; another, William Rudolf of Lunenburg, decided not to oppose the adaptation of the political institutions to responsible government. Finally, when the council approved the judges' bill by 10 to 9, "the place became too hot"[2] for its venerable president Simon Bradstreet Robie who, once decidedly liberal, had moved gradually to the Tories and found the new political environment altogether uncongenial. His resignation enabled the Reformers to name Michael Tobin president of the council and he cast the deciding votes in favour of the civil list and departmental bills on April 6 and 7.

The battle over in Nova Scotia, it moved to Britain, where a stream of protests, petitions, and remonstrances from Nova Scotia's Tories almost inundated the colonial secretary. Howe hoped that he would sweep them out of the way with a firm hand, but it was not to be. In June Lord Grey objected to the departmental bill for its treatment of Fairbanks and for its contemplating two financial officers holding their places by a political tenure. In his opinion, only the financial secretary, like the chancellor of the exchequer in Britain, should be political. His strictures against the civil list bill were even sterner; he objected, especially, because Lieutenant-Governor Sir John Harvey was the only officer who would receive a salary greater than the bill of 1844 provided and because the other officers would not have their salaries maintained nor their arrearages fully recognized. On this bill Grey remained adamant, but he relented on the departmental bill because of a forceful presentation written mainly by Howe. "The inherent vice of old Colonial Governments," he was told, "was the absence of adequate control . . . over the Departments by which the whole Executive machinery was moved." Nevertheless, the Reformers were demanding only seven offices, "the smallest number . . . by the aid of which, it could ever have been sup[p]osed, that Responsible government could be carried on."[3] Conceding that Nova Scotians should determine the principles of their internal government, Grey promised to accept the departmental bill if, after reconsideration, the legislature confirmed it.

The last gasp of the old establishment occurred on February 14, 1849, the most exciting day in the entire history of the legislative council. When the Reform councillor William McKeen was delayed by a snowstorm "unexampled . . . for half a century," the Tories pressed an address denouncing the departmental bill. To stave off defeat, the president Michael Tobin followed the practice of the lord chancellor in the House of Lords, but hitherto unused in Nova Scotia, and voted like other councillors. The result was a tie and the defeat of the Tories' address. The battle for the institutionalization of responsible government was over; the Reformers had got the departmental bill in the form they wanted. In one respect, however, Nova Scotia did not follow the British model since it did not put the sole right to initiate money votes in the executive. Apparently the assemblymen still refused to give up their prerogatives relating to the expenditure of road moneys. It would take another dozen years to establish the British practice.

Throughout 1848 and 1849 the Reform government, or at least Howe, stoutly resisted any attempt to introduce the principle of "to the victors belong the spoils." Refusing a Bridgetown Liberal's request to drive an opponent off a school board, Howe wrote: "if you [were] . . . my brother I would not permit your interests to weigh [a] feather against a trust so sacred as I believe our public school system to be."[4] He continued to insist that Nova Scotia follow the British example in the matter of patronage and it was not until after he left the ministry that the spoils system came to be introduced by stages. Only in the appointment of magistrates (or justices of the peace) did the government appear to depart from its professed principles. On coming to office, it discovered that Reformers had been systematically excluded as magistrates in most counties and in its new commission of the peace it sought to redress the balance. As a result, the colonial secretary expressed indignation that Sir John Harvey was allowing the appointing power of the Crown to be used for party purposes. In public Howe argued the clear need to reduce the overwhelming preponderance of Tory magistrates, but it had been done rather badly and in private he referred with distaste to the "miserable apology . . . [he] was driven to make for the Magisterial lists."[5]

To the Tories the magistrates' affair was simply the last of a series of incidents in which a corrupt government had violated the most sacred interests of society. As J.W. Johnston perceived it, Nova Scotia now possessed the most debased system of government imaginable: "that sustained by a clique and an oligarchy operated upon by the corrupting influences of bitter party feeling." For that reason, "true Conservatism must hereafter consist of a well adjusted, well regulated system of Democratic Institutions."[6] Accordingly, for a period of seven years Johnston became the advocate of such democratic un-Tory devices as universal suffrage, an elective legislative council, and elective municipal institutions.

Until 1851 the basic qualification for voting was the possession of a forty-shilling freehold. Then, on the urging of Lawrence O'Connor Doyle to do away "with the moth-eaten habits of the Saxon settlers," the legislature added a second qualification, the payment of county or poor rates. In its operation it led to such corruption of the electoral process that Johnston could argue convincingly for universal suffrage. Howe, never an out-and-out democrat, did not wish to go that far, but he was unable to devise a middle course and Johnston had his way in 1854. In proposing elective municipal institutions Johnston's aim was to take away the power in local government from the magistrates in sessions, the nominees of a partisan executive council. In 1855 he managed to persuade the legislature to allow four counties to incorporate themselves at their discretion, the next year to extend the act to the rest of the province, again on an optional basis. But practically the act was stillborn. Only Yarmouth Township used its provisions and then not for long. When in its first year of operation the cost of local government rose from £190 to £250 with prospects of much larger increases to come, the township quickly voted to deincorporate itself. Although the act survived until 1879 it remained unwanted and unused. The deeply rooted fear of direct taxation had totally thwarted Johnston's intentions.

He had even less success with his proposals for an elective legislative council, which were also inspired by his desire to strip a partisan executive council of its power to appoint the members of the upper house. In Howe's absence he forced a hard-pressed Reform ministry to accept the principle of an elective council, but Howe could always carry the day with arguments that the proposal would do as much good as sticking "the tail of a dog on the back of a lion" and that the British constitution constituted the "safest and best course" to follow. While heading the government in 1858 Johnston made another attempt only to discover that he had not even the united support of his usual followers. Perhaps a well regulated system of democratic institutions appeared more attractive from the opposition benches than from the seats of power.

The institutionalization of responsible government largely accomplished, Howe hoped to raise Nova Scotia above "the little pedling muddy pool of politics" by pressing any government of which he was a member to "take the initiative . . . in every noble enterprise."[7] But for all his pleading in 1850 he could get the legislature to provide only half the money for the railway line already surveyed from Halifax to Windsor, none of it to be advanced until the remainder had been secured through private sources. About the same time Lord Grey, the colonial secretary, was offering no encouragement to two other railway projects, the line from Halifax to Quebec and the European and North American Railway from Halifax to Portland, Maine. So in November 1850 the executive council sent a "well qualified" man, Joseph Howe, to arrange a loan of $800,000 for the province's railways from British capitalists with or without the British government's guarantee. During his six-month trip Howe — impelled by one of his "flashes" — used his fertile imagination to make the railway projects the base upon which to devise a vigorous colonial policy which, among other things, included representation in Parliament by two executive councillors from each colony operating under responsible government and an immigration and colonization scheme which would relieve the British poor rate. Although Grey looked askance upon much of it, Howe was elated when, through his propagandizing talents, he secured (or so he thought) British guarantees for both the Quebec and Portland lines.

Back in Halifax Howe's first task was the unpleasant one of effecting the removal of executive councillor George Young who, never "quite right" since falling from his horse on his head on a hard road, had been embarrassing the government by his statements on railways. Then Howe the propagandist went to work on behalf of his railway project. "Aid me in this good work," he told Haligonians, and "British North America will rise to [have] . . . all the organization and attributes of a nation"[8] Next, it was on to New Brunswick and Canada, where the response was all he could have hoped. Finally, he sought a favourable outcome in the general election of August 28, 1851. His concern for the project led him to leave his safe seat in Halifax for a more dubious one in Cumberland. In the new house the government generally had the support of 30 or 31 of the 53 members, but not for its railway proposals. In the rural counties, distant from the proposed route, the reaction to them had been lukewarm. This was especially true in western Nova Scotia where, because of the abandonment of the line to Windsor, the Liberals elected only ten of the twenty-seven members, and some of the ten, like Thomas Killam of Yarmouth and Dr. E.L. Brown of Kings, would reject railway proposals of any kind.

Nevertheless, Howe had no difficulty in getting his railway bills accepted in November. When Johnston objected to proposals which permitted Nova Scotia to borrow up to £1,000,000 and, in effect, required it to build not only its own section of the line, but 22 miles of the New Brunswick and 65 miles of the Canadian sections as well, he could muster no more than ten votes. Two bills to promote emigration and colonization completed Howe's somewhat grandiose plan of provincial development. Then, on December 11, the blow struck with the arrival of Grey's dispatch of November 27 insisting that the guarantee had been intended only for the intercolonial line and not for the interconnecting line to Portland. Howe had considerable evidence to show that he had not been mistaken, but for the moment he preferred not to enter into a debating match. Later he would say that self-serving British interests operating behind the scenes had caused the British government to modify the guarantee.

Charles Tupper   1864-7

Courtesy of P.A.N.S.

Terribly chagrined that he had raised hopes so high only to have them dashed so completely, Howe told the other provinces to initiate new proposals on their own. Previously New Brunswick had agreed to a line to Quebec along its east coast because of the guarantee for the Portland line. Now, as Howe expected, it insisted on one through the Saint John Valley which was much less favourable to Nova Scotian interests. Nonetheless, he agreed in January 1852 to Nova Scotia's paying for 159 miles or a quarter of the line. When Johnston upbraided him for favouring New Brunswick at his own province's expense, he did not mince words: "in God's name what is New Brunswick? A Foreign nation, under a foreign Crown with hostile interests and feelings to our own? No, but a Province under the same sceptre, and descended from the same stock."[9] Nevertheless, he found all sorts of excuses for not accompanying the other provinces' delegates to London, and when they failed to secure a guarantee for the line by the Saint John, the Canadian Francis Hincks never forgave him.

The Nova Scotia government was now in a position to proceed with its own lines and in the autumn of 1852 Howe was again in Britain getting questions answered about their financing. The sequel was his introduction the following spring of proposals for the building of 320 miles of railway from Halifax to Windsor, Pictou, and the New Brunswick border. Because of their sweeping nature, Johnston accused him of inoculating "the public mind with extravagant and unrestrained ideas" only to have Howe reply that he was seeking to elevate his countrymen to "something more enobling, exalting and inspiring."[10] Mainly he had to counter arguments against public works being built and owned by government. His defence was that to give a company of speculators entire control over them would produce a monopoly that would dominate the assemblymen and "wrest from them every particle of power." Much to his surprise he found the assembly deadlocked on his bills. Like the Irish brigade in the Commons, a small group of western county Liberals, which tended to oppose all railways, was checkmating both the Liberal majority and the Tories.

Yielding to "compulsion not conviction," Howe accepted for the moment the principle of company railroads. But in the choice of a committee to draft new bills he made sure that its majority thought about railways much as he did. It, in turn, ensured that no speculator would make a killing out of Nova Scotia's railways; indeed, the terms were so hard that Howe was certain that no private company would build them. He was right. So in 1854 he was ready again to proceed with his own proposals. Basically they provided for the appointment of six commissioners by the governor and council, limited to an annual expenditure of

£200,000, to build a government-owned line, starting with the section common to both the trunk line and the branches to Windsor and Pictou. Howe proceeded confidently knowing that his old political enemy and the new Tory member for Windsor, L.M. Wilkins, Jr., had declared that he would sacrifice his party to get on with the railroad. Even so, he carried his bills by only one in the council and three in the assembly. Because of the defection of Bourneuf and Comeau, two Acadian Liberals from western Nova Scotia, he could not have done without the votes of Wilkins and three other Tories from Hants at the terminus of the line to Windsor. Nova Scotia could at last enter the railway age. By 1857 trains would be running to Windsor; by the next year to Truro.

April 4, 1854 saw significant changes in political leadership. On that day J.B. Uniacke, "fairly used up and unfit for public business," gave way as leader of the government to Speaker William Young, who had been biding his time waiting for the position that would likely lead to the main prize, the chief justiceship. The corrosive effect of the railway question on parties manifested itself in the appointment of two former Tories to the ministry: L.M. Wilkins as provincial secretary and Stephen Fulton without departmental duties. The same day saw the appointment of a bi-partisan Railway Board with Howe as chief commissioner. It proceeded so rapidly that before the year was out it had awarded contracts for building almost seventeen miles from the terminus at Richmond to the head of Bedford Basin. Howe reported the lieutenant-governor Sir Gaspard le Marchant as being so amazed that he "swears that I would undertake the building of a Line of Battle Ship, and lay the keel in 24 hours."[11]

William Young soon discovered that the premiership was not a bed of roses. Shortly after assuming it, he agreed to join the Governor General Lord Elgin at a convention in Washington on reciprocity and the fisheries. When the time came Canada and New Brunswick were represented, but through some slip up (Howe suggested that the fine hand of Francis Hincks might have been at work) Young received no specific invitation and the Reciprocity Treaty of 1854 went into effect without Nova Scotia's participation. In the assembly Howe and Johnston, normally an unlikely combination, were outraged that the province would have its fisheries sacrificed for insufficient compensation without its consent, but only three Liberals and twelve Conservatives

Hiram Blanchard   1867

supported them. Apparently most assemblymen believed that the prospects which the treaty offered for Nova Scotian trade far outweighed its undesirable features.

On the whole the session of 1854-5 was a somewhat barren one although it saw the abolition of the Court of Chancery. In part,

Young sought by his bill to oust the Reformer's former *bête noire*, Alexander Stewart, master of the rolls. But it drew immediate criticism from his own supporters for its generous retiring provisions to Stewart, and later from legal students who contended that its framers "had not grasped the basis on which the fusion of law and equity could be brought about," the result being a serious muddle in the administration of justice.[12] In 1855, however, the events of most significance for Nova Scotia's politics did not occur in the legislature. When the British war secretary, unable to recruit sufficient volunteers for the armed forces in the Crimea, asked Sir Gaspard le Marchant to communicate with John F. Crampton, the British ambassador in Washington, on the practicability of sending volunteers from the United States to Halifax, he little realized the profound repercussions his request would have in Nova Scotia. Since no executive councillor would go, le Marchant sent a most willing Joseph Howe to expedite matters with Crampton.

For Howe, stout Briton as he was, there was no need to inquire into the justification of the war; it was enough that it was a British war and Britain needed reinforcements. So for eight weeks between March and May 1855 he was engaged in activities that altogether outmatched all the other activities of a highly adventurous career. Not only did he violate both the spirit and letter of the American neutrality laws, but he became involved with the greatest of scoundrels among the foreign-born; he went into hiding, assumed a disguise, changed names several times, and only escaped arrest through the most fortuitous of circumstances, all with indifferent success in the recuitment of volunteers. He returned home still not realizing that he had sown seeds which would affect markedly the course of provincial politics.

On his arrival he found the assembly dissolved and an election set for May 22. The omens being favourable for the government, Young had sought to catch the Conservatives by surprise. The campaign turned out to be inordinately negative in character. Young argued basically that a Tory victory would mean the immediate cessation of railway-building; had not Thomas Killam, "The Lord of the West," declared that the railway should be halted at once to save Nova Scotia from bankruptcy? Although Johnston continued to advocate a well regulated system of democratic institutions, he and his party concentrated on charging the government with serious misconduct. In effect, the election became a series of constituency contests in which the Liberals appeared to have the better of it in 33 of the 53 seats. The campaign did nothing to lessen the disillusionment of the *Acadian Recorder* and others with party government:

> At the present juncture . . . it would nonplus the shrewdest politician to invent any cogent reason for the division of the Representatives of Nova Scotia into two parties, regularly organised for the annihilation of each other, in the halls of our Legislature. We are not aware of a single public question, of the least consequence to any class, being in suspense.[13]

Significant was Howe's electoral defeat, his first, at the hands of Dr. Charles Tupper in Cumberland. Howe had met the doctor during a by election in 1852 when he had treated him as "a naturalist would an insect of extraordinary size or color, sticking a pin through it" and had told him that if his "physic was no better than his politics, his patients were very much to be pitied."[14] Since that time Tupper had begun to establish his hegemony in Cumberland and he would shortly assume the real, if not the nominal, Tory leadership in the legislature.

In 1856 William Young demonstrated clearly that he could not manage men. Compounding his woes was Tupper, who provoked a major constitutional debate when Young refused either to confirm or deny that "to the victor belongs the spoils." He dared not because, unlike Howe, he had followed the line of least resistance and taken Nova Scotia a major step towards the full introduction of the spoils system. Of much greater consequences for the Liberals, however, was the first sign of their rift with the Catholics. It began when James McLeod, one of the two Catholic ministers, resigned after alleging a "want of candor" towards him in the making of appointments. Later assemblyman John Tobin complained that he could not serve his fellow Catholics and his political leaders faithfully at the same time. But the worst was still to come. On Young's bill to support common schools by compulsory assessment, he bowed to his Catholic members and agreed to add a clause providing for separate schools. Protestant spokesmen were up in arms at once, protesting an action which allegedly taxed the whole country to permit Catholic dogma to be taught to Catholic children. Indignantly Young withdrew his bill. He became even more bitter when, despite his attempts to accommodate the Catholics, his second Catholic minister, Michael Tobin, also resigned. He was fearful, too, that Catholic James McKeagney, once a Liberal, but now independent if not a Conservative, might further inflame the other Catholic back-benchers against a government dependent on them.

It took the Gourlay Shanty riots to precipitate religious warfare. For some time Scottish Presbyterians working on the Nova Scotia Railway had been taunting the Irish navvies about their religious beliefs. On May 26, in retaliation, the latter made a preconcerted attack on Gourlay's Shanty, located on the Windsor branch, and assailed fifteen to twenty Presbyterians from the eastern counties with pick handles. Then in Halifax on June 5, at a meeting to honour John F. Crampton, who had been forced out as British ambassador in Washington for his part in the recruiting mission, a group of Irishmen contended that he had richly deserved dismissal. Allegedly Howe responded with a merciless tongue-lashing of Irishmen. Once a foremost advocate of Irish causes, he had found it hard to restrain himself against the Irish priests who since 1854 had been backing the Halifax *Catholic* as it conducted a vigorous campaign against Protestantism and Britain, and as it chuckled at every British reverse in the Crimea. Even worse, he had learned that William Condon, President of the Charitable Irish Society, had sent telegrams to Boston and New York making known his mission and endangering his safety. Allegedly, too, Condon and his friends had tampered with the Irish whom Howe had recruited in the United States and induced them to state that they had come to work on the railway.

To be fair to Condon, he made an honest presentation of a case based on premises at opposite poles from those of Howe. For him the loyalty "mania" in Halifax was incomprehensible, even though it was harmless in itself. Yet, because of the office he held, he had considered it his duty to put the Irish in the United States on their guard against "recruiters" who were breaking the neutrality law and to protect the "entrapped" Irish who had arrived in Nova Scotia. At this stage the Halifax Irish were receiving no support from the Scottish Catholics. Bishop Colin MacKinnon of Arichat told Howe that his recent denunciation of the editors of the *Catholic* had given "great satisfaction in this quarter," while his brother, a Liberal assemblyman, told Howe not to be disturbed by "the Irish *howl* . . . the Scotch and French of the Diozies [sic] of Arichat are your friends."[15]

The uneasy calm lasted until December when nine alleged railway rioters escaped conviction by juries which divided almost completely along religious lines. Publicly for the first time a gloating *Catholic* explained the causes of the riots. Protestants, it declared, had no right to make fun of Catholic practices knowing how sensitive the Irish were to anything which affected their religion. Angrily Howe replied that "the right to discuss all questions or doctrines . . . to laugh at what we believe to be absurd, is the common right of every Novascotian"; nor could any number of mercurial people "trample it out of our hearts, or of our homesteads."[16] Throughout January Howe and Condon engaged in an angry exchange of letters, by the end of which Howe had alienated all the Catholics, Irish, Scottish, and Acadian. He appalled all of them by his suggestions that Protestants had the right to scorn their most cherished beliefs and that they were seeking to propagate their faith by the bludgeon.

As the 1857 legislative session approached, William Young began to receive disturbing reports from his backbenchers about the likely secession of his Catholic members. The day after it opened Condon was dismissed — the price of Howe's continued support of the government — and the fat was in the fire. Two Irish Catholics, John Tobin and Peter Smyth, deserted the Liberals forthwith, but the government might have clung precariously to office if its Acadian and Scotish Catholic members had remained firm. It was not to be. Through the defection of eight Catholics and two Protestants representing seats with large Catholic populations it lost a non-confidence vote by 28 to 22.

The reaction of Howe and the Liberals was extreme and some of it they wished later to forget. To Howe the chief villain in the government's fall was William Walsh, the Archbishop of Halifax. The Acadian and Scottish Catholic members, he said, had agreed to Condon's dismissal and had left the Liberals reluctantly only because "the Catholic Archbishop so willed." For him the incident was simply part of an aggressive papal policy being pursued elsewhere. Hence, since the Liberal and Conservative parties had fulfilled their missions, he and his friends had decided to work towards an independent Protestant majority. Otherwise, he argued, the Catholic members, by shifting from side to side, could rule the province.

Declaring it was "no light thing to turn out a government," the *Chronicle* appealed to all who distrusted the insidious advance of Catholic power to join an organization, the nucleus of which was a large committee drawn from both branches of the legislature. Meanwhile Howe had sent Hibbert Binney, the Church of England bishop, a copy of a Protestant platform and asked him to nominate two or three of his leading laymen who might be consulted on the next steps. Some writers have suggested that Howe was acting momentarily from a fit of uncontrollable temper. But it was much more than that, for "in the working out of a genuinely traumatic situation . . . several of his basic convictions — including his immense loyalty to Britain and his profound distrust of organized religion"[17] had come into play. And so his decision to do nothing more to further the proposals for a Protestant alliance probably resulted from his realization of their impracticability. If it ever existed, the large committee of legislative members evaporated overnight. Bishop Binney took pleasure in telling Howe that the Liberals had been largely responsible for augmenting Catholic power, while never missing the opportunity of "attacking and robbing us [i.e., the Anglicans] whenever they could do so with advantage to themselves."[18] A Protestant Association of Nova Scotia was formed, headed mainly by Free Church Presbyterian ministers, but the politicians appear to have ignored it and its influence was slight. Nevertheless, Howe remained confident that the Protestants "will do their work yet." The fact "that one-fifth of the assemblymen could change their political allegiance overnight and maintain another party in power without sacrificing their principles demonstrated the lack of meaning of [Nova Scotian] Liberalism and Conservatism."[19]

The manner in which J.W. Johnston and the Conservatives came to power left a backlog of bitterness which at times caused the assembly to resemble a bear-garden. According to the *Acadian Recorder*, it was a place of "silly gossip," "unmitigated twaddle," "malicious malignity," and meaningless contentions between two conglomerations having no right to names more definite than "Ins" and "Outs."[20] Excessive partisanship manifested itself, especially during the session of 1858 when the Conservatives hoist themselves by their own petard and the Liberals came close to doing it. In a measure directly aimed at Jonathan McCully, the Liberal leader in the legislative council, the Conservatives excluded judges of probate and prothonotaries from the legislature. In retaliation, William Annand secured the adoption of the Canadian practice which banned anyone holding an office of profit. But although the major office-holders were to forfeit £10, recoverable in the courts, for each day's violation of the law, the others would incur no pecuniary penalty. "The Liberals were soon to regret their zeal in promoting 'an act for securing the independence of the Legislature,' and the Conservative Attorney-General his failure to insist upon adequate means of enforcing it."[21]

The one positive accomplishment of the session of 1858 was an arrangement for settling the long-standing mines and mineral question. In the 1820s, the General Mining Association, as creditors of the Duke of York and through its own devices, had secured a virtual monopoly of the province's coal mines, but because of its failure to develop them, the province's royalties had been meagre. For years William Young had fought against the improvident arrangement and in 1856 he had actually got the legislature to approve terms for the elimination of the monopoly. But when the time came to send a negotiator from each party to London, Johnston was in office and he invited Adams G. Archibald, a Liberal much less obnoxious to him than Young, to accompany him. In the legislature Young, supported by Howe, argued with good reason against the terms which they had accepted: much of the original monopoly would remain for another twenty-five years and the province would make heavy sacrifices in royalties. But knowing the British government's attitude towards the protection of vested rights, the legislature quickly confirmed the agreement.

Otherwise it was a session of great bitterness revolving mainly around the religious controversy and the extension of the spoils system. Revolting in the extreme were the exchanges between the major rivals in the House, Howe and Tupper. Once Tupper regretted that Howe was not the richer for his efforts since he did not think that Nova Scotia was much the richer for them.

Referring to recent innuendo relating to Tupper, Howe replied that no member of the Protestant Association had "gained his education by a fraud of the basest character" and almost caused a "general 'set to'." Under these circumstances the session of 1859, a pre-election one, was predictable in its nastiness. Following the dismissal of the Nova Scotia Railway's chief engineer, James R. Forman, allegedly because of his connection with the Protestant Association, Howe set the tone by declaring that Catholics must be shown that they were "not the omnipotent dictators they assume themselves to be," and that eight or nine Catholic members, "dragooned by a foreign ecclesiastic," should not be able to "make or unmake an administration in an hour."[22]

The major religious confrontation took place on the government's representation bill, which was intended, and came close, to equalizing the representation within counties. From the outset the Liberals dubbed it the "Roman Catholic Representation bill" and William Young prophesied that the crafty division of counties would permit sixteen Catholics to be elected. Arguably Hants County's loss of a seat and the addition of one seat to both Inverness and the western district of Halifax had the object of electing additional Catholics; perhaps the purpose of merging Catholic Clare with the rest of Digby was to let Catholic voters determine the county's three members. But even these changes had some justification and it was the prevailing atmosphere which provoked the extreme reaction. Howe himself reminded his colleagues that "there were only so many plums in the pudding."

In the election of May 12, 1859 the Conservatives emphasized the delinquencies of the Young government, while the Liberals heaped scorn on Johnston for leaving unfilled the promises of half a life. But actually this election was the only one in provincial history primarily fought and decided on the religious question. Aiding the Liberals was a flood of publications from religious sources, some invoking the wrath of God upon anyone voting for a government connected with the Church of Rome. Although Howe made it known that he did not want to be considered "a Champion of Protestantism," he did expect help from Protestant ministers, since, as he put it, if largely Protestant counties returned those who condoned outrage and disloyalty, the Liberals might as well quit the field. The aid was forthcoming, particularly from Free Church Presbyterian ministers, and it helped the Liberals to win 29 of the 55 seats. Exultantly the *Chronicle* proclaimed that Nova Scotia had "thrown off the yoke of tyranny . . . Nova Scotia, Protestant Nova Scotia, is free."[23]

Although Catholics had given almost solid support to the Conservatives, an even larger number of Protestants had switched to the Liberals. The Acadian vote had enabled the Conservatives to win all six seats in Yarmouth and Digby counties; the Catholic vote had led to the resounding defeat of the Liberals in Cape Breton County and they did not even contest Catholic Sydney County. They also lost the three seats in the western district of Halifax even though they polled about 2,100 of 2,500 Protestant votes. But in largely Protestant seats the Conservatives were usually beaten or hard pressed. In Victoria County Free Church ministers helped to defeat Executive Councillor C. J. Campbell by 500 votes, while in Annapolis County so many Baptists deserted Johnston that he won by a scant 17 votes.

Once again the Liberals had to wait months to assume office. But even before the assembly met late in January 1860 the first glimmer of a highly contentious issue had appeared. Should Lord Mulgrave, the lieutenant-governor, acquiesce in the defeat of the Johnston government by the votes of assemblymen who allegedly held offices of emolument while running for election? Mulgrave had already referred the matter to both the provincial and English law officers, and had received contradictory opinions. The English officers, unlike their Nova Scotian counterparts, held that the oath of qualification which might be required of any member applied only to the want of a property qualification. Hence there was no way to prevent a member allegedly infringing Annand's Law from taking his seat at least temporarily and helping to vote out the government. Howe and Young realized at once that they would be "unapt scholars" if they "did not know how to lead [their] troops now."[24]

Thereafter everything turned in their favour. Defeated in a non-confidence vote, Johnston requested a dissolution only to be told by Mulgrave that, although the Liberals might have "pressed matters somewhat to extremes," they had done nothing unconstitutional. Because of his refusal, the Tories alleged that he had reduced himself to "a cipher, a puppet with the semblance of power, and of no use whatever." They then did their utmost to defeat the new executive councillors at their ministerial elections, only to be thwarted again. To their indignation the premier, William Young, avoided an election by conferring upon himself the hitherto non-existent and unpaid office of president of the council. The three ministers with paid offices easily won re-election.

The fate of Young's government depended on the assembly committees drawn by lot to try controverted elections in accordance with the Nova Scotia version of the English Grenville Act. Well in advance the Liberals argued that the intent of Annand's Law was not to disqualify coroners receiving forty shillings a year or way office keepers earning little more. Hence they insisted that these members not lose their seats if they had not been appointed to their offices precisely as the law required. As it turned out, the luck of the draw favoured them. But they were also fortunate in not striking Conservative John Hatfield of Argyle off any of the seven committees on which he was drawn. "A genial retired master mariner, he simply did not have it in him to vacate the seats of members who came within Annand's Law by a mere technicality."[25] A second Conservative, Colin Campbell of Digby, adopted much the same position and both he and Hatfield were, in effect, read out of the party.

The outcome was that no member had his seat vacated for office-holding. The outrage of the Tories knew no bounds. With alacrity they joined Tupper in describing themselves as Constitutionalists and their opponents as Usurpers. Aggravating the bitterness was the disposition of the chief justiceship, likely to become vacant soon because of the failing health of Sir Brenton Halliburton. For the first time the colonial secretary would accept without question the nominee of the executive council. Both Johnston and Young wanted it to crown their long careers in public life, while their heirs-apparent, Tupper and Howe, aspired to the premiership. The one positive accomplishment of the 1860 session — to place, at long last, the initiation of money votes in the executive council — was actually a proposal of the Johnston government implemented by its successor. Howe, who had long favoured it, promised to use the new power "with courtesy and . . . a due regard to those in opposition." Otherwise the session was largely sterile, marked by recrimination over the escalating dismissal of office-holders. Almost with remorse Howe agreed to replace the chief railway commissioner, James McNab, his wife's cousin and for many years his personal and political friend. Thinking that the Liberals were shipwrecked for decades to come, he had committed the unforgivable sin of deserting to the Conservatives in 1857.

Late in July 1860 Albert Edward, Prince of Wales, and the colonial secretary, the Duke of Newcastle, arrived in Halifax. Even their visit stilled for barely a moment the controversy which followed the death of the chief justice. Coming out in mourning, the *Acadian Recorder* protested the likely succession of William Young, whom it charged with outraging all the proprieties of public life. Nevertheless, the executive council recommended his appointment and the colonial secretary confirmed it despite a stream of addresses sent across the Atlantic. So, when Howe finally became premier, it brought little exhilaration since the politics of the day was "deficient in the great themes upon which the Tribune of the People liked to expound eloquently to the Freeholders of Nova Scotia."[26]

The session of 1861 did not improve the situation for him. Although his opponents described his speeches as "laboured, halting, tedious," the synoptic debates reveal that he could still use his elephantine memory to make his opponents writhe in frustration. Subjected to continual onslaughts by the boisterous Tupper, he replied that to blast the reputation of a human being was neither a political virtue nor, in nine cases out of ten, a political necessity. Quite unexpectedly, he found his support in the assembly challenged. His majority, only three after the election, had risen to nine following the unseating of a Conservative and the defection of Hatfield and Campbell, and then fallen to five after two by election losses on the last day of 1860. He told Mulgrave that he could probably carry on, but if not, he would attempt a reconstruction or advise a dissolution. Mulgrave, in turn, informed Newcastle, in words he would not be allowed to forget, that "any further diminution of . . . strength would necessitate either a reconstruction of the Government, or an appeal to the country."[27] Between January 10 and 21, 1861 Tupper was off to Argyle and Digby, the seats of Hatfield and Campbell, drumming up resolutions and addresses condemning the two members' conduct and demanding a dissolution. The intent was to demonstrate the growing weakness of the government and hence force Mulgrave to give effect to his dispatch, but as Howe pointed out, diminution of strength meant a reduction of the government's majority in the assembly. No attention, he said, should be paid to "a cartload of Petitions manufactured . . . by disappointed politicians."

Parliamentary work in 1861 being exasperating, exhausting, and often ineffectual, Howe was glad to turn to something more exhilarating. A year earlier, after the discovery of gold on the Tangier River in Halifax County, he had written it off, saying that all the gold he had seen "put together would scarcely fill a lady's thimble." In 1861, however, after further finds at Tangier, at the Ovens near Lunenburg, at Lawrencetown and Waverley near Halifax, and at Wine Harbour and Isaac's Harbour on the eastern shore, he began to believe that they might contribute to the province's development even if the newcomers turned to other pursuits. Even more interesting to him, however, were railways for which he never lost his fascination. At the request of the British MP Joseph Nelson, he had persuaded the legislature to adopt an address favouring an intercolonial line, while renouncing any intention to participate personally in further delegations. But in September he was in Quebec City at an inter-provincial conference which agreed that each province contribute £20,000 a year towards the railroad, and in November he was in Britain where, to his disappointment, the government refused to provide a guarantee of an equal amount.

Equally futile to him was the session of 1862. Overhanging it was the American Civil War and the utter derangement of commerce which it produced. Almost all the large budgetary deficit of $125,000 was due to the decrease in revenue from duties on imports and the increased expenditures on the militia in a time of insecurity. In the time-honoured way Howe's administration sought to make up the deficiency by temporary increases in the general tariff from ten to twelve percent and in the duties on luxuries, none of which constituted a serious burden in a lightly taxed province. But Tupper, capitalizing upon the usual hostility to increased taxation, caught the public eye with retrenchment proposals designed to save £79,648. Since most of the savings would come through cuts in the salaries guaranteed in the agreement for the surrender of the casual revenues, Howe suggested scornfully that Nova Scotia would have to go on its knees to the British government and ask its permission to violate the bargain of 1849. Retrenchment might have died a natural death had not the recent convert, Colin Campbell of Digby, bound by previous pledges to cut costs, retired from the executive council and, in effect, from the party. As a result, the government could defeat Tupper's proposal by a mere two votes, a diminution in strength that brought Mulgrave's dispatch into play.

Howe's response was that he would try first to renew the expiring revenue laws, then seek to reconstruct the government, and in the event of failure take appropriate action. Johnston, believing that no Conservative member would co-operate in strengthening the ministry, declared a dissolution to be inevitable once Howe had conceded that he would not continue with a majority of two. But Tupper over-reached himself. In seeking to reduce the indemnities of assemblymen and to eliminate the lieutenant-governor's private secretary, he failed by three and four votes because of the defection in one case of Colin Campbell, and in both cases of Moses Shaw, Johnston's colleague from Annapolis County. In Shaw Howe had found the opposition's weakest link. Treated with scant respect by the Conservative leadership and fearful of being discarded at the next election, he promised, either by his vote or abstention, to protect the government in the current session and to give it full support in 1863.

The immediate result was to restore the confidence of the badly shaken Liberals. In private Howe told Mulgrave that Johnston was not in a position to reduce his majority below that of the past year. Towards the end of the session he pointed out that " no rule of the constitution" named "any certain number as the majority which a government must have to carry on." Although admitting that the government's position was varied somewhat by the governor's dispatch, he insisted that he had put himself in a position to meet its terms. Accordingly he would hereafter "take my own steps, and my own time, and do my work in my own way."[28] When the Tories realized that a dissolution would not take place, they vented their fury on Mulgrave himself, referring to him as the "unfortunate imbecile called a Lieutenant Governor." Meanwhile Mulgrave was telling the colonial secretary of the great harm being done by the feuding of the parties even though no great political question divided them and though the matters in dispute were ones of men, not measures. But in suggesting the possibility of party amalgamation he was incredibly naive.

Howe was hoping to strengthen his government in a more effective way than through the defection of Moses Shaw. A year earlier he had said jocularly that the Catholics had left him foolishly and "like little Bo-peep . . . I let them alone till they . . . come home, wagging their tails behind them." Knowing that the Scottish Catholics had departed reluctantly, he proposed to re-establish "the kindly relations out of which so much of public advantage resulted in times past" by offering a legislative councillorship to the bishop's brother, John McKinnon, and the solicitor generalship, a ministerial position, to Hugh McDonald. But the latter refused; how, he asked, could a life-long Conservative like himself abandon his party "without any change in the persons or in the public policy of the Govt."?

Between the sessions of 1862 and 1863 Howe was again in Britain hoping to bring the intercolonial railway question to a successful conclusion, only to be frustrated by the Canadian government and its delegates. The episode added to his growing distrust of Canadian politicians which would reach its zenith during the Confederation question. But his trip to Britain did get him an Imperial office, although not the one he wanted, a fishery commissionership under the Reciprocity Treaty of 1854. That added a touch of unreality to the session of 1863, for although Howe still led the government, he would be leaving it at its conclusion. Once again he enjoined Tupper to give up his "little, perpetual, peddling, snarling assaults on all subjects, and on all occasions." But it was the legislative councillor H.G. Pineo, once a Conservative, but more recently a Liberal supporter, who most damaged the government. His vote defeated the representation bill which purported to undo the alleged injustice of the 1859 act. Much more consequential was the franchise bill, which supposedly arrested the province's downward tendency towards democracy and republicanism by returning to a property qualification. Never friendly to universal suffrage, Howe almost begged the assembly to "relieve ourselves from the charge of being the only British Colony, save Australia, governed through universal suffrage." Once again, however, Pineo cast the deciding vote which prevented the property qualification from becoming operative until after the next election.[29]

Whatever the outcome of the election which followed the direction of Nova Scotian politics would be falling into new hands. Because of Johnston's indifferent health, Tupper dominated the Tory campaign with his usual vigour. When he called the speeches and writings of Howe no less fabulous than the tales of Munchausen, the *Chronicle* compared him to "a bayou, stagnant and full of crocodiles, alligators, lizards, and creeping, slimy reptiles." Howe, reluctant to leave the assembly, let himself be persuaded to run in Lunenburg. Because his likely successor, Adams G. Archibald, was busy in Colchester, legislative councillor Jonathan McCully took on the task of countering Tupper.

May 28, 1863 brought a crushing defeat to the Liberals. Howe suffered the worse of his two personal losses and the Liberals won only fourteen seats to the Conservatives' forty. The remaining seat went to William Miller, an independent from Richmond, who would shortly play an important role in the Confederation issue. Howe blamed much of the defeat on the inability to put the franchise bill into effect at once; supposedly those to be disfranchised in future voted *en masse* against the authors of their reduced status. But there was much more to it than that. "After winning every election since 1848, the Liberal party was in a pronounced state of disarray. Its credibility had been gradually eroded by the never-ending attacks of Tupper; it went into the election without even letting the public know who was to lead it; it could not attract candidates and let nine Conservatives win by acclamation."[30] The major difference in the election results this time was the overwhelming nature of the Tory victory. Despite the personal appeal of Howe the Liberal successes in every election since 1847 had been by comparatively small margins. Their overwhelming defeat in 1863 led to their giving way immediately instead of waiting to be voted out the following spring, a course that would in future be the unvarying practice. The new government's large majority in the assembly also meant that it need not fear the defection of a few members and hence not be excessively cautious in introducing far-reaching changes.

A curious mistake which has been continued to the present day occurred in the labelling of this General Assembly. Though it was actually the Twentieth-Second, in the latter part of its life the *Journals* of both houses labelled it the Twentieth-Third. In due course the next General Assembly became the Twentieth-Fourth, and since that time each has been ascribed a number greater by one than the actual. This volume, at least in this respect, conforms to historical accuracy.

As Howe left the assembly, he could hardly have believed that he had made Nova Scotia a normal school for the other colonies to follow. Undoubtedly he could boast of the successful institutionalization of responsible government immediately after 1848. But since the early 1850s the attempt to work a full-fledged party system in a small province marked by bitter struggles over the control of patronage, by religious conflict, and even by marked sectional differences had, more often than not, made the political process anything but an exemplar worthy of imitation.

CHAPTER 7

"This Crazy Confederacy": Rejection and Acceptance

On June 11, 1863 J. W. Johnston took over the government of Nova Scotia for the third time, but only until he could secure an appropriate non-political office. From the beginning Tupper assumed the dominant role in the new administration. Fortune favoured him since reviving trade had put the province's finances in good shape and he could conveniently forget his retrenchment proposals. When the assembly met in 1864 it was, in a sense, a new Tupper, for though no less vigorous than before, even combative when necessary, he seldom resorted to the petty, snarling, personal interjections which had irritated Howe.

The government's major proposal, the Free School bill, earned its name by abolishing fees for attendance at public schools. It also established the basic administrative structure of the educational system for many years to come. Because it put education under a Council of Public Instruction, that is, the executive council with the Superintendent of Education as its secretary, it received criticism from Adams G. Archibald, who generally followed a moderate course in leading his small band of Liberals, but who feared that this provision would lead to political domination of the educational process. He also opposed the continued reliance on subscriptions, rather than compulsory assessment, for the support of schools. Reminding Tupper of the government's overwhelming majority, he pointed out that it stood "in a position that no Government has ever stood in this country . . . to deal with this question in a vigorous manner." But

Tupper replied that it would be neither wise nor politic to adopt compulsory assessment at once; he had, however, framed his bill to "render that system as gradually acceptable to the people as it is possible."[1]

Somewhat apologetically, J.W. Johnston announced the decision to continue the building of railways as government works. Although personally still dubious of the policy, he held that it had been "constitutionally settled . . . by the representatives of the people" and he had no choice but to abide by that decision. Because there was "no present probability" of proceeding with the Intercolonial Railway (ICR), he proposed an extension of the provincial railway from Truro to Pictou Harbour, the funds to be provided by a loan from the Provincial Savings Bank and the issue of six per cent debentures not exceeding $1,600,000. Not unexpectedly, five members from Shelburne and Yarmouth, far from the Pictou branch, together with the inveterate foe of government railways, Dr. E.L. Brown of Kings, opposed the measure at every stage.

Fraught with the greatest significance for the province, however, was Tupper's resolution to appoint delegates to consider the possibility of union of the maritime provinces. Prominent among his arguments was the reduction of political acrimony which, he said, increased inversely to the size of the country. Enlarging the sphere of action, he was certain, would "tend to decrease the personal element in our political discussions, and to rest the claims of our men more upon the advocacy of public question[s]."[2] Perhaps because of the feeling that the resolution would lead to nothing, it passed with little debate and no opposition.

Embarrassing even to Tupper was his attempt to create a place for Johnston. The device was an Equity Court bill providing for a chief justice in equity with a rank equal to that of the chief justice. Although Archibald agreed that someone who had served his country for a quarter of a century was "entitled to anything his party can legitimately give him," it ought not to use "an act of such personal legislation as the one now before us."[3] Because of the opposition Tupper appeared to change position in midstream. From a bill necessitated by the heavy work load of the Supreme Court judges, it became one to reduce the burden on ailing Mr. Justice Bliss, who would not be replaced when he

William Annand   1867-75

Courtesy of P.A.N.S.

retired. At that Johnston himself took umbrage, insisting that the bill was not of a temporary character and that the duties falling under the Equity Court judge would tax anyone's talents to the full. Liberal Hiram Blanchard had another objection: "create this double headed monster," he said, "and you will excite perpetual jealousies and bickerings between the two Chief Justices."[4] Largely for that reason the legislative council reduced the title and status of the new judge in equity to little more than that of a puisne judge.

Things moved rapidly in the recess. Excuse or not, Howe pleaded his duties as imperial fishery commissioner not to become a delegate to the Charlottetown Conference, but Liberals A.G. Archibald and Jonathan McCully were delegates and became enthusiastic and unwavering supporters of the Charlottetown and Quebec Resolutions. At first the Confederates had everything going for them: the most fluent speakers, the majority of the Halifax newspapers, and control of the political patronage. But throughout November 1864 a genuine grass-roots movement developed against the union without benefit of leaders of prominence. It started in western Nova Scotia and quickly spread to Halifax and the rest of the province. Coastal areas relying on trade saw no benefit from closer ties with the backwoods of Canada. A political culture that had already congealed also worked against the acceptance of radical change. Howe's imperial office handcuffed him for the moment. But in January 1865 he found a way to state his opinion on the Quebec Resolutions when Annand's *Morning Chronicle* began to publish his "Botheration Letters" anonymously. Some have said that they were a major rallying force against union. Actually their chief effect was to reinforce opinions already held since the weight of evidence is that Nova Scotians had already made up their minds.

The cause of union experienced a serious rebuff on March 6 with the defeat of Leonard Tilley's Confederates in New Brunswick. As a result, Tupper proposed two weeks later that the legislature revert to discussing a maritime province union. Obviously it was a stop-gap since his speech was largely an explanation and justification of the Quebec Resolutions. He had an even stronger reason for not wanting to divide the house on the matter since at least half a dozen Conservatives and independent William Miller opposed the larger union. Isaac LeVesconte of Richmond expressed horror that "Nova Scotia's most gifted sons should be found to have entered into the unholy compact to destroy our political existence".[5]

In contrast, Tupper carried his second controversial measure, compulsory assessment for education, to a successful conclusion without undue difficulty. Although generally satisfied with the operation of the previous year's act — only 213 sections had failed to hold meetings under its provisions — he proposed, "with great diffidence and reluctance" he said, to fulfil an even more solemn duty for his country. His bill increased the government grant for education from $58,000 to $90,000 and required each county to raise by assessment an amount equal to two thirds of that grant, the total proceeds to be distributed to the sections on the basis of school populations. In addition, each section would have to raise by assessment any sum it voted for the lease, purchase, or erection of a school building. In the debate a myriad of opinions appeared: one member wanted schools to be supported out of general revenue; another asked for the inclusion of clauses which would have permitted separate schools; fully a third of the house preferred to rely on fees and subscriptions. But it was not a great act of political courage on Tupper's part. Because of his massive majority, he had no fear of defeat. Moreover, defections on both sides of the house balanced themselves off in the final division. Over the next few years, however, pronounced opposition to compulsory assessment developed and the Conservatives might well have lost the election of 1867 on this question had not a larger issue dominated it.

Fate conspired in every way to assist the Nova Scotian Confederates in the months that followed. When Governor Sir Richard Graves MacDonnell refused to become a tool in pressing union, the British government — uncompromising in its support of the Quebec scheme — sent him off to Hong Kong and installed in his place the native Nova Scotian Sir Fenwick Williams with the sole mission of securing union. Henceforth wining and dining at Government House played a key role in over-all Unionist strategy. But it was the Fenians who precipitated action. When the General Assembly opened on February 22, 1866, the speech from the Throne made no mention of union. Then, on March 7, the Canadian government called out the militia because of the Fenian scare. Ten days later Williams followed suit and all Halifax became excited as a combined army-navy force under General Doyle and Admiral Hope prepared to protect New

Brunswick against the Fenians gathering at Eastport, Maine under Doran Killian.

Howe, his mouth closed up to this time, arrived back in Halifax and quickly made up his mind. Annand, fearing that he might not get a share of the "loaves and fishes" if union took place without his participation, had been flirting with Tupper's suggestion that he propose another conference on union. With Howe's return there was an immediate end to "intrigue". But forces had already started to operate which would resist all of his efforts. Professedly influenced by the Fenian danger, William Miller "made Annand's motion" an April 3. Following it up a week later, Tupper proposed the appointment of delegates to "arrange with the Imperial Government a scheme of union which [would] effectually ensure just provision for the rights and interests" of Nova Scotia. It quickly became apparent that behind-the-scenes manoeuvring and cajolery had done their work when, on April 17, Miller and six Conservatives who had previously opposed the larger union provided the votes to carry Tupper's resolution by 31 to 19. Typical was C.J. Campbell of Victoria, who stated that his earlier objections "vanished like smoke" because of the need to "save us from annexation or from invasion."[6] A few days later the Fenians had evaporated and gone. The evidence seems conclusive that a resolution for union would not have succeeded in 1866 but for the use made of the Fenian scare.

During a five-week speaking tour starting early in May Howe presented his case to the eight western counties. Actually he did not have to win minds, for he "could not find five hundred Confederates on the whole tour." But he did have an opportunity to present his three objections to union: as one interested in Nova Scotia's economic development, he doubted its value to a sea-going province; as a liberal, he opposed it without the prior approval of Nova Scotians in a general election; as a stout Briton, he feared that it would defeat the proposals which he had long advocated for the organization of the Empire. In July he was off to Britain under instructions from the Anti-Confederation League to demand that union not be proceeded with until approved by the provincial electorate. He expected to be away four months; it was nearly ten before he returned. He found that Derby's Tory government had replaced that of Russell, but it did him no good since the colonial secretaries in both administrations, Edward Cardwell and the Earl of Carnarvon, were both committed to union.

For weeks Howe, Annand, Hugh McDonald, and William Garvie mounted a propaganda campaign such as no colonials had ever before launched in Britain. But on January 29, 1867 Carnarvon told Howe he would proceed with union as expeditiously as possible and the Nova Scotians had the impossible task of winning over the parliamentary backbenchers in opposition to the leaders of both parties. For Howe, who had always had an abiding faith in Parliament, the debates in both houses were nothing less than traumatic. Only Carnarvon in the Lords and Cardwell in the Commons showed real knowledge of the subject and some members were nothing less than ludicrous in their support of Confederation.[7] British men, wrote Howe, thought only of themselves and, "having made up their minds that the Provinces are a source of peril and expense to them — the prevailing idea is to set them adrift, to gradually withdraw British troops from them . . . to leave them . . . pass into the [American] Union if they prefer that solution of their difficulties."[8]

Meanwhile the Nova Scotia legislature was concluding its last session under the old order. It revised the terms for building the Windsor to Annapolis line to get an English group to construct the province's first privately owned railroad: in lieu of a subvention per mile it would, in effect, receive £188,600 stg. for building the line and £32,000 for the Avon River Bridge. Because of difficulties in the construction of the Pictou Branch the government had granted a new contract to Sandford Fleming. As a result, it incurred stern criticism from Archibald for placing few conditions upon Fleming and for violating the general statute on railways. But at least construction was proceeding rapidly.

Although the legislature had become powerless to do anything more about union, the subject intruded itself, no matter how irrelevantly, into every debate. That was particularly true of the bills designed to take account of the province's lessened responsibilities under Confederation. One effected a major change in the shape of the executive council: the attorney general would take over the duties of the solicitor general, the provincial secretary those of the financial secretary; the receiver general would become the provincial treasurer; and a new departmental officer, the

commissioner of public works and mines, would assume the
duties of the Board of Works and the chief commissioner of mines.
Thus Nova Scotia would enter Confederation having four
executive councillors with office. These changes evoked little
criticism, but not so those which reduced the assembly from fifty-
five to thirty-eight members and gave Halifax and Pictou three
members each, all the other counties two. "The Provincial
Secretary [Tupper] had almost assumed the position of an
autocrat," said John Locke of Shelburne. When Annand suggested that a newly elected assembly deal with the matter, Tupper
refused. Any future assembly, he pointed out, could change the
representation again if conditions warranted it. Unlike the early
practice in Ontario, the legislature also took steps to prevent any
member of the Senate or House of Commons from sitting in the
legislative council or the House of Assembly. An oddity of the
session was that the Confederate A.G. Archibald continued to lead
the Liberals even though Annand had tried to supplant him.
That said a good deal about Annand's personal attractiveness
within his own party.

Because Tupper had decided to enter federal politics, a
reorganization of the provincial ministry took place on July 4,
1867. Hiram Blanchard, a Liberal turned Confederate, was
generally regarded as the leader of the new government, but it was
sometimes referred to as the Blanchard-Hill administration to
give recognition to its leading Conservative member, Philip
Carteret Hill, a newcomer to provincial politics.

For the time being the anti-Confederates had not decided on a
precise course of action other than to punish the traitorous
assemblymen who, Howe said, deserved the halter or the axe.
Starting with a meeting in Mason's Hall, Halifax on May 9 he
waged what amounted to a four-month election campaign.
Confederation had submerged completely any remnants of past
bitterness with the Catholics, but he still found it difficult to cope
with Archbishop Connolly of Halifax, an ardent Unionist.
Although he urged the archbishop to remain "above the range of
mere political controversy," he knew that his public intervention
in the campaign was certain. When the anti-Confederates of
Cumberland found it difficult to secure a suitable candidate to
oppose Tupper for the federal seat, he got them to accept William

Annand, his friend of thirty-five years, and then spoke on his behalf in almost every hamlet in the county. Otherwise, he ventured little outside of his own constituency of Hants so certain did the outcome seem to be. In fact, his major difficulty arose from a multiplicity of prospective candidates eager to run on the anti-Confederate ticket. Perhaps his greatest accomplishment was to induce the Liberals of Pictou to accept their old enemy Martin Wilkins, an unreconstructed Tory.

The results of the federal and provincial elections of September 18 were almost all that the Antis wanted. Tupper defeated Annand by a mere ninety-seven votes and his coat tails pulled in H.G. Pineo, Jr., a provincial running mate; Unionist Hiram Blanchard won a personal victory for an assembly seat in Inverness. Otherwise, the victors were all Antis, 18 MPs and 36 MPPs. Although Archbishop Connolly's intervention enabled the Unionists to carry the city of Halifax by 400 votes, they lost the whole county by 200. In explaining away their defeat, they contended that anti-Confederation became a cave of Adullam to which all the discontented and distressed flocked. They had in mind particularly the dissatisfaction arising from the imposition of compulsory assessment for education. Actually, however, "the election of 1867, more than any other, was a referendum on one question — Confederation."[9] The Unionists also sought to minimize the extent of their defeat. Only 20,000 of 52,000 voters, they argued, had voted for the Antis, while 32,000 had either supported union or stayed at home. But, as Howe pointed out, his party had carried four counties by acclamation and ten others by extraordinary majorities. What had happened in broad terms was that only a relatively small number of Liberals had voted for union, while an immensely larger number of Conservatives had moved to the Liberals, and many of them remained. As a result, the Liberals dominated provincial politics for the next ninety years. One historian, Delphin A. Muise, suggests that Unionist support, such as it was, centred in areas benefiting from the new economy based on railroads and coal mines, while the Antis did best in areas "most intensively committed to the older economy of wood, wind and sail."[10] But perhaps his analysis is more applicable to succeeding elections. In 1867 one issue, reinforced or counteracted to a small degree by other considerations, was the only thing that mattered.

When the Anti members, federal and provincial, met in Halifax in October, they decided both to authorize the MPs to go to Ottawa and to seek repeal of the BNA Act. Meanwhile the disposition of the Nova Scotia government awaited the departure of Sir Fenwick Williams, who, mission accomplished, wished to leave no less quickly than the Antis wanted it. His successor would be Sir Hastings Doyle, commander of the troops in Halifax, who had already pleaded with his friend Howe not to "kick" the Confederates when they were down. In Ottawa John A. Macdonald was receiving misleading information about the strength of anti-Confederate feeling in Nova Scotia from Archbishop Connolly, Jonathan McCully, and others, who told him that Howe could easily be "tickled by something worth acceptance under the Dominion." Accordingly he suggested, somewhat preposterously, to Philip Carteret Hill, co-leader of the government with Hiram Blanchard, not to resign until he was voted out. But for a ministry to cling to office when it had only one executive councillor and one backbencher in the assembly was to invite disaster. So its first act, after Doyle became governor on October 25, was to offer its resignation. On Howe's advice, the governor asked R.A. McHeffey, the only Liberal Anti member with ministerial experience, to head the government. Since the Anti caucus considered him too moderate to meet the needs of the day, it chose in his stead William Annand. Former Conservative Martin Wilkins became his principal colleague and attorney general.

At Ottawa the Anti MPs found their position highly uncomfortable. They could not form an alliance with other opponents of the government because most of them favoured Confederation; they could not establish a meeting of minds with the Ontario Grits who, they quickly concluded, saw everything through Ontario eyes. They lost Stewart Campbell, the member for Guysborough, who went over to the enemy. But they suffered their worst blow in December when the new duties bore out all their dire prophecies. The general tariff, previously ten per cent in Nova Scotia, became the Canadian rate of fifteen per cent, accompanied by stamp duties, taxes on newspapers, and duties on flour, corn, and cornmeal, allegedly designed to protect the Ontario producers. By the end of December Doyle reported to Macdonald that the province was "boiling over with Anti Confederate bile . . . A

Philip Carteret Hill   1867(?); 1875-8

Courtesy of P.A.N.S.

feeling of annexation *they tell me* is gaining ground . . . since the tariff arrived, and the food of the poor became taxed.''[11]

What were the Antis to do now? Once Howe had felt that "a man with a manly, honest case" could "obtain fair play" from the British Parliament, but no longer. But perhaps it should have a chance to rise above its "insular apathy and indifference" and "repair the wrong" to Nova Scotia. So, in mid-February, he was on his way to Britain, instructed by a minute of council, later reinforced by an address and resolutions of the legislature, to seek nothing but repeal. In London he found Disraeli's Tory government in office, but tottering from the start and having an eye to little more than the most controversial of issues, Irish Church disestablishment. After hearing the pleas of Howe and his three associates, Disraeli's colonial secretary, the Duke of Buckingham and Chandos, gave his decision on June 4: Nova Scotia should recognize that the union was "important to the interests of the whole empire" and the Dominion Parliament should "relax or modify any arrangements [on taxation, regulation of trade, and fisheries] which may prejudice the peculiar interests of Nova Scotia, and of the Maritime portion of the Dominion."

Parliament had still to pronounce on Nova Scotia's plea. In 1867 John Bright was only one of several MPs who had assisted the Nova Scotians; in 1867 he was their main adviser and spokesman. Accepting his advice and disregarding their instructions, the delegates agreed that the only practicable course was to ask for a parliamentary investigation of the province's grievances. None was surprised when the House of Commons turned them down by 183 to 87. Howe could only take solace that some of the best intellects in a moribund Parliament had shown sufficient independence to vote against their party leaders.

The result was to place the anti-Confederates in an even greater quandary. But at least John A. Macdonald had come to realize that he had received bad advice about Nova Scotia. The other major teething problems of the federation being resolved, he intended to give Nova Scotia his active attention. Horrified to learn that Tupper was planning a speaking tour throughout Nova Scotia, he told him to cancel it. Instead, he turned to Tilley and Archibald, who advised him to visit Halifax in early August to consult Howe and others when the anti-Confederates were meeting in convention prior to the opening of the legislature. Asked for suggestions at the convention, Howe told the assembly-men and executive councillors that if they agreed to "strike work, resign their offices and repudiate the [BNA] act I would resign and go to the Country with them!" He received no response and later some would question the seriousness of his offer. After two days neither the convention nor the committee which it appointed to make proposals had anything to suggest. Following persuasion by Howe the committee agreed to hear Macdonald, who stated generally what he was prepared to do and expressed his willingness to consider any specific propositions. In private, Howe told Macdonald that he would continue to press for repeal so long as there was any chance of success. In turn Macdonald promised that after prorogation he would send Howe a letter containing terms upon which the two might agree, and that although "marked private" Howe might show it to his friends with the hope of winning them over, provided, of course, that Howe had agreed to accept federal office.

Both Macdonald and Howe were uneasy that, after a year of Confederation, the legislature had not dealt with a single item of normal government business, but only with repeal. That would continue for a while longer in the form of assembly resolutions and minutes of council which, according to the *British Colonist*, were typical of the style of the Jacobin clubs in the worst period of the French Revolution. Most of the arguments were those of Attorney General Martin Wilkins, the author of a peculiar brand of constitutional law which held that the British Parliament had not the legal right to enact the BNA Act. He went too far, however, with his threat that if his proposal to have Nova Scotia collect its own customs duties failed, "we'll appeal to another nation." On Doyle's intervention he declared himself incapable of uttering disloyal sentiments. When Provincial Secretary W.B. Vail at long last presented the estimates, they provided further ammunition for the extremists. It was apparent that the financial bargain of Confederation arranged by Tupper had left the province in a precarious financial position. Even after cutting expenditures to the bone, including the road grant from $240,000 to $100,000, Vail still forecast a deficit of $13,000. Both Macdonald and Howe must have breathed a sigh of relief when the legislature prorogued on September 21.

Throughout the month Macdonald had been writing to Howe that Nova Scotia's interests were suffering because of his keeping important offices open until Howe was in a position to make recommendations. He was also warning Tupper, Archibald and McCully that, because of the "slumbering volcano" that was Nova Scotia, they must forego their own claims to prevent Howe from having "an opportunity of throwing himself back again into the arms of the violent Antis." After prorogation he sent Howe the "private" letter he had promised, but by its very nature it could contain nothing in the way of specific undertakings. The Nova Scotian MPs, it stated, would have to take up constitutional matters in the Commons, but Sir John Rose, the federal minister of finance, would treat with Howe, Annand, and others on financial, taxation, and commercial questions "not in a rigid but in the most liberal spirit."[12]

Throughout the autumn Howe's position became more and more difficult. To those who asked if he had "accepted the situation," he insisted that he was still for repeal if it could be got. But he was convinced that Gladstone would win the forthcoming election and he had twice voted against Nova Scotia. More and more his differences with the "locals" were coming into the open. Now and again the *Recorder* and *Chronicle* published, sometimes covert, sometimes direct, attacks on him. For a time he patched it up with them, but when 82-year old, retired judge John George Marshall broke the truce, Howe thought that he would be "a dastard and a fool to allow this system of bullying and defamation to go on."[13] So between November 6 and 27 he justified his conduct to the public in letters to the *Morning Chronicle*. Basically he argued that in corresponding with Macdonald he was simply testing the Canadians' sincerity and hence seeking an alternative to fall back on if repeal should fail. When he also suggested that the executive councillors who responded nega-tively to his proposal at the convention in August "wanted to hold their offices, cry out for repeal, and throw the responsiblity of a compromize on the Dominion men," he raised a veritable hornets' nest.

By December Howe knew that repeal was out of the question. Except for Bright, the incoming Gladstone government consisted largely of proponents of Confederation. Accordingly on Janu-ary 4 he, in effect, "accepted the situation" by agreeing to meet Sir John Rose at Portland, Maine and to play a major role in awarding federal patronage in Nova Scotia. Ten days later, after the Gladstone government had indicated by telegram that it would not entertain demands for repeal, he was on his way to Portland and a few days later to Ottawa. By the 28th he could report that he and Colchester MP A.W. McLelan had reached an agreement with Rose. Although the "better terms" meant that Nova Scotia got no more than New Brunswick had received by way of subsidy and debt allowance in 1867, it did add substantially to the province's revenues. On January 30, the day on which the British government's dispatch reached Ottawa, Howe entered the federal cabinet as president of the council. Macdonald had "struck off the tallest head of the anti-Confederates" and Howe had accepted a major role in the pacification of Nova Scotia. He might have found the task a good deal easier if he had been more flexible and extended an invitation to the moderate Vail to accompany him to Portland, or if after reaching agreement he had returned at once to Halifax as he had promised, laid his cards on the table, and appeared to let his associates share in the decision. In that case he might have split the moderates off from the extremists. Instead, most Antis would "accept the situation" only after a process of slow attrition. In Halifax Doyle could hardly describe the bitter feelings of Howe's old associates, who felt that they had been "dragged . . . into the mud and left sticking there."

By early February Howe found himself in a ministerial election which turned out to be one of the most celebrated by elections in provincial history. Clearly the electors of Hants County faced a dilemma. "The old Conservatives were being asked to vote for a man whom many of them believed was 'less likely to do right than the devil himself'. The old Liberals found it equally hard to support someone whom two years earlier they had elected to 'whale Confederates'."[14] Night after night, he fought "a whole batch of fellows" in almost every polling district in the county and, as he told Macdonald, the question was: "Could I stand the strain of this severe work in mid winter?" At Nine Mile River, sick and exhausted, he wrapped himself in a sleigh blanket and lay at the back of the platform until it was his turn to speak. Then he collapsed and needed five weeks to recuperate before he could continue. At least "the sinews of war" were forthcoming, especially from Ottawa, and one historian estimates that Howe's campaign cost as much as $30,000. Although the merchants of

Halifax were also profligate in their efforts to defeat him, his majority was still a comfortable 383. But he never recovered fully from the mid-winter campaign in Hants.

In quality the post-Confederation assembly was decidedly inferior to its predecessors because the leading men of both parties had opted for federal politics or office. That fact more than anything enabled William Annand to hold the post of premier for seven and a half years. A poor speaker, enjoying little respect among the party rank and file, he had created the impression that his business interests ranked first among his priorities. But a political vacuum needed to be filled and he was there to fill it. Still, it is astonishing that a premier could sit for this prolonged period in the legislative council as provincial treasurer. Admittedly the policy-making function in matters of finance belonged to the provincial secretary, but nonetheless the electorate seems not to have been demanding at a time when anti-Confederate issues dominated everything else. Actually Annand kept the lowest of profiles as leader of the government and left the limelight to erratic, unpredictable, but not unintelligent Attorney General Martin Wilkins and to moderate, capable, and efficient Provincial Secretary W.B. Vail who, more than anyone, kept the government on the rail.

Between 1869 and 1871 the only non-Confederation issue of consequence was the Rand affair. What had prompted the dismissal of Theodore Harding Rand as Superintendent of Education? Was it because he had conspired with his Confederate friends against the government which paid him? Or, as the government's opponents alleged, was it because he had dared to investigate charges that the public schools in Arichat, Richmond County, were Roman Catholic schools in disguise? The two opposition members could get little information in the assembly, but outside they had the vociferous support of the *Presbyterian Witness* and the Baptist *Christian Messenger*. Whatever else, the issue worked towards making the Catholics a basic core of the Liberal party.

Over the next few years the most difficult problem of the executive council was to make it appear that it was as anxious to get the province out of the federation as the extremist Antis were. In 1869, when Wilkins moved resolutions agreeing to accept "better terms" as a first instalment that was due Nova Scotia, demanding the relaxation of the Dominion's taxation policies, and declaring that no settlement could be final unless accepted by the people, the fat was in the fire. Seven Anti members accused him of accepting the situation and expressed indignation at this radical departure from recently established anti-Confederate policy. Five of the seven, Dr. E.L. Brown, Robert Chambers of Colchester, William Kidston of Victoria, Dr. George Murray of Pictou, and John Ryerson of Yarmouth, would turn out to be die-hard extremists. Chambers expressed a willingness to use any means, honourable or dishonourable, to get the province out of the union: "I would prefer annexation a thousand times, yes, ten thousand times over, to Confederation." Dr. Murray argued that, if Nova Scotia could not be brought safely into port again, the best thing would be to "go down with her, with . . . colors flying, fighting for the rights of which we have been shorn."[15]

The government was not yet done with Murray, whom it regarded as a "wild man," even though he was a respected physician in New Glasgow, one of the few Nova Scotian surgeons who performed operations for cataracts, and the first to operate successfully for harelip. Quite dissatisfied with the government's action, he proposed an address to the Crown asking for the release of Nova Scotians from their allegiance so that, as "a free and independent people," they could adopt institutions "most conducive to . . . happiness and prosperity." The proposal being considered disloyal, Vail moved the previous question and cut off debate. When the legislature met in 1870, it quickly became clear that the government intended to do nothing substantive on the Confederation question. But when Dr. Murray drew up his own set of resolutions, it reached an agreement with him by which it accepted most of them, made a few additions, and presented the new version as its own, disjointed though it was. Nevertheless, the extremists remained convinced that the government had abandoned its main objective. To Kidston it was "seeking to stick together by any and every means" and forgetting the reason for its existence; to Murray it appeared to have accepted the situation and had not "the manliness to say so."[16]

By the time the assembly met in 1871 some of the steam had gone out of the extremists. Not that they ceased to vent their usual venom against the régime at Ottawa. Nor, despite the absence of bitter, provocative resolutions, did they fail to express their dissatisfaction with Annand and his more submissive followers. Robert Chambers, for one, accused them of keeping up the cry of "Repeal and Anticonfederate," while selling the country for personal pelf and gain. At least outwardly, however, the ministry lost no opportunity to worsen its relations with Ottawa or extol its own performance as guardian of Nova Scotian interests. When, as a result of "better terms," it was able to restore some of the cuts in the road and bridge services and forecast small surpluses in 1870 and 1871, it boasted that forceful Anti action had enabled Tupper's bad financial bargain to be partially rectified. Whatever the faults of the Annand government, Vail saw to it that the provincial finances were in good shape.

Despite a balanced budget, the government lacked the means to extend the system of provincial railways. The Pictou branch had started operations in 1867, the Windsor and Annapolis in 1869, but that left much of the province still unserved by railways. In 1870 the assembly approved Vail's resolution that, since the province had surrendered its main revenue sources, the Dominion government had the duty to assume the major responsibility for extending the railways east and west.[17] Perhaps he was anticipating the deluge of requests for railway surveys in all parts of the province which flooded the legislature in 1871. It was the beginning of a concern with railway-building which would test the ingenuity of all governments for almost four decades.

In 1870 the two levels of government found another source of contention in the building which Nova Scotia had begun to construct before July 1867, largely for the post office, and which it had since completed at a cost of $66,385. The questions were: Was it a building which under section 108 of the BNA Act was to be handed over to the Dominion? If it was, should the province be reimbursed for its expenditures since Confederation? Had there been goodwill on both sides arbitration might quickly have settled the dispute. Instead, the rhetoric on both sides rose to a crescendo and the building continued to be locked to the public. The British Colonist was especially indignant that its only use was as "a caucus hall for Government cliques and semi-defunct Annexation and Repeal Leagues," while Halifax had to put up with "the worst and meanest Post Office in America." But if the Antis could not have their way on this question, they could at

Simon Hugh Holmes   1878-82

Courtesy of P.A.N.S.

least arrange some of the political institutions to suit their own needs and interests. Because of the tactics alleged to have been used in the Hants by election, Antis of all shades pressed successfully to have the secret ballot introduced in 1870. Moderate

J.C. Troop called it necessary because the federal government "will not shrink from a final attempt upon the independence of Nova Scotia"; extremist Kidston said that without it "our enemies will triumph, and will call us dead Indians." Alas for the Antis! The ballot failed its first test in a Halifax by election in November 1870 when Confederate Philip Carteret Hill beat out William Garvie, albeit by a mere fourteen votes. Declaring the ballot "entirely useless," the assembly passed bills to repeal it in 1871 and 1873, but "the Legislative Council declined to allow the Legislature to look ridiculous by abandoning it without a fair trial."[18]

Perhaps fearing his own fate, Hill, in one of his first acts as an assemblyman, sought to have the trial of controverted elections transferred from assembly committees to the courts as the British Parliament recently had done. A typical Anti reaction was that of Thomas F. Morrison of Colchester, who contended that the judges came from "the loins of the partisan and despotic political institutions of Canada . . . they are the creatures of Canada . . . I want no grovelling political judges" to try these cases.[19] Foiled in his proposal, Hill awaited a certain fate at the hands of an election committee of seven Liberals headed by Attorney General Wilkins. Before large crowds his opponents produced all sorts of evidence — bribery, impersonation, and the voting of dead men and penniless minors — against his election workers, while the iniquities of the other side remained largely undisclosed. In the end Hill could at least say that he had led a small opposition rather effectively through most of the session of 1871.

That year the most contentious measure was one supposedly intended to secure the independence of the legislature by denying most federal office-holders the right to vote in provincial elections and hence prevent them from "from being walked up to the polls and voting whether [they] asked or not." Its sponsors declared Nova Scotia to be more in danger than any other province because of the large number of employees in the Department of Marine and Fisheries and the Customs Department. But the *British Colonist* condemned the "disfranchising bill" as surpassing in iniquity all the Antis' other evil-doing, calling it the first attempt in Nova Scotia history to proscribe a class supposed to belong to the opposition. Clearly designed for a general election only a few months away, the act may have had its greatest effect in an incident which followed in its wake. Early in April the Anti press carried sensational stories of a "diabolical" attempt by leading Tories — Dr. Tupper, James McDonald, Dr. Wickwire, M.B. Daly, and Dr. Parker — to induce the veteran Legislative Councillor James McNab to vote against the disfranchising bill by promise of a federal appointment to his son Peter. The Tories told a different story of Peter, a complete ne'er-do-well of dubious sanity. According to them, kind-hearted members of their party, when begged to give him a last chance, promised in writing to get federal preferment for him. Governor Doyle, annoyed that the Confederates were caught up in the affair, took comfort that there were "two sides to this question," that Tupper *et al.* were "only *out bidding* offers, that had been made . . . by my immaculate Premier [Annand] and his brother Executive Councillor, Mr. McHeffy."[20] When Peter handed over the letters of the Halifax Tories to the Antis, the latter published them and put their opponents completely on the defensive before a public already ill-disposed to them.

While the "local" Antis were badly split among themselves, Howe was doing his best to pacify the Anti MPs. To many of them the Grits of Edward Blake and Alexander Mackenzie seemed no less objectionable than John A. Macdonald's Tories. On "better terms" they had given the government such a bad time that it carried one division by a majority of only nineteen even with the support of fourteen Nova Scotian MPs. When Edward Blake insisted that the better terms were "final and irrevocable," an indignant *Morning Chronicle* told the Anti MPs to be "careful ere they discharge King Wolf, that King Tiger is not about to mount his throne." Meanwhile Howe was making effective use of patronage in the pacification process. Major appointments like senatorships and judgeships were not the most useful to him since the claimants for them were so numerous that the outcome was sometimes divisive. Rather the smaller offices served him best. By requesting and accepting the recommendations of the Nova Scotian members who were reasonably co-operative, he established at least civil relations with most of them. So much so that in January 1870 he gave Postmaster General Alexander Campbell the names of ten Nova Scotian MPs whose advice he might take on appointments without reference to himself. By year's end all but James Carmichael of Pictou and A.G. Jones and Patrick Power of Halifax were co-operating with him. More and more he was "becoming convinced that his policy of maintaining a reasonable rapport with the Dominion members while letting the 'locals' stew in their frustration would win out in the end. For the Anti members to give a 'fair support' to the Macdonald administration in return for the disposition of patronage automatically meant a separation of sorts from the 'locals,' and for their followers to turn to them for Dominion offices meant an ever-widening acceptance of the federal régime."[21]

As Doyle prorogued the General Assembly in April 1871 prior to dissolution, he was pleased on several counts. His advisers had permitted the word "Dominion" to appear in a speech from the Throne for the first time, indicating that the steam had gone further out of the Anti movement. He was delighted, too, to be saying farewell to "a number of Scoundrels . . . whose faces I never hope to see again!"[22] One was Martin Wilkins, whom John A. Macdonald had not appointed to the Supreme Court but "played like a trout," and who would go to perhaps the most lucrative of provincial offices, the prothonotaryship of Halifax. Following prorogation Annand reconstructed his cabinet in preparation for the election of May 16. Doyle called the new ministers a "decided improvement upon the old ones." They were capable but undistinguished Henry W. Smith as attorney general; brilliant and articulate William Garvie as commissioner of public works and mines; and E.P Flynn of Arichat Schools notoriety as commissioner of crown lands, a new ministerial office — the fifth — which had been created at the most recent session of the legislature.

It was not a repeal election. The *Acadian Recorder*, always highly militant on that subject, conceded that the union was "fixed, settled and irrevocable." Yet, directly or indirectly, almost everything discussed in the campaign related to Confederation and the *British Colonist* would say that the government's only policies were "detestation of Canada" and "eternal hate to Canada." For the Antis the McNab case was a trump card and they never gave up their lambasting of Hill, Daly, McDonald, and Wickwire as Tupper's bribers. None of the old Tory "sins" escaped their condemnation, but they had a new one as well, the fisheries clauses of the Treaty of Washington, which were only becoming known during the election. To them this surrender of colonial, and especially Nova Scotian, interests was another indication of the British decision to withdraw from North America and might well presage the political absorption of Canada into the United States.

The Conservatives seized upon arguments of this kind to picture Annand as being in league with Benjamin Butler, the chief American advocate of annexation: "Annand is Premier and leads the Local Government: and Ben Butler leads Annand." Otherwise, they concentrated on Liberal "iniquities" such as the retention of the provincial building and the disfranchising act, and on denunciation of Annand as "a great loon, a great cheat, a great corruptionist, a great impostor, a great humbug," whose most ardent admirers were unable to discover a single good measure originated by his cabinet. A more negative campaign would be difficult to imagine and Joseph Howe's intervention did not make it less so. Seriously unwell, he contented himself with five letters to the *British Colonist* and *Express* which administered "a skinning" to Annand, Wilkins, and "the little knot of worthies" about them. Wilkins, he said, by accepting the prothonotaryship could "pass the rest of his days in swearing witnesses to do what he never did himself — 'to tell the truth, the whole truth, and nothing but the truth'."[23] Howe's opponents dismissed the letters as "a voice from the grave," the "last infirmity of [a] noble mind."

The outcome was the election of twenty-four Liberals and fourteen Conservatives. The *Recorder* was right in part in attributing the government's loss of twelve seats since 1867 to "the wear and tear of political management"; few governments, it pointed out, retained their strength after four years. Annand and his ministers had at least the consolation that they would no longer have the "wild men" to harass them: Chambers had chosen not to run and Brown, Kidston, Murray, and Ryerson all lost. Their failure throws further light upon Nova Scotians' dislike of extremism. For the Conservatives the biggest disappointment was their inability to win any of the three seats in Halifax. Seemingly they could not blame the disfranchsing act since Hill trailed the third Liberal by almost two hundred votes. But they could console themselves in their taking about 45 percent of the popular vote and making themselves much more competitive.

The period of the Twenty-Fourth General Assembly (1871-4) continued and completed the absorption of Nova Scotia into the Canadian political system. In the federal election of mid-1872 the Liberals admitted to serious difficulties. Although the government at Ottawa recognized Nova Scotia's pre-1867 election law and held all its elections in the province on the same day, elsewhere they staged them earlier in seats which they expected to win "and thus strengthen[ed] their weak-kneed supporters" in places like Nova Scotia. Even more perturbing to the *Chronicle* was the conduct of the province's MPs who, "going up to Ottawa as red-hot Antis," had been "successively wheedled" into giving almost unbroken support to a government containing Howe and Tupper. But in again urging the voters to punish the traitors who sold the province into Confederation it failed, for the eighteen Antis of nineteen in 1867 appeared to become only eleven of twenty-one in 1872. "Repeal, Annexation, Gritism, bogus Reform, Rougism, are all wiped out," exulted the *British Colonist*. Conceding that "the question of Union or Anti-Union is dead," the *Chronicle* urged its readers to join "the cause of those noble statesmen, Mackenzie and Blake" and unite with the other Liberal parties of Canada to ensure "an honest, economical, honorable and Liberal government."[24]

Six months earlier, when the Twenty-Fourth General Assembly met for the first time, William Garvie, seriously ill with consumption, was not there. Two days later he appeared at the request of Annand to respond to the rejuvenated opposition. Speaking at the time was D.B. Woodworth, a Conservative from Kings, who for the next seven years disturbed the tranquillity of the assembly as no one else has ever done. When Woodworth referred to ministers "who sit like dumbdogs and have not a word to say," Garvie replied in a speech which, for "the brilliancy of its wit, the sting of its sarcasm, the intensity of its invective, . . . the wealth of historical illustration and literary allusion," made it "one of the finest pieces of parliamentary oratory ever heard" in Nova Scotia.[25] Tragically Garvie's maiden speech would be his last. He died later in the year on his way to the south of France, where he had hoped to regain his health.

The result was to leave Vail the undoubted leader of a mediocre government in the assembly against a vigorous opposition eager to take it over. No General Assembly has ever produced so little in the way of substantive legislation. In 1873 only five public bills became law — the smallest number in provincial history — and the major one — to limit the expenditure on common schools to $117,000 — was anything but positive in character. The Conservatives denounced it for turning the clock back and for lowering the quality of education. Yet the period from 1871 to 1874 did mark the first tentative steps towards the resumption of railway building — a response to continual pressure from the areas without railways which would continue unabated for many years. Vail could make a start because of an increase in population which led to an additional $46,000 in the federal subsidy. But his proposals to build the railways from Annapolis to Yarmouth (Western Counties Railway), Springhill to Parrsboro, and New Glasgow to the Strait of Canso (Eastern Extension) and on to Louisburg, involved relatively little in the way of money. The companies building the three lines would all get extensive grants of Crown lands; those building the last two would get half the royalties on the coal from the mines which they opened up; only the company building the first would get cash grants amounting to $30,000 a year for twenty years.

Critics called the proposals, especially those relating to the third line, "a delusion and a snare." Although some discussion with contractors took place on the first two, interest in the Eastern Extension was "as barren as the desert sands." The government was silent on railways in 1873, but it tried again in 1874 following an increase of about $75,000 in its annual revenue because of an addition to its debt allowance. Leaving the Crown lands grants intact, Vail proposed, in addition, a subsidy of $6,000 a mile for the first line and $5,000 a mile for the other two. He defended the differential on the ground that "there was no worse country in the world for railroad operations than the country between Annapolis and Digby."

Partly because of the lack of consequential business, the assembly was at its rancorous worst in these years. The Liberals were described as the "brainless rump" of a once powerful party, a gang of "bunglers and cheats"; in turn they accused Hiram Blanchard, the Conservative leader, of growing "only the reverse of wiser as he grows older"; lambasted James McDonald for believing that his bullying, browbeating tactics would make him cock o' the walk; and dismissed Woodworth as "a noisy creature" who performed best when he remained seated. In 1872 rancor manifested itself on such old issues as the provincial building and the disfranchising act; in 1873 it centred around the growing Liberal antipathy for Douglas Woodworth. By the end of the session Vail would tell him that no ten-year old would be guilty of the nonsense which he inflicted on the house.

In 1874 the assembly met in a different political context. Brought to power on the Pacific Scandal without benefit of an election, Alexander Mackenzie and the federal Liberals decided to hold one early in the year. Nova Scotia Liberals agreed that "the era of reform [should] be inaugurated with a pure House of Commons as well as a pure government." It was hardly a contest in Nova Scotia. On the defensive from the start, the Conservatives won only three of twenty-one seats. Overshadowing everything else were the extraordinary events in Halifax. There the incumbent Conservatives, facing certain defeat, chose not to run but contrived to put forward mechanic Andrew Robb, although he called himself a Workingman's candidate. An outraged *Chronicle* was aghast at tactics aimed particularly at Liberal candidate A.G. Jones. Any attempt to set up one class against another, it said, was "Communism — nothing more or less" and, if successful, could not "fail to shake the foundations of society." Robb fared badly, but the repercussions of the incident would be far-reaching. When P.C. Hill publicly condemned his party's opposition to Jones, the Tory *Colonist* alleged a conspiracy devised by Jones himself. Supposedly Vail was to give up the provincial secretaryship to Hill and, as the member for Digby, assume a portfolio at Ottawa. A slip-up had occurred in Digby but Hill's coming into print meant that he was fulfilling his part of the bargain. Alas! said the *Colonist*, "we silvered him over with brilliant glitter, but the base pewter would ever reveal itself."[26] By the end of the year it was clear that it knew whereof it wrote.

The advent of the federal Liberals to office changed much of the focus of provincial politics even though some old issues re-

John S. D. Thompson   1882

Courtesy of P.A.N.S.

mained. The shoe on the other foot, the provincial Conservatives
hailed with delight the chance to assail a Liberal government at
Ottawa. Opposing them at every turn was Thomas Fletcher
Morrison of Colchester, as strong a partisan who ever sat in the
provincial assembly and who only a year before had called
Canadians the "scum of the earth." Whether it was due to the
"eccentric pulpit oratory of 'Father Taylor' which he had heard in
Boston," the "ranting and roaring" of the temperance quacks, or

the long and constant use of his voice amidst the swelling of the waves, he had won the soubriquet of "Rolling Billows."[27] The *British Colonist* even told him that he ought to be in charge of a fog trumpet at the mouth of the Bay of Fundy.

But his treatment of the Conservatives was as nothing compared with Woodworth's harassment of the Liberals. He began by presenting a petition from Peter McNab for release from the Lunatic Asylum and by insinuating that the Liberals had been the real culprits in his case three years earlier. The wretched McNab, after being given money by the Liberals and a provincial position with few duties attached to it, had stabbed a man and been confined, first in jail and later in the asylum. Unable to get a full investigation of the unsavoury affair, Woodworth turned on Vail, whom he accused of ordering erasures in the Crown lands books after the lieutenant-governor had approved specific grants. Although *prima facie* evidence existed for the charges, a plausible explanation was forthcoming. Determined to have their own innings, the Liberals got the house to adjudge Woodworth guilty of violating its privileges and order an apology. Blanchard called it "an exercise of power not equalled by the Star Chamber." Woodworth refused to apologize and the sergeant at arms forcibly ejected him. Later he would have his vengeance before the courts. It took a non-party newspaper like the *Presbyterian Witness* to deplore the sorry state into which the Nova Scotia assembly had degenerated: even in the "worst 'bowie knife and revolver assemblies' of the States, [one] would not find anything . . . more low and vulgar in language, more ungentlemanly in conduct, more majority despotical; in short more unlike the days of Fairbanks, Robie, Johnston and Howe."[28]

The provincial Liberals soon discovered that the installation of their party at Ottawa had its disadvantages as well as its benefits. In particular, many of their leading men could not resist the good things which the Mackenzie government was in a position to offer. Vail left in September 1874 to become minister of militia and defence; Attorney General Smith wanted the vacant place on the provincial Supreme Court; Annand himself, now sixty-six, craved the comfortable berth of Canada's agent general in London. Because the provincial cabinet was about to be decimated and suitable replacements were unavailable within Liberal ranks, a desperate remedy was needed. The public got an inkling of what it was on November 19 when the *British Colonist* launched a tirade at P.C. Hill for becoming "one of the most active tools and agents of [the] present, most imbecile, corrupt and unprincipled Local Government." Hill, it said, had helped to get Jones elected in Halifax and was to be repaid in kind. Within days its prophecy was borne out. For on November 26, only one day after the dissolution of the General Assembly, he agreed to run for the Liberals in Halifax. Six days later he became provincial secretary and would apparently move to the top since Annand announced "his intention when the contest . . . was over . . . to retire altogether from active affairs." Most of the Tory press was unrestrained in its criticism of a man whom it accused of sapping the foundations of his party by burrowing in secret for months and then selling himself completely to the enemy. Hill replied that, Confederation no longer being the question at issue, he cordially approved fully of the government's policy. "What the Local Government most require[d] at the present time was hard-working, painstaking and efficient men in the Departmental offices."[29]

It was the shortest of campaigns, only three and a half weeks. Annand spoke only at the Liberal nominating convention in Halifax and later drew derision for not even issuing a party manifesto. For the Liberals the issue was simple: Should a government of seven years labouring under "not a ghost of a charge" be sustained or should it be "recklessly overturned and give place to a batch of untried, inexperienced, and irresponsible men"? Because they had few specific accomplishments of which to boast, they concentrated on denouncing the opposition as a petty faction. The Conservative leader in the assembly, Hiram Blanchard, did not run and died on election day before the results were known. His chief lieutenant, Simon Holmes, did not venture beyond his own county of Pictou and it was left to the recently formed Liberal Conservative Association of Halifax and its secretary Robert Sedgewick, both candidates for Halifax, to issue the party's manifesto, written for the most part by the third candidate, Martin Griffin, the youthful, highly literate, but more than a little arrogant, editor of the *Express*.

Generally the Conservatives levelled charges in intemperate terms against the government's "system of jobbery and fraud" and the attempts to prevent inquiry into its activities. They also lambasted the Mackenzie government for its increase in tariffs on the Intercolonial Railway and prophesied that Nova Scotians would become "the slaves of Ontario's Grits." They had one positive proposal too. Because the Liberals had failed to meet any of the demands for the railroads, they proposed to capitalize $250,000 of the province's annual revenues and to use the $4.5 millions of borrowed funds to complete railways to the Strait of Canso and Louisburg, and to Yarmouth with branch lines to Lunenburg, Bridgewater, Liverpool and Shelburne.

To the disappointment of the Conservatives they again lost all three seats in Halifax. When Martin Griffin footed the poll, he compared himself to the horse-racer who, coming last, stated that he had pushed all the others before him. Outside Halifax, the results were not so certain since most of the Cape Breton candidates appeared to put the railroad before the party. But it was disappointment again for the Conservatives, for when the members finally established firm allegiances the standing was twenty-four Liberals to fourteen Conservatives, the same as in 1871. The Liberals would continue to run Nova Scotia for another four years.

CHAPTER 8

Political Misfits: Hill and Holmes

The Twenty-Fifth General Assembly started its first session in 1875 with new leadership in the lower house. By seniority, if not for demonstrated ability, Pictonian Simon Hugh Holmes succeeded Blanchard as Conservative leader almost as a matter of course. Facing him, in the process of being groomed for the premiership, was Provincial Secretary Philip Carteret Hill. Time would prove that neither possessed the talents needed to be a successful leader in the politics of the day. It was not quite true that Hill was "to the manor born," but it was almost so. His father had left the army to become cashier of the Halifax Banking Company where, like the bank itself, his fortunes had flourished. In short order the Hill family became identified with the Tory-Anglican establishment and Philip Carteret did his own cause no harm when he married Margaretta Collins, daughter of Enos, later reputed to be the richest man in British North America.

Though admitted to the bar, he had no need to practise law to earn a living and the *Chronicle* once stated that if he ever gave a legal opinion or addressed a jury, "it must have been a remote time to which the memory of man runneth not."[1] His penchant for the conservative's concept of an ordered society became clear in an address following a visit to the United States in the late 1850s. Dismissing the uninhibited expectations of young Americans, he told ordinary Nova Scotians to imitate the Englishman who, cast in a subordinate role, carried out his duties conscientiously and uncomplainingly. The true test for everyone was the faithful exercise of the trust committed to him, though it was but a minor one.

Hill's entrance into partisan politics had begun on July 4, 1867 when, almost like a bolt from the blue, he became provincial secretary in the Blanchard-Hill administration. Defeat came quickly, as it did to most Confederates. Although victorious in a by election in 1870, he had his seat vacated before he served out the session. Various accounts seek to explain his move from the Tory to the Liberal camp — his friendship with federal Liberal A.G. Jones; his abhorrence of the Pacific Scandal; his desire, as a man of leisure, to have a political career and his choice of the Liberals as the only vehicle offering any chance of success. Perhaps all three factors played a part.

From the start Hill had a new, formidable opponent arrayed against him. Appearing for the first time on January 14, 1875 was *The Morning Herald and Commercial Advertiser,* which under various names has remained to this day a major provincial newspaper. Established by leading young Conservatives, it promised to be "a faithful exponent of the policy of the Liberal Conservative party, in the administration of public affairs, whether coming under the cognizance of the Dominion or the Local Government." While offering every encouragement to enterprise and industry it would also advocate a careful husbandry of the public resources and "maintain under all circumstances the integrity of the Empire, the continuance of British connection and fealty to the Crown of England." In a very real sense it succeeded the *British Colonist,* the principal Conservative paper for twenty-seven years, whose proprietor, Alpin Grant, had disposed of his interests to the founders of the *Herald.* Disappearing also at this time was the Conservative *Express* and before long its editor, Martin Griffin, would assume the same position at the *Herald.* When he left in 1878, eventually to become Librarian of Parliament, his successor was John James Stewart who, as the *Herald's* editor for almost three decades, did as much as anyone to determine Conservative party policy.

Hoping to evoke a friendly response from his opponents both at the *Herald* and in the assembly, Hill started off in 1875 by expressing regret over the passing of Blanchard in the prime of life — *ut flos succisus aratro,* as he put it — but the too ostentatious display of his classical knowledge won him no plaudits. Neither did his resort to some recent words of Disraeli that even when "political passions run high . . . sentiments of

William T. Pipes   1882-4

Courtesy of P.A.N.S.

courtesy" might continue. Nova Scotia's Tories, he was told, could hardly be expected to follow the course of Disraeli and Gladstone, who respected one another for being true to their parties' traditions, while he had "bartered away consistency and political honor for the sake of office."² Despite Hill's self-pitying complaints of unfair treatment, he was taunted inside and outside the assembly with names from *"the* son-in-law" to "ass" and "traitor." In the house he met a barrage of attacks, especially from Holmes; Avard Longley, nicknamed the "bird of Paradise" because of his place of residence in Annapolis County; and Douglas Woodworth, who was normally turbulence itself. To Hill, the classical scholar and "elegant man of exquisite taste," it was a new and disquieting experience to be subjected continually to a mélange of half-truths and unfounded charges. Incapable of matching his opponents' rhetoric, he generally replied in short, factual, reasoned speeches more suited to an Oxford debating society than to the Nova Scotia assembly of the mid-seventies.

Strange as it may seem, the Conservatives started the session with the hope of supplanting the Liberals. It rested on their belief that all the Cape Breton members attached less importance to party than to the railway, "the one all-absorbing topic with the people in the East." Accordingly twelve Conservative members secretively circulated a paper — their opponents called it a round robin — which promised $6,000 a mile to construct the line eastward to Louisburg. Hill countered with a better offer: $5,000 a mile; 300,000 acres of Crown lands, including mineral rights in half of them; and $5,000 towards a ferry at the Strait of Canso. It was enough; even E.T. Moseley, the most outspoken of the islanders, agreed that Hill could have got nothing more from the legislature. In the end only one of the eight Cape Breton members — Dr. Murdoch McRae of Inverness County — supported the Conservatives.

When Holmes finally got round to introducing a non-confidence motion, he placed great emphasis on a long-standing ill which caused Hill no little trouble. Three Liberal newspapers, the *Chronicle,* controlled by the premier; the *Citizen,* partly owned by former Provincial Secretary Vail; and the *Acadian Recorder,* whose proprietor had been Queen's printer, were each receiving about $5,000 annually from public printing without tenders being called. After an assembly committee headed by the "bird of Paradise" found the amounts to be excessive, Hill replied lamely that it had gone only part way and relied too heavily on the evidence of prejudiced smaller printers. Otherwise frustrated, the Conservatives vented their displeasure in what the *Recorder* called "the roughest, most unnecessary piece of business ever perpetrated in a deliberative assembly," Woodworth's motion calling on the speaker to resign. In a very real sense the government was paying for its sins. To ensure the support of John Barnhill Dickie of Colchester it had made him speaker even though he was new to the house. Evidently he had performed badly since seven Liberals joined thirteen Conservatives to carry Woodworth's motion against twelve Liberals, who included all the members of the executive council. To the *Herald* it was meet justice for a member who had run on an anti-government ticket and then betrayed his constituents. "Revenge," it wrote, "is a sweet morsel at times."[3] For Hill the session had been a rough initiation. He had won approbation only for his transference of the trial of controverted elections to the courts and he had ended up by appearing to have lost control over his backbenchers.

The session over, Annand quickly gave way to Hill. Because of the weakness of his cabinet and the need to cope with an intractable opposition, Hill resorted to expediency and in November appointed Otto Schwartz Weeks as his attorney general. Popular with his colleagues, talented as a lawyer, articulate and argumentative, Weeks would certainly be able to meet a fractious opposition at its own level. But his intemperate habits and erratic behaviour might also mean that Hill was borrowing trouble for the future. The synoptic debates for 1876 tend to create the impression that Weeks was very much the leader *de facto*. It led Woodworth to wonder who really headed the government. Perhaps, he said, they might settle it in the manner of the Tycoon and the Mikado, the one having the semblance, the other the reality of power.

This session Woodworth was less intemperate than usual, elated perhaps because the Supreme Court of Nova Scotia had awarded him $500 against the Liberal members who had had him ejected from the assembly in 1874. Eventually the Supreme Court of Canada would concur that no member could be removed unless he was causing an immediate obstruction to the house. Unwilling to await its decision and leave themselves at the mercy of Woodworth and others like him, Hill and his colleagues got the assembly to abandon its reliance upon self-preservative inherent powers for a complete statutory guarantee of its privileges, powers, and immunities based upon earlier acts of Quebec and

Ontario. Strangely, Woodworth and the Conservatives made no attempt to obstruct the bill. Again Hill won commendation for only one act in 1876, his opening of the public printing to tender. But he showed not a little courage in moving tentatively towards a provincial university, long one of his pet projects. For at least five years the denominational colleges would continue to receive government grants, while preliminary steps were taken to establish the institution which he had in mind under the title of University of Halifax. The Conservatives, long the defenders of denominational colleges, complained that these institutions had been given five years' notice to quit, much "like the Aztecs, who attended and feasted the victims they destined to slaughter."[4]

Dominating everything else in 1876, however, was the seemingly everlasting railway question. When the government made it known that it had received no offers to build the Eastern Extension and Cape Breton lines, it was too much for E.T. Moseley and he moved to the other side of the house. As its railway policy, the Hill government introduced two bills: one to encourage the construction of a line from Nictaux and Middleton to the Atlantic, the other to increase the subsidy for the Eastern Extension to $8,000 a mile. Simon Holmes, already showing the keen interest in railways that would become an obsession, suggested going back to building them as government works. Such a "wild" and "reckless" proposal, replied Hill, would "pitchfork" the province into a debt of $3,000,000 and annual interest payments of $150,000.

Otto Weeks had done much to ease Hill through the session of 1876. When sober, he had ability to spare. But much of the time he was not and shortly after the session his intemperateness resulted in long absences from his office. This was natural for a man who at times exhibited all sorts of eccentricities, including a careless use of firearms. Once, allegedly, he took aim at his wife and a stray pellet struck her in the leg; on another occasion, while lying in bed, he diverted himself by firing shots into the ceiling of his hotel room. After the session of 1876 he was repeatedly absent from his office over long periods of time without making provision for the transaction of his department's business, often at a time when important matters needed to be discussed. Worse still, "the air was full of charges against his character," which he made no attempt to answer and which his colleagues felt that they could no longer ignore. Asked to resign in the fall of 1876, he refused and on the unanimous recommendation of the Executive Council, the lieutenant-governor removed him from office, the only incident of its kind in Nova Scotia. Over the next two sessions Weeks pursued a somewhat independent course, on occasion siding with the opposition and otherwise adopting an anti-government stance.

Apparently Hill had difficulty in filling the vacancy and not till the session of 1877 was about to begin did Alonzo J. White, the commissioner of crown lands, become attorney general as well. Whatever his other abilities, White could not cope nearly as effectively with the opposition as Weeks and if ever Hill had doubts about the wisdom of changing parties to become premier he must have had them in 1877 when he was constantly beset, especially on the Great Seal question. In 1869 the province had received a new seal and was ordered to return the old one. Told that Nova Scotians wanted no change, the Dominion government referred the matter to Britain. No reply having been received, the old seal remained in use. Apprized of the situation seven or eight years later, the Conservatives contended that the seal had no validity, that appointments and conveyances of land under it were invalid, and that even the legislature and government were illegally constituted. Woodworth did so much "blowing," said the *Chronicle*, that it appeared to be the "great porpoise" rather than the Great Seal question. Hill called it "monstrous" to alarm the people needlessly.[5] Then, after weeks of contention, it proved to be a case of much ado about nothing.

But the impending financial crisis did not fizzle out. Making it worse was the economic downturn which, beginning late in 1875, had ripened into a full-scale recession. It occurred at a time when the "better terms" payments of $82,698 a year for ten years were coming to an end. Although Hill had warned Prime Minister Mackenzie and Finance Minister Richard Cartwright that their loss would force Nova Scotia to resort to direct taxation, he was told that they could not be continued unless the other provinces received *pro rata* payments and that was out of the question in a period of financial stringency. Because the guarantees to the Western Counties Railway (WCR), the Nictaux and Atlantic, and the Eastern Extension would exhaust the province's debt account at Ottawa, the situation was all the worse. Indeed, the overall result would be to reduce the province's annual revenue by $180,000, a large proportion of the total.

To save money, Hill raised the old question of maritime union. "It would seem . . . quite as proper," he said, "to employ one of Narmyth's steam hammers to crush an egg-shell as to employ such an [inordinate] amount of machinery" to govern three small provinces."[6] But E.T. Moseley told him to put his own financial house in order before sending a delegation to New Brunswick as "beggars" and Weeks, seemingly intent on embarrassing both Hill and the government, insisted that any conference on maritime union take place in Nova Scotia. Much the same situation developed on Hill's second money-saving proposal: a reduction in the number of ministers with office from five to four by combining the offices of attorney general and commissioner of crown lands. This time Weeks heaped scorn upon so "curious and incongruous an amalgamation," while the Conservatives scoffed at a change that would save no more than $2,000 a year.

Other than the letting, at long last, of a contract for the Eastern Extension, the government's railway programme had made little headway. On the WCR progress had been slow, especially on the difficult 18.2-mile section between Annapolis and Digby; part of it would become the celebrated "missing link." Resuming his old aggressivenes, Woodworth charged that this line had been "built largely of brush and logs" and that "the sky [might soon be] filled with smoke from the conflagration of the Western Counties Railway."[7] Counter-attacking, the *Chronicle* took it out on its party's tormentor by accusing him of receiving $900 for navigation securities in Kings County under false pretences. As it turned out, he had spent $308.14 on wharves and breakwaters, and placed the remainder in a Kentville bank, apparently to be applied to its proper purpose the following year. Always fair, Hill cut the ground from under his own supporters by admitting that Woodworth had done nothing which other members would not have done with perfect propriety under similar circumstances.

This was quite unacceptable to liberal backbencher Dr. E.M. Farrell, who had developed an intense loathing for Woodworth. When he insisted on a committee to investigate the conduct of his *bête noire*, the exchanges between the two, lasting to prorogation, almost turned the assembly into a bear-garden. On one occasion Farrell accused Woodworth of "keeping agencies for servant girls at the Halifax Hotel," while the latter charged Farrell with perpetrating an indignity upon a dead man after placing stones and refuse in his coffin. Farrell, said Woodworth, was "a little man," whom Almighty Providence had given, as to little animals generally, "a certain disagreeableness to compensate for their insignificance."[8] Clearly the assembly of 1877 was not a congenial place for Hill, the man of exquisite taste. More than ever, his government seemed to lack leadership and direction, and its position deteriorated even further between sessions. In December 1877 it lost a by election in Antigonish to John Sparrow David Thompson and two months later its candidate Thomas Robertson went down to defeat in Shelburne. "The Stuarts have disappeared from the ranks of royalty; so have the Guises and Bonapartes," wrote the *Herald*; now, hopefully, the Robertsons of Shelburne had received their quietus.[9] Suddenly the government's position in the assembly, previously so secure, was a little precarious: a majority of only three with a Liberal speaker in the chair.

Hill dressed up the speech from the Throne as best he could in 1878, but he could not hide the prevailing gloom. Admittedly the Eastern Extension was progressing, but unpaid labourers' claims were becoming a thorny issue on that line. A similar problem had led to a complete halt in building the Nictaux and Atlantic. Work on the WCR had not resumed after a year's stoppage and Woodworth lamented the spending of a million dollars with nothing to show for it but "rails rusted, . . . sleepers rotten and everything in the most shameful state." Worse still for Hill, following the federal government's transference of the Windsor Branch to the WCR from the Windsor and Annapolis, the latter made no attempt to ensure a smooth transfer of passengers and freight at Windsor and encouraged the movement of goods to Saint John rather than to Halifax. Almost in despair, Hill bewailed the lack of legal power to intervene; "if anything could be done by . . . moral suasion," he would do it.[10]

Nothing that Hill attempted in 1878 escaped harsh criticism. To cut expenditures in a time of financial stringency he took steps to reduce the number of ministers with office to three by having the provincial secretary assume the duties of the provincial treasurer. But, according to Holmes, not only were the savings miniscule, but the necessary check which the provincial secretary acting as a financial secretary exercised upon the provincial treasurer would disappear. Harassed by charges of gross misman-agement in the lunatic asylum, Hill proposed a Board of Commissioners of Public Charities to manage that institution, only to be accused of departing from the principles of responsible government. Painting the blackest picture possible, the *Herald* declared his "prestige as a leader completely broken, his personal honor sullied, his Government a combination of irreconcilables and incurables, the country a mass of ruins."[11] Although grossly unfair, it was right that the courtly, polished Hill lacked the temperament to act decisively in many matters. The previous session the opposition had demanded action against the counties which had been overspending their road allocations. Neverthe-less, these advances had risen from $81,000 to $152,000 during the year and in Inverness alone they had reached $32,000. Even so, it took the combined efforts of the opposition and Weeks to secure a resolution requiring each county to pay one quarter of its advances out of the current year's allocation.

By 1878 even Hill was seeking to put Woodworth on the defensive. According to the *Herald*, a commission which he appointed to investigate the spending of road moneys in Kings County held a Court of Star Chamber at Jaw Bone Corner (actually Lower Canard) and condemned both Kings County members. But an assembly committee which dealt finally with the matter brought in contradictory majority and minority reports and Woodworth had, in effect, escaped again.

Naturally he would have his innings. Supposedly on the basis of new evidence, he sought to renew his seven-year old charges against former Provincial Secretary Vail for his treatment of Crown land grants only to have Hill point out that no precedent existed for reviewing the act of a committee of a previous legislature upon relatively trivial grounds. Woodworth got even more into the limelight on March 14 when a news story in the *Chronicle* alleged that he had sought to bring down the govern-ment through a bribe of $1,000 to a Liberal member. Appearing outraged, Woodworth secured an investigation by the assembly's committee of privileges and then stopped it from reaching a definitive conclusion, first by delaying its proceedings and later by refusing to testify under oath. It was clear, nonetheless, that John A. Fraser of Victoria had received $1,000 from Woodworth one day, paid it back the next, and then left Halifax before he could be called upon to testify.

The episode brought into the public eye William Stevens Fielding, who described himself as "one of the editors" of the *Chronicle*. Prevented from appearing before the committee because of prorogation, he presented evidence damaging to Woodworth in affidavit form in his newspaper. In these proceedings both Holmes and John S.D. Thompson sought to distance themselves from Woodworth. To them it must have seemed incomprehensible that anyone would seek to bring down a government by unseemly means on the eve of dissolution. Indeed, their reaction may have induced him to move to federal politics. That action would come too late to relieve Hill of his principal tormentor.

Hill's last political act of consequence was to choose the date of the election. At least astute enough to realize the unpopularity of his own government, he deluded himself into believing that he might ride back into office on the coat tails of the federal Liberal government. In this respect he was only less deluded than Prime Minister Mackenzie himself, whose biographer states that he was "the last to know how he really rated with the public."[12] In any case federal election day, September 17, also became the provincial, and federal issues altogether dominated the campaign in Nova Scotia, especially in the Liberal newspapers. For them, the first, last, and foremost issue was the protective tariff advocated by the Conservatives; that monster "protection — the foulest blot in history on the fair name of British institutions" — was certain to wreak hardship on Nova Scotian producers and consumers even as it benefited Ontario producers.[13] Although supporting the "National Policy" (N.P.) the *Herald* did not eulogize it to the extent that the Liberal press damned it; rather it condemned Mackenzie's unrelenting hostility to Nova Scotia.

Provincially, it ran a series of editorials entitled "Eleven Years of Jobbery and Ruin" in which it catalogued every conceivable fault of the Annand and Hill governments, and described their legacy as "a Treasury absolutely bankrupt; two or three lines of rubbish heaps called railways . . . endless country debts."[14] Hill's major election activity took the form of a lengthy letter to the people of Nova Scotia in which he claimed to be a good housekeeper and boasted of his success in extending the railways eastward and westward. The letter demonstrates that he had become something of a politician for, although the facts were accurate, they exaggerated his government's rather meagre accomplishments and glossed over the problems which it left unresolved.

If Hill did not have troubles enough, Weeks managed to add to them. Losing the party nomination in Guysborough, he ran nonetheless, calling himself a Liberal and intimating that Hill had remained silent about his removal because he lacked good grounds to justify it. That led Hill to adopt the extraordinary course of having a letter published in the *Morning Chronicle* on September 4 outlining publicly for the first time the reason for Weeks' dismissal. But Weeks, always popular in Guysborough, polled 502 votes, as many as the second Liberal candidate, and was principally responsible for the defeat of the party's two candidates in the county.

Elsewhere recession was the major determinant of the election and it led to massive victories for the Conservatives both provincially and federally. Of the twenty-one federal seats the Conservatives added eleven to the three which they had won in 1874 and took 51.8 per cent of the vote to the Liberals' 45.0. Provincially the Conservatives won thirty of the thirty-eight seats and their popular vote was 51.7 per cent to their opponents' 45.1. Defeated personally in Halifax, Hill's political career was over. Four years later he moved to Tunbridge Wells, England, where for a dozen years he revived his literary interests, especially in the discussion of religious subjects. Likely these were happier days than those he spent as premier of Nova Scotia. The weight of evidence suggests that his entrance into politics was not so much a case of *noblesse oblige* as it was a craving for recognition. For being a turncoat he paid a heavy price. Perhaps his greatest failing was that he could not bring himself to resort to many of the normal devices of the politician even though he sat in the most intemperate assembly in provincial history. Basically he remained his cultivated, urbane, dignified self, who employed reason and logic instead of verbiage and rhetoric, and who, whatever the provocation, refused to stoop to innuendo or name-calling. Not even a Douglas Woodworth could make him change his ways.

The new Conservative government of Simon Holmes took office on October 22, 1878. Holmes became provincial secretary; Legislative Councillor Samuel Creelman, "Upper Stewiacke's most illustrious son," commissioner of public works and mines; and John S.D. Thompson attorney general. Thompson, a reluctant politician, had won his by election and general election contests with the assistance of Bishop John Cameron of Arichat, although the bishop professed only a modest share in his successes: "You were a stranger to the County of Antigonish, and I simply introduced you to my friends . . . That the Catholics of the County attached more importance to my words than to the raving of the *Chronicle* and its selfish or bigoted disciples, is only what might have been expected, the moment they saw you and your rivals face to face." Making no bones about his Conservative leanings the bishop told Holmes that "there were few, if any, who rejoiced more than myself at this happy turn of events both on public and personal grounds . . . the amplest measure of success and glory in your strenuous efforts to cleanse the Augean stables."[15]

Holmes may not have inherited the Augean stables, but he had fallen heir to interrelated railway and financial problems which were almost insoluble. In making the first of many pleas to Ottawa early in 1879,[16] he pointed out that the province had an accumulated deficit of $316,000 and that its expenditures of $450,000 for the year would exceed its revenues by at least $200,000. Seeking to refute Richard Cartwright's contention that Nova Scotia was spending large sums on education and highways, which other provinces met by direct local taxation, he argued forcefully that Nova Scotia could hardly be accused of extravagance since its outgo on these services was $60,000 less than before Confederation. In contradicting Alexander Mackenzie's argument that any concessions to Nova Scotia would have to be made *pro rata* to the other provinces, he based his case primarily on fiscal need, much as his successors would do decades later. Surely if the revenue of four provinces was "*pro rata* far in excess of that of the fifth" and the federal subsidy to the fifth was altogether inadequate, its claim for aid became a claim of right which ought to be allowed "in a large and liberal sense." Since Canada had received $5.5 millions for allowing the Americans to take fish in eastern waters, half of which were caught off Nova Scotia, was it too much to ask that the province might receive an additional $100,000 annually?

Only a few days earlier Holmes had made a submission on railways and he and Thompson followed it up with a visit to Ottawa in mid-February 1879.[17] They had a sad story to tell. Construction of the Nictaux and Atlantic (later called the Nova Scotia Central Railway), which had been stopped several times earlier, was again at a standstill. The same was true of the WCR, which had not a single mile of its own road in operation and was "in fact, rotting under the eyes of the whole country." These difficulties, however, paled in comparison with those of the Eastern Extension. In 1876 Harry Abbott had agreed to build the line from New Glasgow to the Strait and to a point on Bras d'Or Lake for a cash subsidy, a grant of Crown lands, and, when he met specific conditions, the Pictou Branch. He quickly transferred his contract to the Halifax and Cape Breton Railway and Coal Company, which entered into a construction contract with the Canada Improvement Company. It, in turn, employed C.C. Gregory to build the line. In 1877, when Abbott sought less restrictive terms on the bonds of the Halifax and Cape Breton Railway and Coal Company, Gregory, who was to be paid partly in the company's bonds, objected.

Lashing out at the government's monumental stupidity, the *Herald* wrote with some justification that "such a swarm of wickedly knavish abortions as they have called into existence, never before existed outside the walls of a parish workhouse." On coming to office, Holmes discovered that the Halifax and Cape Breton Railway and Coal Company was not even a valid corporation. Nevertheless, he did agree to pay Abbott any moneys due him provided that he furnished security for completing the contract. But he also put pressure on the federal government not to transfer the Pictou Branch on the ground that Abbott had not yet made the required expenditure on his own line. To hand it over, he said, would simply be repeating the mistake made in the case of the WCR and render railway extension "unsuccessful and abortive".

Those were the financial and railway situations facing Holmes when the legislature met in March 1879. As a precaution, he had secretly requested Charles J. Townshend, a minister without portfolio, to prepare a bill for the incorporation of counties. Basically it transferred the non-judicial functions of the courts of sessions and grand juries to elective county and district councils. But it also gave the new bodies an additional power, the distribution and expenditure of road moneys. If Ottawa had hearkened quickly to Holmes's pleas, the bill would probably not have been introduced, but no early reply was forthcoming. So Holmes bit the bullet and on April 4 — almost like a bolt from the blue — the County Incorporation Act saw the light of day. The forthright Thompson freely admitted that a principal objective was to "compel the Counties to tax themselves directly to keep up their roads and bridges . . . you will have to face the melancholy fact that additional taxation stares you in the face."[18] That fact became clear when Holmes budgeted only $85,000 for roads instead of the previous year's $175,000. It was a courageous act since the Conservatives were taking their political life in their hands by forcing the local communities to resort to the direct taxation which they abhorred.

Throughout the session the eight Liberal assemblymen provided little opposition and certainly not a united opposition. When Albert Gayton, the only former executive councillor, refused the seat normally occupied by the leader of the opposition, the Herald called it "the end of the great Anti-Confederate-Repeal-Annexationist Party!" But the government had more opposition than it wanted from a legislative council which harassed it as it harassed no other ministry. Directing it was the old Tory baiter, T.F. Morrison, the *de facto* leader of Liberals outnumbering the Conservatives by two to one. In 1879 he set his sights on Holmes's attempt to deal with the debt. Having no funded debt, the province was paying an inordinately high rate of interest on its overdraft at the banks. Because that sum would grow as substantial railway subsidies became payable, the government requested authority to borrow up to $800,000, a seemingly reasonable proposition. But the Liberal councillors took the position that Holmes ought not to be entrusted with any greater borrowing power than was absolutely necessary and rejected the bill. When they went further and refused to renew the lapsed Cape Breton railway bills, originally those of the Hill government, their conduct became even more indefensible. The government replied by showing its contempt for the council.

Taking the position that an upper house was no longer necessary now that the federal government was conducting most of the public business and that the council had destroyed its usefulness in any case by failing to appreciate its position and functions, it introduced an abolition bill. But although approved unanimously in the assembly, the proposal failed in the council by twelve to six. On this occasion the *Herald* told Morrison that he had eclipsed all his "previous efforts at playing the harlequin."

The Holmes government ended its first session with its credibility high, indeed the highest it would ever be. It then turned again to finances and railways. What is puzzling throughout its entire life is the lack of sympathetic consideration by the Macdonald government. Between Holmes and his fellow Pictonian, James McDonald, the minister of justice, the rapport was good. But Charles Tupper, the minister of railways, appeared to act as if he neither needed nor wanted Holmes's good will. In November, still awaiting a reply to his memorandum of ten months earlier, Holmes pointed out to the prime minister and the minister of finance, Leonard Tilley, that he could not meet the legislature next winter without "some evidence of having energetically pressed for justice." Even after eliminating navigation securities and cutting road grants to $85,000, he said, the province's cash deficiency had increased by $75,000.

Meanwhile he was having the same headaches with railways that had tormented Hill. To permit work on the WCR to proceed, he had obtained authority from the legislature to guarantee its bonds. An unhappy C.J. Townshend had second thoughts, fearing that "this wretched undertaking" would be thrown on the government's hands, "a burden too heavy for the Province to bear."[19] Subsequently, however, construction proceeded rapidly and on October 1 the WCR opened the sixty-seven miles from Digby to Yarmouth. But later in the year, when a court decision required the federal government to hand back the Windsor branch to the Windsor and Annapolis, the WCR suspended all its operations. Traffic on a largely unballasted stretch of the Eastern Extension thirty miles in length had opened on September 18. Tupper, wanting to use the rolling stock of the Pictou Branch on the ICR, again sought to hand the line over to Abbott, but met strong resistance from Nova Scotia's second federal minister, James McDonald, acting on Holmes's behalf. Because of the unsatisfactory state of the Eastern Extension and the dismal prospects of extending it to meet Cape Breton's needs, Holmes was pondering the completion of the work by the government and late in the year was enlisting expert opinion to determine if the Eastern Extension in conjunction with the Pictou Branch could operate at a profit.

Focusing his main attention on getting out of the financial and railway morasses he had inherited, Holmes gave the legislative council little opportunity to embarrass him in 1880. In the circumstances he had done remarkably well in reducing the province's deficit position to $38,000; "the wonder," wrote the *Herald*, "is how he managed to keep within [his] means." But despite his extensive lobbying of federal friends, he had been unable to pry additional funds out of Ottawa. Not until January 1880, after a year's delay, did he receive a flat rejection of his first memorial. Nova Scotia, said J.M. Courtney, the deputy minister of finance, would not be in financial distress, if it had managed its affairs properly: it had not employed its debt allowance for the "construction of remunerative public works"; it should reduce the education grants to the counties; it could maintain the roads in their existing state for less money. Courtney would not be the first distant bureaucrat at Ottawa to know more about the province's affairs than the administrators on the spot. John Costley, the province's deputy provincial secretary, was quick to point out that, after the road grant had been halved in 1879, it had been necessary to increase it twice; otherwise the roads in several counties would have been impassable and mail distribution brought to a standstill. Further, the education grant of $200,000 was hardly extravagant since it had been $165,000 for a smaller population in 1865 and since it was significantly less per capita than the expenditures in New Brunswick and Prince Edward Island.[20]

Nothing daunted, Holmes called on the legislature in 1880 to demand a share of the award provided by the Washington Treaty for American use of the province's fishery. Resounding approval came from both sides of the assembly. Conservative John Pugh threatened not to support his federal counterparts "an hour . . . if they did not give us a fair proportion of the Award, or its equivalent." But the *Chronicle* only scoffed at the treatment accorded Holmes by his friends at Ottawa: "the whine of a street mendicant" could have drawn "no greater contempt."[21] Actually Holmes had become more forceful even before these taunts. In a telegram to James McDonald he introduced a threatening note by suggesting that if Nova Scotia did not receive either a share of the fishery award or financial parity with the other provinces, his backbenchers and the people generally were likely to unite against the federal government. For once Ottawa seemed a little perturbed. McDonald replied at once that he could not "see what advantage either the house or people can propose to achieve by such a course."[22] But it took Tilley, the minister of finance, more than a month to provide only the most meagre of crumbs, $32,340 for the value with interest of Nova Scotian stores taken over by Ottawa in 1867.

Still undaunted, Holmes appealed to Tupper on April 30 for justice, which he equated with the principle that each province should receive moneys "sufficient to meet its local wants in fair and equal proportions." To him Edward Blake's resolution that Nova Scotia's "better terms" constituted a final and unalterable settlement not only derogated from the power of Parliament but was "a mere piece of clap trap" which Blake himself conveniently forgot when Ontario and Quebec received large additions to their debt allowances. Holmes was also critical of the annual payment of $160,000 made to New Brunswick in lieu of the export tax on timber which it had levied before 1867. In his opinion either it should have received no compensation or the other provinces should have had an equivalent, which in Nova Scotia's case would have been $200,000. Holmes concluded that without assistance the alternatives for his province were bleak: let the roads go to wrack and ruin and abandon the principle of free schools; or enter into heavy direct taxation; or admit bankruptcy.

Tupper took Holmes's pleas to the prime minister, but it was again Courtney who applied the philosophy from which he would not retreat. Through all of Nova Scotia's submissions, he said, ran the fallacious argument that because a province suffered financial embarrassment it ought to be rescued. If that idea became prevalent, "it would materially help to destroy any economical tendency in Provincial Legislatures." As for the alleged preferential treatment to New Brunswick, "I cannot see why if A and B both receive money from C, and A gets more than B, that necessarily B is wronged." Costley made one final effort to answer Courtney's contention that the province's revenue, if properly managed, could meet its needs. Experience, he said, had shown that it could barely carry on even with an impairment of services. "Policy, as well as justice, demands that each province should have enough to maintain in efficiency its local services."[23] Realizing that his bargaining power on finances in general was minimal, Holmes confined his future pleas to assistance for railways.

By early 1880 he wanted to take over the Eastern Extension but his limited financial resources deterred him. Keeping the option open, however, he renewed the company's contract on the condition that, within two years of the line's completion, the government might possess it by reimbursing the company for its outlay. By year's end the line was operating to the Strait of Canso although ballasting remained uncompleted. As part of a larger, over-all plan, the government had placed strict conditions on the Nictaux and Atlantic. Should it fail to pay for its right of way or satisfy its unpaid labourers it would also be subject to a take over. The government was also in a position to acquire the WCR, which had not completed the "missing link" and was not making repairs on the rest of its line. Kept in the dark and fearful that the Dominion's railway policy might run counter to his own, Holmes complained bitterly to Tupper: "Already half of our term of office is about over and if we leave things as bad as we got them we may say good-bye to our chances of being returned."[24] His unaccustomed vehemence was a reaction against the possibility of being thwarted in his objective — soon to become an obsession — to consolidate all the province's railways not controlled by the Dominion.

By this time he had put plans in place to acquire the WCR, Windsor and Annapolis, Eastern Extension, and probably the Windsor Branch and, as the Provincial Engineer pointed out, it was fortuitous that these lines, although built piecemeal, without order, or without thought of establishing a single system, "should nevertheless constitute so perfect a Trunk line of communication through the whole length of the Peninsula." For Holmes consolidation would let him get rid of his railway burden and through the moneys received from the consolidating company relieve his financial burden, in other words, solve his two major problems at one fell swoop. In October 1880 he was inviting offers from capitalists for railways costing $10 millions, $7 millions provided as provincial subsidies. But in not keeping his fellow ministers adequately informed of his plans he was damaging his own position.

In its first two years the government had the usual, but no serious, problems with patronage. Office holders who had worked electorally for the Liberals received short shrift. Local committees usually made the recommendations for minor offices, but sometimes it was not possible to ignore powerful suitors. Bishop Cameron once wrote to Thompson: "somehow I have not the fortitude to resist the solicitation of friends." Although the County Incorporation Act had eliminated the courts of sessions, Nova Scotians still wanted to be magistrates even if the office was only honorific in most cases. From the outset Holmes made it clear he would name no justices of "the same stripe as those appointed almost exclusively for the last eleven years." But the County Incorporation Act had a much greater effect upon patronage in another way. Henceforth the new municipal councils would choose the road commissioners, divide the road moneys, and supervise its expenditure. Conservative assemblymen became highly indignant when they realized that they had lost their most important prerogative in cases where the Liberals controlled the municipal councils. C.A. Smith of Lunenburg told Holmes that if he could not name the commissioners in two or three districts, "our friends will suffer. What I complain of is that we were led to believe that we had the . . . power to protect" fellow Conservatives.[25] But Holmes could only confess that they no longer had that power.

Throughout 1880 Holmes's credibility steadily declined. The public would hardly find attractive a man of little charisma, seemingly obsessed with economy and railroads, and apparently little mindful of the needs of ordinary Nova Scotians. No less serious was his failure to establish a rapport with his colleagues. To them he did too much on his own, sought to settle matters by telegram rather than in cabinet meetings, and was too prone to go on delegations to Ottawa for insufficient reason. Although John Thompson wanted nothing of intrigue, his colleagues confided in him their uneasiness. Summoned to Halifax in December, James Stainforth MacDonald, a minister without office, concluded that a supposed invitation to go to Ottawa on railway business "did not sound much like a 'request' for a delegation." Besides nothing would come of it since "Mr. Holmes has no weight at Ottawa." A little later when Holmes went off to Ottawa accompanied by John F. Stairs, another minister without office, and did not even consult Thompson, MacDonald became even more perturbed. To him the political prospects looked bleak. "Mr. Holmes may keep the confidence of the country while he cannot command the respect of his Colleagues, but I very much doubt it." About the same time C.J. Townshend admitted to sharing in the general dissatisfaction, complaining particularly of being held responsible for railway policies which Holmes had taken into his own hands. Had the time not come when the other ministers "ought to interfere and try and redeem ourselves from the obloquy which is everywhere being thrown upon us"?[26]

The session of 1881 produced no significant legislation, not so much because of the absence of bills as because of the legislative council. To deal with Hill's act on universities which was about to expire, the government sponsored a bill which eliminated the University of Halifax, but sought to upgrade standards by requiring visitations of the Superintendent of Education as a condition to each of six universities receiving annual grants of $1,400. Only one assemblyman opposed the bill, but the situation was different in the council not because of T.F. Morrison, but because of the existence of widely disparate groups: Presbyterians who felt that Dalhousie was receiving unfair treatment; Anglicans who objected to the inspection of King's College; some who opposed grants to two Catholic colleges and others who wanted to retain the University of Halifax. As a result, the bill did not pass and the colleges remained without government grants for more than seventy years. Morrison did play a prominent role in the rejection of the government's bridge bill. Designed to wipe out the road advances to some counties by providing compensatory grants which would put the counties on an equality, the bill proposed the borrowing of $393,000 for bridges over the next twenty years, the whole to be liquidated through amounts deducted annually from the ordinary road and bridge allocation. Calling the councillors "dying freaks," the *Herald* declared that the Council of Twelve, in its palmiest days, "never acted worse or thwarted the popular branch more frequently or defiantly . . . we have the battle of responsible government to fight over again."[27]

Behind the scenes Holmes's obsession with railways grew ever greater in 1881. To his satisfaction E.W. Plunkett, a former contractor and part owner of the WCR, was forming a syndicate to take over all the Nova Scotian railways except the federally-owned ICR. Starting in March the correspondence between the two was never-ending. Holmes was also addressing the prime minister "in the common interest of our party," telling him that he could put $1,500,000 in the provincial treasury, "provided we can get certain privileges from the Dominion which it can give and lose nothing." He did get promises of two things, the transfer of the Windsor Branch to the syndicate and the granting of running rights over the ICR. But he had much greater difficulty with his request to have the province's payment from the syndicate placed in its debt account drawing the usual return of five per cent at a time when the prevailing rate was four per cent. "As you know," he told Plunkett, "it is hard work to get the beggars to do anything sensible."[28]

Having concluded an agreement with Plunkett,⋅ Holmes introduced a bill late in January 1882 which, he said, had "not been exceeded [in importance] by . . . any measure introduced . . . since Confederation." As a guarantee of the intentions of the syndicate, now acting as the Nova Scotia Railway Company, to fulfil its contract, Baring Brothers had already paid $52,000 into the provincial treasury. The company would also give the province $1,350,000 for its right in the railways and provide a sinking fund of $4,500,000 to be paid out proportionately as it acquired the various lines. In addition to completing these lines, including the "missing link," the company, upon the provision of specific subsidies, would build a twenty-six mile line from the Pictou Branch to Pictou town; a ten-mile line from Windsor Junction to Dartmouth; and an eighty-mile line from the Strait of Canso to a point near Louisburg. In return, the province would guarantee the interest on the company's outlay to the extent of $225,000 a year for forty-one years. Because this provision would use up a large proportion of the provincial revenue, it required a detailed justification by Holmes. The province, he pointed out, would receive annual interest of $67,500 on $1,350,000 at five per cent; in addition, it would rid itself of an annual obligation of $30,000 in connection with the Windsor and Annapolis Railway as well as commitments of $54,278 to the other lines.

Badly divided on the syndicate bill, the Liberal assemblymen could provide little opposition. So it was Fielding who led the attack in the *Chronicle* and in the process developed his financial expertise. To him the bill created a "bogus company" whose promoters had invested not a dollar of their own capital and who would use the sinking fund security to convert the worthless bonds of the WCR into bonds guaranteed by the province and the provincial guarantee to carry on stock-jobbing operations in London. Worst of all, the outcome would be a gigantic monopoly against which the province would be defenceless. Much of this criticism was unfair and John Thompson easily refuted most of it. The money in the sinking fund, he pointed out, was not to be used exclusively for the WCR but was to be paid over proportionately as the lines were acquired. On the charge that the company would not need to use its own funds he showed that, since the province, in effect, guaranteed interest on only $4,500,000 at five per cent, the company would have to invest at least $1,000,000 of its own money. To the charges of monopoly he replied that, if the company's tolls proved to be excessive, the government could set up a commission to regulate them. Because the bill let the province secure at least $1,000,000 for its roads and bridges, Thompson was certain that it would usher in a new day.[29] Only three assemblymen opposed the bill and, despite T.F. Morrison, the legislative council passed it by eleven to nine.

A second government bill of significance was a new version of the bridge bill. Again the council refused to pass it, this time on the ground that it had insufficient time before prorogation. All Grittism, said the *Herald*, was "destructive and unprogressive," but the Grittism of the legislative council was "beyond question the worst of the class."* A little earlier the government had requested the appropriate authorities in Britain to appoint sufficient legislative councillors to effect abolition only to be told that it had not proved that a change in the constitution was necessary. When the council defeated the government's direct attempt at abolition by twelve to nine, the *Chronicle* charged that it had violated the privileges of the upper house by having the bill introduced in the assembly. At prorogation Holmes and Thompson boasted that they had reduced the deficit to $17,374 and the balance against the province to $23,564, partly, they admitted, because of greater revenue from coal royalties. The *Herald* prophesied that they would do even better, now that they had got rid of the financial mess left by the Hill government, but the *Chronicle* was certain they were going to their political grave, "unwept, unhallowed and unsung."

As a general election approached pressure mounted on Holmes to get out. In April a party committee sought unsuccessfully to secure his resignation and a reconstruction of the government. About the same time Bishop Cameron was telling Thompson that for the good of the party and the province he must take over the ministry, while James Stainforth MacDonald was suggesting that the cabinet had to do "some unpleasant work."[30] Seldom has a political leader stood so alone, so lacking in friends, as Holmes. Meanwhile the Liberal press was reporting threats of mutiny in Conservative ranks and further weakening Holmes by its personal attacks. Had his "masterful inactivity" not permitted the roads to degenerate into quagmires? Had he not been unconvincing in his demands on Ottawa? Might he not "have been as well employed in going about whistling with his hands in his pockets as in discharging the duties of the Provincial Secretary"?

The time for decision arrived on May 18 with the dissolution of Parliament and the calling of a federal election for June 20. Clearly the Conservatives' best hope for a victory in Nova Scotia was to let themselves be pulled in by their federal counterparts. Receiving reports that the *Herald*, never kindly disposed towards him, would not support him, Holmes wrote its president on May 20 and apparently received a reply not to his liking.[31] Three days later he resigned using the stereotyped excuse that "the state of my health at present calls for a rest." But it was a reluctant departure accompanied by a promise to return if the necessity arose. He had, however, looked after his own future since the lucrative office of prothonotary and clerk of the Crown for Halifax County was waiting for him. That office he would hold until his death thirty-seven years later, coming close to outliving a forty-three year old Liberal government. Perhaps he deserved sympathy for having had to face almost insoluble problems from the outset of his premiership. But like Hill before him his failures resulted basically from personal traits. He was a political misfit, totally incapable of acting as captain of a team.

Thompson was more reluctant to succeed to the leadership than Holmes was to give it up. Tired of politics and likely to be going to the bench before long, he wondered about the ethics of taking over the government in these circumstances. But Bishop Cameron told him that his proper course was to strengthen his government and prepare it to shift for itself after he became a judge.[32] Although not fully convinced, Thompson remained in politics, setting the provincial election for the same day as the federal. Seldom has a ministry been more decimated. Because Samuel Creelman was in London completing the syndicate agreement, Thompson and Adam Bell, Holmes's successor as provincial secretary, were the only ministers with office who took part in the election. Of six ministers without office, John F. Stairs and James S. MacDonald had resigned and H.F. McDougall and N.W. White were contesting the federal election. Leaving the vacancies unfilled was a glaring sign of weakness.

The election was a little unreal in another way. Without leadership, the Liberals could not even say who would become premier if they were successful. Once again Fielding and the *Chronicle* outlined their party's position. Federally they found the very name of protection no less odious than before since, despite heavy taxation by way of duties, manufacturing had not prospered in Nova Scotia. The recent duty on salt was simply "another turn of the screw" which would harm Nova Scotians to benefit the Tories interested in the salt works at Goderich, Ontario. Provincially, the *Chronicle* lamented the legacy of the syndicate scheme: if any valid reason "could be found for escaping from [it] . . . it would be for the advantage of the Province to use it." It was a much-told story, but the *Chronicle* did it forcefully and dramatically.

For the *Herald* the federal contest was the crucial one and almost daily it produced panegyrics on the goodness of protection. "The only vital issue before the electors," it said, "is the National Policy . . . infusing life and vigor into every avenue of trade and commerce . . . The sheet anchor of all hopes of progress," it had already borne fruit in a sugar refinery in Halifax and a cotton mill was to follow. Charles Tupper arrived early on the scene and made his presence widely known throughout the province; John Thompson kept so low a profile that it was difficult to tell who was leading the provincial Conservatives. Early in the campaign he went to Antigonish, where he devoted almost all his attention to winning his own seat. Although the

William Stevens Fielding   1884-96

Courtesy of P.A.N.S.

Herald's interest in the provincial contest was only secondary, it gave fulsome support to Thompson, whom it described as the real as well as the official head of the bar, "an ornament of his profession." It also lauded the provincial Conservatives for the "gradual and steady restoration of the ground lost" under the Hill government and proclaimed that "the Syndicate scheme has not failed, and has never . . . been for a moment in jeopardy."

Federally the Conservatives won no less decisively than in 1878: fourteen of twenty-one seats and 51.4 per cent of the popular vote compared to the Liberals' 45.0 per cent. But on the same day the voters reversed themselves at the provincial level, where the Conservatives polled only 46.9 per cent of the vote to the Liberals' 51.8 per cent and won only fourteen seats to their opponents' twenty-four. Perhaps their greatest success was in holding Fielding to an eleven-vote majority in Halifax. In nine counties the voters returned a split ticket, a number not nearly equalled before or since and an indication that many voters were supporting a candidate rather than a party. The Conservatives suffered because of the rough hands which the County Incorporation Act had laid upon the traditional method of distributing road moneys in the rural areas. But they lost much more because of the return to their old love of the Liberal-oriented voters of Nova Scotia, altogether disenchanted with four years of the unattractive, lacklustre Holmes. Meanwhile the vigorous, combative Tupper was making a strong, positive appeal at a time when it still appeared as if the National Policy might have a favourable effect upon provincial development.

Despite the returns the *Herald* still contended that the Liberals were a long way from the treasury benches. It thought in terms of a disorganized Liberal party, half of whose members had supported the major proposals of the government. Thompson had that in mind when he invited Liberal Albert Gayton to enter into a coalition. The differences between the provincial parties, he argued, were slight and the province needed a ministry of all the talents to deal with the railway question. Adam Bell went eastward with a similar message to independent-minded members like Dr D.J. Campbell of Inverness and A.J. White of Cape Breton. That all three took time to consider the proposal may have indicated the possibility of success, but party considerations prevailed in the end [33] and Thompson resigned on July 18 after a premiership of only fifty-four days. Resorting to sour grapes, the *Herald* said that it had "never regarded the possession of the Local Government as of very great importance."[34]

CHAPTER 9

Fielding Establishes Himself

For a time the Liberals feared that Thompson might not get out. Fielding went so far as to have the twenty-four Liberal members sign a round robin petitioning the governor to summon the assembly in case the government failed to acknowledge its defeat. Even after the Conservatives offered their resignation, however, it took the Liberals sixteen days to form a ministry because of the extraordinary circumstances. They were without a leader and fifteen of their twenty-four assemblymen were newcomers. At one time or another Otto Weeks, Alonzo White, and Albert Gayton had served in the executive council and it was the last whom the governor, Adams G. Archibald, empowered to form a government. Lacking credentials as leader and hardly of premiership calibre, Gayton followed the course of R.A. McHeffey in 1867 and summoned the Liberal members into convention on August 1.

It was neither a happy nor a peaceful gathering. Fielding might have had the leadership of the government for the asking because of the general recognition that as editor of the *Chronicle* he had played a key role in the Liberals' electoral triumph. But because of limited financial resources he refused even to consider it. Cabals abounded with their intrigues and jealousies. In the end the three ministerial offices went to White as attorney general and commissioner of crown lands; Gayton as commissioner of public works and mines; and newcomer Charles Church as provincial secretary. Most surprising of all was the choice of "premier," a designation more and more replacing that of "leader of the government." It went to a thirty-two year old freshman member from Cumberland, William Thomas Pipes, who was apparently as surprised as anyone by the unexpected honour. At this time, however, the premier was barely *primus inter pares* and held an office unrecognized in law and hence unpaid. That fact put Pipes in an impossible situation: to support his family, he needed to carry on a law practice in Amherst, while to conduct the business of government he required frequent, sometimes extended, stays in Halifax. Somewhat reticent, he established a genuine rapport with few members other than Fielding, whom he induced to become a minister without office before the year was out.

Pipes's testing would come during the first session of the Twenty-Seventh General Assembly when it met in February 1883. A Liberal backbencher who would soon achieve prominence, James A. Fraser of Guysborough, quickly sized up the leading members. On the Liberal side Fielding was "dogmatic, combative and tyrannical"; James Wilberforce Longley "conceited, unlovable and unbearable"; while the diffident Charles Church did not "do himself justice." His greatest admiration was for the intemperate Otto Weeks, who had again been elected as a Liberal in Guysborough and whom he described as a "prince of good fellows" and the ablest man in the house "so far as real eloquence, knowledge and training is concerned." On the Conservative side, Charles J. Townshend was "a poor stuttering speaker, with not good argumentative power" and the only man of ability, now that Thompson had gone to the bench, was the new leader Adam Bell, whom, were it not for politics, Fraser would have preferred to support rather than Pipes, a "morose and distant man in his disposition."[1]

Morose or not, Pipes had few difficulties with the assembly in 1883. Overshadowing everything else was the railway question, the subject of debate in the *Herald* and *Chronicle* long before the legislature met. The Pipes government had sent W.B. Vail to England to replace Creelman in its dealings with Plunkett. Its opponents quickly alleged that he was even more determined to bring about the collapse of the syndicate scheme than the government itself. Not so, replied Pipes and Fielding, who contended that they would have accepted $5.5 millions, instead of the $6.5 millions which, according to them, the agreement with Holmes had stipulated. But when Plunkett also demanded that

$1.4 millions of the amount go to pay for the WCR, they rejected it outright. To Fielding the Nova Scotia Railway Company was a paper company, whose directors had subscribed none of their own money. "Plunkettism," he declared, had ended with Mr. Plunkett.

For its own railway policy the government proposed a $2.46 million borrowing bill which would, in effect, inaugurate a public debt. Of this amount $1.5 million would go to purchase the Eastern Extension and repair the Pictou Branch; $50,000 to keep the WCR running; and $350,000 to subsidize further the Nictaux and Atlantic. As security, Pipes sought to use the federal subsidy, but Ottawa refused to let the province alienate any part of it on the ground that it would contravene the spirit of the BNA Act. The assembly passed the bill without ado; the legislative council after only ninety minutes of debate. Goaded about his rejection of all the borrowing bills of the Holmes government, T.F. Morrison simply replied: "Oh that was before the freshet. I have changed my mind since the freshet."[2] The *Herald* wondered how any Cape Breton members could support the railway bill, but the *Chronicle* simply replied that, if the profits from the Pictou Branch and the Eastern Extension were as large as expected, they would permit an extension to the island.

Otherwise, the government's programme was slender, mostly because of lack of money. In opposition, the Liberals had condemned the Conservatives as wasteful; in office, they found that Holmes's penny-pinching had been such as to leave little room for further reduction. Hence they contented themselves with two minor savings. Hitherto ministers travelling on government business had received *per diem* and mileage allowances; henceforth — the *Herald* called it "a very little bill" — they would get only out-of-pocket expenses. The more controversial change related to the prothonotary in Halifax who, with fees, received more than a minister with office. In future, the total cost of his office was limited to $3,000 which, according to Fielding, would leave Holmes with the income of the political head of a department even after he paid his expenses. The Conservatives labelled the bill as an attack on a political opponent not in a position to defend himself. But Fielding told them that they were unwise to give prominence to a man whose conduct did not "entitle him to the highest possible consideration from the House." At the time

Holmes was apparently enjoying one of his frequent periods of absenteeism; after this exchange his wife, fearful of his dismissal, substituted for him.

The session of 1883 also ushered in a new method of distributing and spending the road moneys. Henceforth they were to be spent, not under "tender and contract," but by day's work and private contract. When the Conservatives called it "the most wasteful and corrupt method," the government replied that it was the desirable course whenever it was impossible to lay down explicit specifications as was often true of road work. Was it not best, therefore, to leave the expenditures in the hands of experienced municipal councillors who were directly responsible to the people of their districts? During these months the difficulties of Pipes's position had manifested themselves in poignant fashion. Once he wrote Fielding from Amherst describing his wife as "low" and nursing a child of six months, whose cries worried her and lessened her chances of recovery. "I am badly broken up, my children and house are in bad condition." If his presence were indispensable, he would come to Halifax; otherwise Fielding should get J.W. Longley or someone else to assist him. That he relied on a minister without office and a backbencher to act in his stead testifies eloquently to his relations with his ministers with office.

The government's railway proposals turned out to be fruitless. Like Holmes before them, Pipes and Fielding soon found out that their interests always took second place to those of their federal counterparts. When they were about to acquire the Eastern Extension, they discovered that Ottawa was placing conditions upon the transfer of the Pictou Branch which made it financially impracticable. After two trips to Ottawa they finally accepted markedly different arrangements as their best available option. The outcome was that the federal government retained the Pictou Branch and took over the Eastern Extension for $1,200,000, approximately the cost to the province of acquiring it from the Halifax and Cape Breton Railway and Coal Company. To say that any Nova Scotia provincial politician liked these arrangements would be an exaggeration. Otto Weeks called them a gift of two millions to the federal government and defied anyone to point out "a wretched comedy of errors . . . more astonishing than the Syndicate" and its sequel. To add insult to injury, the *Herald* accused Pipes and Fielding of seeking to "cram [a bad deal] down the throats of their supporters."

No less understanding, Adam Bell contended during the 1884 session that a government, which the previous year had been lavish in its promises of railways to Cape Breton, had now cut it off from assistance altogether. C.J. Townshend wondered what the province would have left if the bill passed. "We might . . . sell this building [Province House] and wind up the Legislature — having disposed of or given away everything we had we would almost be without any object in meeting here again." But Fielding, again showing himself the master of detail, argued that, within the limits permitted by Ottawa, "every step taken by the Government had been taken for the advantage of the country." Both he and Pipes found one positive feature in the new arrangements. Although the federal government had made no promise to extend the railway into Cape Breton, they believed that by amalgamating the Eastern Extension with the ICR the federal government had irrevocably committed itself to do it. But that did not satisfy Conservative Murdoch McRae of Richmond County, who bewailed the province's treatment of the island. Was it not contributing $136,417 a year more to the province's revenues than it received? Would Cape Breton not be better off if it separated itself from the peninsula of Nova Scotia?[3]

The general needs of Nova Scotia, however, overshadowed those of Cape Breton. Early in the session of 1884 the government indicated that it would be making demands upon Ottawa for additional funds even though, like the other provinces, it would receive more money through the backdating to 1867 of the changes made in debt allowances in 1873. The *Chronicle* called the additional sum of $23,614 which would come to Nova Scotia annually only "an instalment of better terms." Beating the government to the punch, James A. Fraser of Guysborough moved resolutions demanding redress in vigorous language and telling Ottawa, in effect, to respond favourably or be faced with a secession movement. Contrasted with its earlier position, he said, Nova Scotia was unable to build its railways; its great roads and bridges were going to ruin; and its treasury was verging on bankruptcy. "Should we decide to drift along in poverty, or act like men and demand that our revenue be restored to us? . . . Should we always continue to truckle to the politicians at

Ottawa," unable to go to Her Majesty's "glorious throne [except] through the slums and pitfalls of Canadian politics."[4]

Somewhat reluctantly, Fraser agreed to Pipes's entreaties and withdrew his resolutions so that the province's claims might come from the "whole people of Nova Scotia." As a result, the legislature unanimously agreed to present to the governor general in council a moderately-worded joint address which a committee of seven had drawn up. But Fraser and Weeks were unhappy to have the question approached with "bated breath" and not with the determination which the province's interest demanded. They prophesied that the outcome would not be redress, but "a few letters between the two governments and there it would all end." Actually, much like Holmes, the Liberals had put themselves in a poor position. As a result of strict economy, coal royalties of $122,010 — the largest amount ever collected — and an increase of $8,000 in Crown land revenues, Church had produced a surplus of $26,725 in 1883. Not only that, he was budgeting for another the next year, although one of only $1,761.54 to "wear and haul upon, as the sailors say."

Otherwise, the assembly's bill of fare continued to be meagre in 1884. The Conservatives criticized the government for its failure to re-appoint three sheriffs only to be told that Scott of Queens had been guilty of "culpable carelessness" in the last provincial election; that Robinson of Annapolis, in an "exhibition of temper," had fired at a fleeing prisoner and struck him "in the nethermost part"; and that Dunlop of Victoria had earned the dislike of every municipal councillor in the county. W.F. MacCoy of Shelburne sought to abolish the Nova Scotia version of imprisonment for debt. Instead of putting a debtor in jail, he proposed to take him, from time to time, before a commission, which would compel him to meet the debt in full where possible, or pay a stated amount each month, or assign his property. But a deeply-rooted fear that the bill might somehow harm the business community led to its defeat by a non-party vote of 18 to 14.

Although Pipes had got through the session of 1884 with ease, he remained unhappy. According to Lieutenant-Governor M.H. Richey,[5] he was reticent not only with him, but even with his fellow executive councillors. His strained relations with them had increased when he appointed Fielding to the executive council without consulting them. They were fearful that he wanted ministerial offices with emolument for himself and Fielding, and when he asked Gayton to make way for the latter they generally supported Gayton's refusal. In May 1884 Pipes approached Richey with several hypothetical questions. Asked if his resignation would mean the dissolution of the ministry, Richey replied that it would. Asked if he would accept Pipes's recommendation of a successor, Richey refused a definite answer unless he knew the situation existing at the time of the resignation. But he would undoubtedly take his premier's advice if the government appeared to be acting together and still commanded a majority in the assembly. Weeks later, on July 14, Pipes presented his resignation and on his advice Fielding succeeded him. Although Fielding's task was ostensibly to reorganize the cabinet, Richey made it clear that he regarded the old ministry as having been dissolved.

The result was debate in the public press about the applicability of the British model to Nova Scotia. A letter-writer in the *Herald* argued that it did not apply since the lieutenant-governor in these matters was bound to follow the advice, not of a so-called "premier," an office declared to be non-existent in Nova Scotia, but of a majority of the executive council.[6] Richey also received "a sort of protest" from some executive councillors who expressed surprise at Pipes's recommendation of Fielding. Later two of them told Richey that the resignation of the leader of the government did not dissolve a ministry since the governor was required under the old commissions to act on the advice of an executive council of nine and the BNA Act provided that the Nova Scotia council should continue after Confederation as before. Although Richey admitted to having doubts about his position, he replied that, however cogent these arguments might be for the period prior to the granting of responsible government, he had no choice but to follow, "if at an humble distance, the constitutional usage of the mother country."[7] Later he repeated his doubts about the constitutionality of his course to Sir John Macdonald, but no one would again question the applicability of the entire British analogy to Nova Scotia.

One account, probably apocryphal, suggests that Fielding asked Pipes who his successor was to be and was referred to II Samuel 12:7 — "And Nathan said to David, Thou art the man." Fielding, who had earlier presented his own resignation, did not want the premiership and when Pipes insisted on getting out he sought to induce some senior member of the party like Robert Boak, president of the legislative council, to assume the leadership. Unsuccessful, he found that there was nothing "left but for me to go ahead and take the risks."[8] Because of these "risks and difficulties," it took him from July 15 to 28 to reach some sort of *modus vivendi*. Apparently he sought the attorney generalship for Pipes and the provincial secretaryship for himself, but the same "troublesome fellows" who had bothered Pipes prevented him from getting much more than a minimum of what he wanted. Gayton left the executive council and Church moved to his portfolio; Fielding became provincial secretary and J.W. Longley a minister without office.

From several of Fielding's supporters came expressions of satisfaction that "matters have straightened out." James A. Fraser was delighted that his friend J.W. Longley had been "taken from the dark regions of Grumbledom" and did not regret the departure of Pipes, whom "I like . . . personally but detest . . . politically." Pipes himself was pleased that Fielding had taught the troublesome fellows something of a lesson and agreed that it was right to retain most of them. But if they failed to support Fielding in his ministerial election in Halifax, he would "swear like a pirate at them and tell them they must put you in at all hazards. I can do it. They want none of Pipes 'ruffianism'."[9] The Conservatives put up a strong candidate in merchant John Y. Payzant, but Fielding triumphed by a comfortable margin on August 20. To one polling district chairman he expressed pleasure that Upper Musquodoboit was "in her usual place, as Liberal as in the days of Joseph Howe." But the heaviest blow for the Tories was their defeat in the city, the result of "the personal friendship of many Conservatives" for Fielding.

Victory strengthened Fielding's hands. "Certain parties," who would not have regretted his defeat, he told Edward Blake, were "now among the most loyal." But when he again sought to make Pipes attorney general, he met insoluble difficulties. To make it possible A.J. White would have had to be given the registrarship of deeds for Halifax County and many prominent Halifax Liberals objected because he was an outsider. Fielding would not have minded their displeasure, but he feared the opening of seats in Cumberland and Cape Breton which the arrangement would necessitate. During December and January he considered his options, but, cautious as usual, he finally told Pipes that the changes must "stand over for the present"; would he care to be appointed to the Library Commission?

At this stage Fielding was already displaying the scrupulous adherence to principle which would last throughout his career. To William Geddes of Upper Musquodoboit who tried to exact a promise from him he replied that he could not "make promises that I may not be able to fulfil . . . I believe in the maxim 'Slow to promise, sure to perform'." When pressed to appoint Dr. Angus McLennan of Inverness to the executive council if he crossed the floor of the house, he was appalled. To put an opponent suddenly in the cabinet, he said, would "present a spectacle creditable neither to the Government nor to himself"; it would "not only be indefensible on grounds of political morality, but would be in the end disastrous to the Liberal party."[10]

Federal-provincial financial relations would occupy much of his attention during his early days as premier. Almost at once he told James A. Fraser that he did not differ with him on "what we would like to accomplish," but only on "the practical effect of the methods you wish to employ." In January 1885 he sent Charles Church and T.F. Morrison to Ottawa to discuss better terms, but when the legislature met in mid-February it still had no reply to its address of the previous session. Without consulting anyone, Fraser introduced a motion incorporating the ideas of repeal and maritime union. Clearly in a dilemma, Fielding delayed debate on the motion, desperately hoping for an answer from Ottawa. His financial accounts for 1884 showed only a small deficit even though coal royalties had brought in $20,000 less than the expected $120,000. Additional interest of $39,000 from the increased debt allowance had even enabled him to make a small increase in the road grant and for the year 1885 he estimated a surplus of $2,500. Clearly he was being too prudent for one who wanted better terms from Ottawa.

Causing great controversy in 1885 was a bridge bill which permitted each county's allocation to be increased by fifty per cent, but limited the total expenditure to $500,000. Its opponents argued strongly that the interest on the expenditures would be a charge against the county road grants and that a continuance of the practice would lead to the exhaustion of those grants. But the usually cautious Fielding dismissed outright the fears of the alarmists. "As prudent men we are bound to look ahead, but if we allow foolish fears of the future to prevent us from grappling with the issues and duties of the living present, we shall fail to deserve the confidence of the people."[11] Adam Bell also taxed Fielding with doing nothing for Cape Breton railways in two years. But the premier told him that the island had had enough of "paper railways" and that his government was providing the same incentives there as in western Nova Scotia.

The most important non-financial bill of 1885 extended the franchise, untouched since 1863. It added to the voters' lists the sons of parents whose property was of sufficient value to justify two, three, or more votes. Fielding contended that the bill legalized a practice already in effect. It also followed "the good example" of Ontario, except for the inclusion of an income franchise, which was incapable of adoption in Nova Scotia because it had no income tax. The Conservatives, again more liberal on the franchise than their opponents, doubted the wisdom of encumbering the statute book with "complicated and difficult measures" and favoured a return to universal suffrage. Adam Bell wondered if the bill was intended to let the Liberals "perpetuate their own existence." Did it not enfranchise farmers while leaving out the "intelligent manhood" found among the mining and manufacturing population? But J.W. Longley, speaking like the voice of authority itself, declared that universal suffrage was "not a Liberal measure in any way whatever" and that his party would support a property qualification "until a degree of intelligence is reached that has not been reached yet in this country."[12]

By 1885 the bitter memories of the Confederation era had faded sufficiently to permit the legislature to grant without dissent an annuity of $500 to Mrs. Joseph Howe. Longley called it "a duty which this province had owed for many years to the widow of her most distinguished son"; Fielding described it "a just, if a somewhat tardy measure."

Not until mid-March did Fielding give the go-ahead to debate Fraser's motion, which contended that Nova Scotia would continue to deteriorate so long as it remained part of Canada. For Fraser the question was much broader than that of better financial terms. Because of the protective tariff and the change in the natural and normal trading relations with the United States, he had become convinced that Nova Scotia's future was bleak. Knowing that Fielding meant to introduce substitute resolutions, he asked that someone else do it so that he would not have to oppose a motion of the premier. But it was Fielding himself who proposed the amendment that, if the Dominion Parliament did not put Nova Scotia in a better financial position, the legislature would have to consider political separation at its next session. His stance was again typical of his caution. In recent years, he pointed out, the repeal question had been treated, "perhaps not as dead, but as sleeping." Not a single member had campaigned for it during the election. If the province approached the British Parliament on the tariff, no matter how iniquitous it was, the answer would be that two-thirds of its MPs had supported it. As for himself, he denied that he was "a repealer who would never have anything but repeal." Because of all these circumstances could not Fraser see that Nova Scotia should exhaust its constitutional means of agitation for better terms before it proceeded further? "If we want to fight the repeal question, we can do it just as well afterwards as we can do it now, and much better if the better terms negotiations fail."[13]

Fielding carried his resolutions by 20 to 13 even though Fraser and two other Liberals thought that he was far too moderate. In contrast, Conservative leader Adam Bell assumed the garb of the national statesman, declaring it ridiculous to drag "out of the lumber closet of the past this wooden horse of repeal." Ex-premier Pipes of Cumberland, a county which seemed to be benefiting from N.P., also wanted "an end of this exhibition of tinkling cymbals and sounding brass." Later Fielding, a devoted Liberal federally as well as provincially, had great difficulty in explaining Nova Scotia's position to Edward Blake, still an ardent believer in the words "final and unalterable" which he had forced into the better terms agreement of 1869. Fielding told him that of his twenty-three followers in the assembly only Pipes and Longley were not repealers at heart and they had damaged themselves by their stance. The lack of resources to carry on the provincial business with decency had reinforced the bitter anti-Confederation feelings which had existed since 1867. To suggest that Nova Scotia use direct taxation was sheer folly; it would "almost lead to rebellion." Nova Scotians, who had amply provided for their needs by a low tariff before 1867, would argue that now, following enormous increases in the duties, they should not have to resort to direct taxation. Under existing conditions the main issue in the provincial election of 1886 would be repeal and he wanted to prevent it even though Nova Scotia was never likely to be as happy as it had been before 1867. Simply give the province adequate funds and the strongest argument for repeal would disappear.[14]

To both Blake and J.A. Kirk, the Liberal MP for Guysborough, Fielding outlined a scenario which he thought would be fruitful. Let Kirk raise Nova Scotia's difficulties on a motion for correspondence; then have Blake, if possible, express some sympathy for a reconsideration of the financial terms of Confederation. Once assured that the Ontario Grits did not object, Sir John A. Macdonald might well open the question. But Blake was too deeply committed to principle to bend even a whit. He also stated, almost as unpalatably to Fielding, that for health and other reasons he might be leaving politics and drew the response that it would be "a national calamity" if he did. To complete the bad news, the prime minister told Fielding that if the province had not used its debt allowance unwisely it would not be in financial troubles. Confirming that position was Deputy Minister of Finance J.M. Courtney, who used exactly the same argument which he had employed against Holmes four or five years earlier.

Undaunted in the least, Fielding explained to Blake early in 1886 that Nova Scotia had had no choice but to use its debt allowance to build railways since the federal government had refused to construct them. The result had been calamitous. To pay for fire escapes in the Insane Asylum the province had had to create a capital account; the combined salaries of the ministers with office were barely $6,000; only one civil servant received as much as $3,000 a year; projects such as putting a heating plant of moderate cost in Province House or repairing the walls and sidewalks at Government House were awaiting the availability of funds. Once again he told Blake that the imposition of direct taxation would "unite five sixths of the people in a demand for repeal."[15] If nothing else, the correspondence demonstrated how Ontario-oriented the Liberal party of Canada was under Blake. A Nova Scotia Liberal premier desperately trying to secure some recognition of serious problems ended up with not a whit of sympathy.

In September and October of 1885 Fielding had become involved in federal politics as John S.D. Thompson, the newly appointed Minister of Justice, fought a by election in Antigonish. At the outset he contended that nothing but the influence of Bishop Cameron could save Thompson from overwhelming defeat. But he also advised Liberal newspapers to treat the bishop gingerly. "The people will oppose [him] but they do not want to see him attacked." As the campaign progressed he began to have doubts about a Liberal victory and they increased when early in October Bishop Cameron issued a circular letter supporting Thompson and followed it up with an even stronger one shortly before election day. Meanwhile a large number of parish priests were actively canvassing for Thompson. When he won the election handily, Fielding wanted to have "the undue influence" dealt with in both the civil and church courts. If it went unpunished, "there will be an end to all liberty in Nova Scotia. The election seems to have been a scandal to the church and to politics and I can see no good in hesitating to expose the doings of those who have done the wrong."[16]

Not until the legislature opened in February 1886 did the public learn of Ottawa's rejection of the province's request for better terms. Although the *Chronicle* suggested that Nova Scotia resume the right to levy its own customs and excise duties, Fielding refused to act precipitately. Instead he referred the federal government's reply for analysis to the committee which had drawn up the original memorial two years earlier and went on with other business. Matters relating to transportation and communications took up much of the assembly's time in 1886. To remove the last toll bridge in the province the government took over the privately-owned Avon River bridge, intending to build a new one costing $35,000 on the old foundation. Railways, however, drew more attention. Because the federal government had not assumed the initiative in railway construction and because the claims of Cape Breton were so compelling, the province decided to take special steps to have its railways built. To the company constructing a line to Sydney or Louisburg Fielding's bill offered a subsidy of $3,200 a mile up to $256,000 together with a land grant of 2,000 acres a mile up to 160,000 acres, the latter not to be given until the completion of the line. In addition, the company would receive a free right of way and exemption from municipal taxation for the railway and its stations. Most of these provisions were already on the statute book, but they would now go to a single company. If, however, no company took up the offer, the government might subdivide the benefits to secure the construction of sections of the line, a provision which the opposition called the "lobster clause."

Adam Bell described the bill as "wholly illusory, vague, and false"; his colleagues lambasted "the lobster portion," calling it "a mollusc, a polypus, and all sorts of curious names," but Fielding justified it as a device to have as many miles as possible built by reliable companies. When Bell wondered how the government could expect help from Ottawa as long as the repeal resolutions lay on the table, Fielding replied that repeal required consideration on its own merits. "The moment it becomes necessary for me to go to Ottawa in the spirit of Uriah Heap, that moment I will step aside, and my hon. friend can be the premier of Nova Scotia."[17] He also expressed concern about the railways in the western counties where work on the Nictaux and Atlantic had again halted and the "missing link" remained uncompleted. To him it was unconscionable that the $4,000,000 spent on these lines should not provide "more advantage to the province than we are yet able to enjoy." Two years earlier he had introduced a bill to facilitate the consolidation of the lines, but the proposal had failed because the WCR had no wish to unite. Recently, he said, new efforts offered greater prospects of success.

The session of 1886 made it clear the Fielding was stamping his own views and outlook upon both the government and the assembly. Prudent financing again enabled him to budget for a surplus of $3,000. In several instances his strong views on responsibility came into play. A year earlier he had taken the leading role in abolishing the Central Board of Agriculture and making the government directly responsible for its functions. In 1886 he did the same with the Public Charities Board, which had been set up eight years earlier as an independent authority. As a result, the city assumed responsibility for the poor house and the government for the insane asylum. "Experience has shown," he said, "that with all the faults to which a government is liable, government management is better than an irresponsible management of such institutions." He also successfully resisted the attempts of some Liberal backbenchers to get their counties out of the County Incorporation Act or to repeal the act altogether. "The question is simply whether they are to be governed by the magistrates. Popular government always costs something."

But in regulating the sale of alcohol he could not always carry his backbenchers with him. Taking advantage of a developing temperance movement, Albert Gayton had moved to change the existing law, which empowered the municipalities to issue licences for the sale of liquor. Although a teetotaller, Fielding found two of the proposals highly obnoxious. He said of one, which provided that liquor inspectors not use alcohol as a beverage: "I do not know of such a law in any other province or the world." But he reserved most of his indignation for a provision, specially intended for Halifax, which required a two-thirds majority of ratepayers as a condition for the granting of a licence. "We live, and sometimes we die, politically by majorities." But he was only one of a corporal's guard to take that position.

Not unexpectedly, matters relating to the province's position in the federation became the most significant business of the session. On April 16 the committee analyzing the federal government's reply to the province's request for better terms produced a second memorial rebutting all its arguments. Eleven days later, when the federal government acknowledged the receipt of the memorial without comment, Fielding had reached the end of his tether. Early in May he introduced repeal resolutions stating that the interests of the maritime provinces required their withdrawal from the Canadian federation and their entering into a maritime union; should that prove impossibe Nova Scotia should seek to become once again a province of Great Britain with its own fiscal and tariff laws.

If Ottawa had treated Nova Scotia in a liberal manner, he said, "we should have tried to bear the . . . ills a while longer." So long as Nova Scotia remained in Canada, he would continue to follow Edward Blake; "nevertheless . . . some of [our] evils are deeper down than can be removed by Mr. Blake and Sir John A. Macdonald." Longley, previously dubious, had become an out-and-out repealer. He was now convinced that any attempt to weld the Canadian provinces into a common nationality by act of parliament or by tariffs could not succeed. No advantage would ever accrue to Nova Scotia from trading with Quebec and Ontario because its natural markets were with the United States. Since 1867 "the cormorants of Montreal and Ontario" had been able to infest the province and absorb "the solid cash" as a result of the "fettered trade" with New England. The *Chronicle* agreed with him that Confederation had not brought the people of the provinces any closer together: "a man would make his fortune by exhibiting a Nova Scotian in Ontario and charging spectators five cents apiece." To its knowledge the only Upper Canadian to come to Nova Scotia was the commercial traveller who "has a diamond ring, smokes fat cigars . . . and generally conveys the impression that . . . he is a very superior being . . . He saps our resources, sucks our money, and leaves a lot of shoddy behind him." It concluded that the attempt to build a Canadian nationality had been "the most complete miscarrage . . . in the history of civilized communities."[18]

Adam Bell warned about the danger of Nova Scotia being relegated to the condition of a small helpless province or of being annexed to the United States. Nevertheless, after only a single day of debate, the assembly adopted the resolutions, fifteen Liberals opposing Pipes and five Conservatives. Despite the alleged importance of the question fifteen members had left for home, the vote taking place only two days before prorogation. Within days Fielding had the assembly dissolved. Because he allowed the shortest time permitted by law for the campaign, the *Herald* called it "a scandalous attempt" to prevent the full discussion of the secession resolutions. A little earlier Sir John Macdonald had gone so far as to tell the lieutenant-governor, M.H. Richey, that he had the right to grant or refuse a dissolution and that in matters relating to federal-provincial relations the proper representatives of Nova Scotia were the federal MPs. But Richey realized the danger of accepting Macdonald's contention that a lieutenant-governor was primarily an agent of the Dominion government; besides, elections in Nova Scotia were subject to a Quadrennial Act and almost four years had elapsed since the last one.

Fielding's manifesto fell into two parts; the first and larger part described the previous four years as "marked by upright and economical administration," and by wise and progressive legislation adapted to the requirements of the day; the second called for secession from a union "productive of little good and much evil," in which Nova Scotia had got no more than "a few miles of the Intercolonial Railway," and in which most of the Canadian debt had resulted from works of little interest to it. Perhaps, said Fielding, the federal government itself recognized the injustice since it was now intimating that it would build the main Cape Breton line as part of the ICR.

To the *Chronicle* repeal was "almost as vital to Nova Scotia as repeal of the union and home rule is to Ireland." To the *Herald* the Liberals were like burglars and murderers seeking to destroy the evidence of their guilt by using the secession issue to divert attention from their abysmal record. It described the aim of re-establishing the old province of Nova Scotia as entirely an illusion. Instead, the result would be its dismemberment since Cape Breton, Pictou, Cumberland, and Colchester counties — the first three likely to gain substantially from N.P. — were almost certain to reject repeal. When, at the end of May, Fielding reconstructed his cabinet and made J.W. Longley his attorney general, the *Herald* told him that he had reached the "lowest depth of degradation." Was not Longley simply the *Acadian Recorder* "on legs . . . a compound of everything that is undesirable in politics?"

The *Chronicle* was in ecstasy when June 15 became the Conservatives' Waterloo. The Liberals increased their number of seats from twenty-four to twenty-nine, well distributed throughout the province, while the Conservatives fell from fourteen to eight.[19] The *Herald* was decidedly wrong that four specific counties could not possibly vote for the Liberals and repeal. Cape Breton County did reverse itself and returned two Conservatives, but the Liberals gained one seat in Pictou, two in Colchester, and held on to their seat in Cumberland, admittedly with a non-repealer. When Colin Howell classified the Liberal candidates as confirmed repealers, moderate repealers, and unionists, he found a distinct cleavage in the voting.[20] Of those elected, all eleven repealers and ten moderates came from the western counties and along the southern and eastern shores "where prosperity was dependent upon access to international export markets." In contrast, the little success that the Conservatives had was in the counties experiencing industrial growth in Cape Breton and the northern part of the peninsula. In those areas, too, the Liberal candidates often tended to be hostile or lukewarm to repeal.

Generally the tendency has been to attribute the decisive Liberal victory to the repeal issue. A worried John A. Macdonald told Tupper in London that the Conservatives had lost "on the Secession cry — horse, foot and artillery. Never was there such a rout." But Howell wonders if repeal was an altogether dominant issue. He is undoubtedly correct that even without it Fielding would have won a convincing majority on his record. He also adduces evidence that in Liberal county newspapers and among Liberal candidates great skepticism existed about repeal and that in some counties it was only a peripheral issue. To many voters it may have been a mandate for negotiating better terms; John A. Macdonald suggested as much when he referred to it in terms of "blackmail."

Little doubt exists, however, that Fielding was deadly serious on the repeal question. "The men who forced Nova Scotia into the Union," he told Premier Oliver Mowat of Ontario, "planted the seeds of difficulties which have ever since been bearing fruit." When, in addition, the people laboured under heavy taxation and a neglect of public works and provincial services, it was easy to see why repeal was popular. Although better things were unlikely from Blake and the Ontario Grits, Nova Scotia would join in the fight against Toryism at Ottawa until the province parted company with Canada. When Blake finally wrote to Fielding in August, he agreed that they would never see eye to eye on secession, but he expected to find common ground on many other questions if, as he hoped, the next federal election showed a marked reaction against the bribery and degradation of morality under John A. Macdonald. In reply, Fielding apologized for causing embarrassment. He had tried to make repeal a non-party question only to discover that such a course would divide the Liberals while leaving the Tories united. At least he had avoided that danger: "you are none the weaker in the West on account of our course, and . . . we are stronger here."[21]

Two days after the election the *Herald* told Fielding to "put legs under [repeal]. Let us see it walk, move and have it's [sic] way!" He at least tried. Almost at once he told Premier A.G. Blair of New Brunswick that, although Nova Scotia was prepared to "go it alone for repeal," he hoped that his province would act in concert. About the same time he visited Prince Edward Island where, perhaps because an election was in progress, neither party showed the slightest interest in repeal or maritime union. By September Blair too had made it clear that his "answer would be decidedly in the negative." So for Fielding it had "become a question of whether his own province could secure repeal by itself."[22]

Over the next few months James A. Fraser and his friends pressed him for strong, decisive action. But knowing that his party was not fully united he decided to play a waiting game. "To have half a dozen of the Liberals break away from us on the Repeal question would much weaken the cause." Hence the party's first interest should be maritime union on which all its members could agree and on which, through visits, he could work among the people of the other maritime provinces. "It is not for us to expose our own weak spots."[23] By mid-November 1886 both parties were nominating candidates for the federal election and Fielding missed no opportunity to present his point of view. Everywhere he argued that, when Nova Scotia appealed to the foot of the throne for release from Confederation, none of its representatives should be in a position to counter its request. At the outset he talked in terms of sixteen Liberal seats, but by mid-February — election day was on the twenty-second — he was entering caveats. Because of close fights in some counties, he had grown fearful that a small change in public opinion or a massive expenditure of money might defeat the Liberals.

Whatever the cause his party took only seven of the twenty-one seats, the same as in 1882. Eight seats changed hands, but the gains and losses were equal. The electoral system undoubtedly helped the Conservatives since four of their victories were by combined majorities of fewer than 150 votes. As in the provincial election the Liberals did best in the southern and eastern counties from Yarmouth to Guysborough, where they won five of their seven seats. Likewise, the Conservatives took the northern industrializing seats and many more including twelve seats in the northern half of the province from Digby through the Annapolis Valley and over into Cape Breton. Not surprisingly, Fielding the incorruptible was certain that an honest election would have produced different results. Undoubtedly the Conservatives had much the larger campaign chest, but in treating them as utterly corrupt and his own party as totally pure he was engaging in self-deception. Factors other than money favoured the Conservatives. In Halifax, they benefited greatly from the votes of federal officials disfranchised in provincial elections. As in other elections during this period the ablest and most aspiring Liberals tended to enter and often to remain in provincial politics where they were almost certain of success.

Other things were even more significant. At John A. Macdonald's bidding Charles Tupper had returned to Nova Scotia from Britain to give life and drive to his party, apparently with his usual success. No less helpful to the Conservatives was the lack of unity of purpose within their opponents' ranks. Colin Howell has shown that only four of the Liberal candidates were out-and-out repealers: Kirk of Guysborough, Eisenhauer of Lunenburg, Lovitt of Yarmouth, and Fuller of Halifax. Nine others, including W.T. Pipes of Cumberland and George H. Murray of Cape Breton, were non-repealers; the eight remaining, including A.G. Jones of Halifax and Frederick W. Borden of Kings, were unsympathetic towards repeal, but did not repudiate it because it was official party policy. Of the Liberal newspapers only the Yarmouth *Herald* was militant in its support; the *Morning Chronicle* was much more moderate than in 1886, while the *Eastern Chronicle*, the Liverpool *Advance*, and the *Acadian Recorder* advocated reciprocity and did not deal with repeal.[24] Thus Liberal voters faced the confusing situation in which their national leader dismissed any thought of secession and their provincial leader made it the primary issue notwithstanding the lukewarmness or opposition of many followers.

Despite some opinions to the contrary, Fielding appears to have followed a straightforward course throughout both elections, viewing the repeal movement neither as a device to obtain better terms, nor as the best means of avoiding a split in the provincial party. The outcome left him completely disconsolate. "The people lost — or sold — a grand opportunity to strike a blow for the interests of Nova Scotia," he told James Eisenhauer. With different results, "there would have been a fair chance of winning separation from Canada," he informed John Lovitt of Yarmouth. "What now? The question is not an easy one to answer." But for him the election of 1887 was not yet over. The loss that rankled him most was that of Angus McGillivray to John S.D. Thompson in Antigonish by forty-six votes. The conduct of Bishop Cameron, he said, would be "condemned not only by the election court but also by the tribunal of the church in Rome . . . Such clerical influence . . . should not be tolerated in a free country."[25]

It was too much to expect the Catholics of Antigonish to proceed against their bishop, but elsewhere Fielding was unrelenting in his campaign for electoral purity.[26] Following the unseating of a Conservative in Digby, he told his party to fight the election cleanly and "if they [were] beaten *petition at once.*" Aware that legal proceedings cost money, he offered his bit: "if $20 from me will help let me know and it will be cheerfully given." He was especially elated when the Liberals unseated Postmaster General A.W. McLelan in Colchester, but warned that "half the good results of the trial will be lost if he is not opposed" at the second election. Only by this means could the Liberals "get the honest vote of the country to prevail, and I am satisfied that as a rule it can be on the Liberal side."

Cumberland, however, drew Fielding's greatest attention. Personally he wanted badly to proceed against Charles Tupper, but knowing that the Liberals of that county were likely to compromise, he was prepared to have them withdraw their petition provided that the Conservatives did the same in the case of Liberal Thomas Johnson in Shelburne: "My own opinion is that rather than submit to cross examination [at an election trial] Sir Charles will agree to anything that is proposed." As it turned out, everything went wrong for the Liberals. After the unseating of both Johnson and Tupper, the former increased his majority in Cumberland, while the latter lost out in Shelburne. The Conservatives also won the new elections in Digby and Colchester. Clearly Fielding was more than a little naive in expecting Nova Scotians to vote against a party which had recently carried a general election on the ground that it had resorted to bribery in some constituencies. To them the two parties were not polarized along the lines of good and evil as he perceived them.

Naive or not, Fielding, by his decisive provincial victory in 1886, had established his position within the party beyond challenge. As he would often say, nothing succeeds in politics like success and after 1886 any reference to the "troublesome fellows" is missing entirely from his correspondence. Even before then he must have convinced his correspondents that his tolerance was limited; after that time he was, if anything, more outspoken. With those who were unreasonable, he minced no words. To any who stooped to threats he gave a veritable tongue-lashing. "I will go a long way to help a friend who is fair-minded," he told one, "but [not] those who fall into the error of threatening . . . Nothing is to be gained by submitting to such indignity." To the Liberal members for Colchester who embarrassed him by a public letter relating to the county sheriff he said bluntly that it was "the most extraordinary that I ever received from parties claiming to be friends of the Government."

Fielding did not endear himself to some supporters by his general stance on patronage.[27] "We should aim at permanency in our public offices . . . The mere fact that a man holding [office] has been of the other political party is hardly a sufficient ground for his removal." From both the public and political standpoints he considered it a sound policy not to dismiss a public servant except for charges established by an investigation; otherwise "we cannot expect our successors to continue in office those whom we appointed." That did not mean that he was not a strong party man. Of no use to him was a Liberal who took an entirely independent position in the assembly. "Party government requires agreement. To agree we must all 'give and take' a little — not insist on all our own ideas being adopted." He conceded, however, that in cases where a man had a strong and conscientious objection to party policy he might justifiably oppose it. Though a teetotaller he became annoyed at the fanaticism of temperance advocates: "I cannot help thinking," he told one clergyman, "that they must be illiberal Liberals who deny [the Chronicle's] right to speak its views [on temperance matters] or who hold the Liberal party or even the Provincial Secretary responsible for those views."

Like his predecessors Fielding found expenditures on roads and bridges especially troublesome. Time and again he told correspondents that, except for the larger bridges, the allocations had been the prerogative of the municipal councils since 1879. The council might "have little money for the purpose but . . . I have none." To Father Ronald McGillivray in Antigonish, who demanded a bridge in threatening terms, he replied with equal frankness: Did the father's judgment not tell him that threats were unlikely to have much weight in the mind of a right-thinking man? If a government responded to threats after it did not respond to the merits of the case would it not deserve his contempt?

From all this correspondence emerges a humble, modest man, even though after reading some of Tupper's speeches he once jokingly remarked that he had learned "the unwisdom of modesty." In establishing his leadership securely, he found it a "misfortune" in one respect, since he had got into a position which he could not maintain without going into debt. "If I could quietly step aside, I should be strongly inclined to do so, because as a private citizen I could handle my own affairs with a freedom that is not open to me as Premier of N.S." In five years he had had to run three elections; for two years he had been a minister without office or salary, for two years premier with an inadequate salary. Only because of an increase in pay the previous session could he begin to "overtake arrears," but his debt was still "a constant source of worry to him." Late in 1887 he approached Pipes, from whom he had previously borrowed, offering the security of a life insurance policy. "Pride . . . makes me unwilling to encumber what little property I own." Later he approached another non-Haligonian, stating that he wanted to be free of his Halifax friends, especially those who might do business with the government. Finally, early in 1888, he appealed to John K. Lovitt of Yarmouth, whose kind words in the past made him optimistic.[28] His success in his borrowing ventures is not known. What is certain is that by this time his position within his party was such that many of its members would have moved heaven and earth to keep him in politics.

CHAPTER 10

Fielding: Political Master of the Province

If any doubts existed about Fielding having become the political master of the province, the ease with which he gave the quietus to the repeal question squelched them. A month after the opening of the first session of the Twenty-Eight General Assembly in 1887 he presented resolutions which made it clear that, because of the federal election results in Nova Scotia, he would not press the idea of separation; however, unless the province's financial position improved, he might raise it again in the future. Denying that he had not been active enough for repeal, he showed that before the election he had actively promoted maritime union; that during the election he had campaigned vigorously for repeal in every county except Cumberland, where both candidates opposed it. Only two Liberal diehards objected. Roche of Halifax insisted that the issue was not over; McColl of Pictou wanted to ask the American government to admit Nova Scotia to the American union, but could not find a seconder for his motion. As a result, Fielding easily carried his resolutions by twenty-four to eight and for him the issue was over forever.

Although the *Herald* objected to the house being turned continually into "a political club for the discussion of Dominion issues," this General Assembly probably concerned itself with federal questions more than any other. Could N.P. confer any practical benefits upon Nova Scotia? Would the province gain from a change in trading relations with the United States? Was Portland, Maine rather than Halifax likely to become the winter port of the Dominion under existing federal policies? Could Nova Scotia benefit in any way from the CPR?

It quickly became evident that the government would easily have its way during the four years of the assembly's life. Of the eight Conservatives elected, only three had had previous legislative experience and only two after their leader Adam Bell resigned to contest the federal election. In caucus they chose the sincere, conscientious Dr. William MacKay of Cape Breton County to lead them. But his inexperience, his failure to master detail, and his inability to "go for the jugular" caused the session of 1887 to be largely devoid of party politics. A resident of Reserve Mines, he found it difficult to keep himself *au courant* of public affairs. So, during the next few years, J.J. Stewart, the editor of the *Herald*, and its editorial writers assumed the real leadership of the party to an unprecedented degree. Their editorials provided most of the substance of Conservative speeches in the legislature and the two themes which they stressed in 1887 would be a constant for many years to come and be repeated *ad nauseam* by Conservative assemblymen, if only as a faint echo.

The first was financial mismanagement. Even with revenues increased to $633,000, lamented the *Herald*, the government had incurred a deficit of $25,000 and the provincial debt had mounted to at least $1,000,000. Allegedly "boodlism" marked every page of the financial returns, as evidenced by the large sums paid to Liberal lawyers — "those indefatigable milkmen" — for revising the statutes. Neither education, nor agriculture, nor the road service had profited from the additional revenues received from coal royalties. A bill to borrow $250,000 for permanent bridges — the third of its kind — would do irreparable harm to the municipalities; they should realize that every $100 borrowed under the act meant a permanent loss of $4.50 from the municipal road grants. Fielding, in reply, claimed prudence in every facet of expenditure. "Whenever . . . it becomes necessary in the cause of the public credit, I shall be willing to lay hands, unholy hands you may call them, even on the cause of education."[1]

The *Herald's* second theme was the meagreness of the legislative bill of fare. It had some point in 1887 since the government itself conceded that the session was a housekeeping one. But the *Herald* went further in describing the few bills as dangerous. It condemned Attorney General Longley in particular for yielding to the vicious element of his party and initiating action to exclude Dominion officials from holding municipal office. It also denounced him for a bill permitting him to appoint a Crown prosecutor in every county. Hitherto a Supreme Court judge had designated a Queen's Counsel or senior barrister to perform that function at sessions of the court. To the *Herald* and Dr. MacKay it was simply a case of adding to Liberal patronage and making the administration of justice a part of the political machine.

More typical of most Fielding years, the session of 1888 brought unspectacular, but practical, useful legislation. A Towns' Incorporation Act meant that the legislature would no longer have to deal with individual incorporation bills. A new assessment act included for municipal purposes a mild form of income tax applicable to well-to-do Nova Scotians. Another act took a slight step towards removing imprisonment for debt, but without reducing the penalties for fraudulent transactions. Most novel of all was an act which bound both parties in coal-mining operations to accept arbitration, a provision which favoured miners over operators in the context of that day. But for the *Herald* these were picayune matters compared with those relating to trade relations with the United States.

Since the autumn of 1885 J.W. Longley had been supporting commercial union in *The Week* and the *Acadian Recorder*. Standing for a common Canadian-United States tariff against the rest of the world, it carried with it at least some possibility of political union. Allegedly Longley was not reluctant to apply the term annexationist to himself in Boston late in 1887. Two months earlier the general question had come up at an interprovincial conference convened in Quebec City by Premier Honoré Mercier and attended by five of the seven provincial premiers. After making it clear that he did so without prejudice to future efforts for repeal, Fielding became one of the conference's most active participants. The outcome was pleasing to all the premiers. Mowat of Ontario, engaged in a long constitutional battle with John A. Macdonald, secured agreement for such demands as the abolition of disallowance and the appointment of senators by the provinces; the other premiers won his approval of proposals which would have trebled federal grants to the provincial governments. The five of them agreed, too, on unrestricted reciprocity (u.r.), which would have meant complete free trade with the United States, while allowing both countries to set up their own tariffs against all others.

Shortly before the Nova Scotia legislature met in 1888, the Liberals' financial spokesman at Ottawa, Richard Cartwright, had introduced a resolution in the Commons favouring commercial union, later changing it to u.r. Rising in righteous indignation, the *Herald* declared that "the grit leaders are again coquetting with the Wiman-Butterworth scheme for making Canada a commercial vassal of the United States." Day after day this was its refrain to the exclusion of almost all other editorial comment.[2] Its target changed after April 13 when Longley introduced a resolution in the assembly favouring u.r. Countering the *Herald's* claim that he was trying to make Canada an American vassal, he contended that it was better to adopt the policy of letting trade flow in the channels which God and nature intended rather than one which was an abject failure and laid a heavy burden of debt on the country.

Prorogation took place without a vote on Longley's resolution or on one calling for repeal and u.r. by one of the most persistent of all the repealers, William Roche of Halifax. Fielding did insist, however, that the legislature vote on the Quebec Resolutions despite the *Herald's* taunt that they were a curious mixture of the satisfactory and the ridiculous. The *Chronicle* had its innings when the Conservatives spoke not a word on the resolutions and yet voted *en masse* against them. How, it wondered, could they object to proposals which would increase the province's annual revenue by $162,000? Fielding easily carried the assembly by twenty-two to eleven, but failed in the council when seven Liberals turned against him. Clearly their motivation was self-preservation since one of the resolutions proposed steps to eliminate the second chambers in all the provinces.

This was the second time during the session that the councillors had taken action to protect themselves. Earlier they had had to deal with Fielding's abolition bill, which the assembly had approved by thirty-one to four. Taking the position that the public had never shown any desire to get rid of them and that they performed an indispensable function in perfecting the assembly's bills, they voted against abolition by eleven to eight. One Liberal who had given a written pledge in favour of abolition, Monson Goudge, joined the majority, as did two Conservatives, Samuel

Locke and George Whitman, who had previously pledged themselves verbally.

By 1889 the emphasis had reverted to Nova Scotia politics, although federal questions sporadically gained the public's attention. To its long-time federal hero, Charles Tupper, the *Herald* added John S.D. Thompson for his justification of the government's conduct on Jesuits' estates. Naturally it blasted Richard Cartwright for proposing that Canada have the right to negotiate its own commercial treaties. Meanwhile the *Chronicle* was condemning it for seeing annexation in everything. On provincial questions the Conservative asemblymen were considerably more lively in 1889 although that pleased the *Chronicle* no more that their previous reticence. Dr. MacKay, it said, had "no aptitude for politics and no judgment whatever." By his own admission he got his ideas from the *Herald*, where "idiocy and unveracity seem to be enthroned." His followers were not much better, indeed, "a humiliation to the province." In no other legislature in the civilized world did a political party "cut such a ridiculous figure."[3]

This year the Conservatives launched their major assault on the government's road policy. Taking the position that the bridges were at last in reasonable shape, Fielding decided to deal directly with roads, which were suffering from the natural tendency of the municipal councils to spread the road moneys in small amounts among the various polling districts. Accordingly he proposed to borrow $300,000 for new roads, and roads in largely unsettled districts. As in the case of the bridge bills, the interest on these expenditures was to be deducted from each county's regular road grants. MacKay proposed, instead, that the government limit itself for the moment to only essential expenditures on roads while it made two studies: one on the adequacy of the forty-year old scale for the division of the road moneys among counties; the other on combining the provincial and municipal road moneys and statutory labour to the best advantage. But although the proposals made some sense, the government refused even to consider them.

The year 1889 saw another liberalization of the franchise. As usual, the Conservatives proposed universal male suffrage and, as usual, Attorney General Longley declared that it would bring in "the dregs," who supported the Tories. In the end the Conservatives claimed a moral victory for forcing the government to broaden its original proposals. The outcome was to add an annual income of $250 as a qualification for voting and to let fishermen vote under the federal qualifications. The assembly also debated again the disfranchisement of Dominion officials in provincial and municipal elections. But the attempt of Liberal Joseph Matheson of Richmond to remove the restrictions in municipal elections failed, although only by a single vote. No less adamant than before, the *Chronicle* held that federal servants were not free agents, but "mere instruments . . . for carrying out the will of the most unjust, unscrupulous and tyrannical government that ever cursed a country supposed to be possessed of free institutions."[4]

As usual, the legislature abounded in recrimination on railways. Even when the federal government decided to build the "missing link," the provincial government was still dissatisfied. Why did Ottawa not acquire the Windsor and Annapolis, and make possible the convenience of a single line instead of three between Halifax and Yarmouth? In their turn, the Conservatives railed at Fielding's "do-nothing" railway policy. In Queens and Shelburne the people had "railway charters innumerable, but no railway"; Cape Breton would have no railways at all if the federal government had not decided to extend the ICR to Sydney; Fielding had even refused a subsidy to the Inverness and Richmond Railway Company until the Dominion first provided one.

In 1890 the debate was free from trade issues, but not from federal issues. Great was the *Chronicle's* lament at a fifty per cent increase in the duty on flour from 50 to 75 cents a barrel, which it was certain would bear primarily on the maritime provinces. Why, asked the *Herald*, was the Dominion spending $1,500,000 on railways in Cape Breton, the province little or nothing? Dr. MacKay compared Fielding's policy in non-railway counties to Jules Verne's journey to the moon: "There is a great deal of moonshine about it." Throughout the session both parties had an eye to the election which would come later in the year. When the *Herald* called for the abolition of the legislative council, the government quickly responded with a bill to that effect. Since three recent appointees had pledged themselves to abolition in writing, it appeared as if the upper house might be doomed. But its devices to protect itself were limitless. Its committee of privileges simply declared that the introduction of the bill in the assembly violated its privileges, an opinion that all the councillors could support without breaking their pledges.

But the real debate in 1890 was on finances. Both MacKay and J.J. Stewart of the *Herald* agreed that the best way to fight the election was to damage the government's credibility on its spending record. So when Fielding proposed to remove the limit on temporary government borrowings from the banks, the *Herald* called it a scheme to overwhelm the province with debt without the public knowing it. The *Chronicle* replied scornfully that J.J. Stewart could see further into a millstone than any other person on earth. The main financial target, however, was the government's road bill which, for the second year in a row, proposed to borrow $300,000 for capital expenditures on highways. Because the expenditures were to be made without tender, the opposition called it "the $300,000 Boodle Bill." Highly sensitive to charges of this kind, Fielding had a large chest brought into the house containing accounts and vouchers for the expenditure of every dollar of the road money during the previous year. A second major objection to the bill was that the interest on these expenditures would again be met by reducing the counties' road moneys, a process that would lead to their exhaustion. It was "neither statesmanlike nor honest," said the *Herald*, "to take their money, — the money that the province virtually pledged to them at the time of municipal incorporation — and hand it over to party hacks and heelers to be used as a corruption fund."[5]

Above all, the Conservatives attacked their opponents for piling up a debt beyond the resources of the province to meet. The *Herald* sought to show that the federal government would have to increase the national debt to about $135,000,000 (it was then $20,000,000) to match the province's. Longley and the *Chronicle* had figures of their own to counter this argument. Their calculations indicated the per capita net debt of the Dominion to be $47.00, that of Halifax $50.00, and that of Nova Scotia a modest $1.25. Meanwhile Fielding was stating his basic principles in finance: "We are desirous of making liberal grants, but we have a higher duty to perform . . . to make both ends meet and to place the credit of the province in a safe and solid position." Increased coal royalties — he estimated them at $185,000, the highest on record — would, he hoped, contribute materially to that end.

Thus months before the election the Conservatives had mapped out their election strategy. All the evidence points to its being planned and directed from the offices of the *Morning Herald*. As the *Chronicle* put it bluntly, MacKay — limited in political talents and lacking assistance within the assembly — "sought inspiration from certain disreputable sources outside." Certainly his election manifesto in the *Herald* of April 24 was a summary of that paper's editorials. Members of the *Herald* office had also seen to it that the county Conservatives had got into high gear months earlier. By the time of calling the election they had nominated candidates in every county but Hants and Kings, and they included Stewart, the *Herald's* editor, in Halifax and C.H. Cahan, one of its editorial writers, in Shelburne. The indictment of the government by MacKay's manifesto was extensive and detailed. After alleging gross mismanagement in every facet of the public service, it contended that any useful legislation resulted from pressure by the Conservative party and "the educated public opinion of this province." Again the basic emphasis was on the ministry's financial record — "calamitous" the manifesto called it — and the *Herald* followed it up with editorials headed "Misman-agement of the Finance"; "Mortgaging the Future", and "Direct Taxation at Hand."

Fielding's manifesto two days later resembled his speeches in overwhelming its readers with detail on every matter which could possibly be of advantage to his government. It blamed its failure to progress with railway-building on the obstructive tactics of the federal government. It sought, in answer to the opposition's main attack, to demonstrate that the government had spent the moneys efficiently and faithfully, and quoted financial circulars that "no other province east or west of Ontario had such good security as Nova Scotia." As the campaign progressed the *Chronicle* resorted more and more to the personal argument. Who would be premier if the Conservatives won? "Dr. MacKay? What responsible man can contemplate this with calmness?" Who might be his associates: Cahan, J.J. Stewart, David Hearn, and Dr. McLennan? "What a tribe of worthies we have here. The people of Nova Scotia will have no such folly."

Mid-way through the election Fielding prophesied the outcome as twenty-seven Liberals to eleven Conservatives. The day before the election, however, he admitted that it was "a matter of uncertainty. Politics is a lottery in which there are blanks for somebody. Some of these days the blanks will come to me."[6] But for Fielding the blanks would not come for another twenty-one years. Although the Liberals' popular vote fell by 2.5 per cent, they won twenty-eight seats, only one fewer than in 1886. Up to his old tricks, Otto Weeks ran unofficially as a Liberal in Guysborough and brought about the defeat of the two official Liberals, one of them James A. Fraser. Neither Fraser nor Weeks would ever sit in the assembly again, although Fraser would long serve the Liberal cause as editor of the *Eastern Chronicle* in New Glasgow.

For the Conservatives the election began a phenomenon that would plague them for many years: the loss of their leader, in this case Dr. MacKay. Although C.H. Cahan won by nine votes in Shelburne, the *Herald's* editor, J.J. Stewart, was at the foot of the poll in Halifax. But it was unrepentant. It lamented the approval of the wretched policy of borrowing for current purposes and promised to continue the fight against mortgaging the future. For Fielding there were some surprises, some disappointments, seats which he expected to win but lost, and the reverse. He was especially pleased with the results in Yarmouth, where he feared that the Conservatives' nomination of an Acadian might hurt his party, and in Annapolis, where Longley's opponents had lavished their financial resources to beat him. Always thinking of his federal counterparts, he told Premier Blair that the victory should infuse them with "a determination to win," although he admitted to Arthur Hardy of Ontario that their success could not be as great since many who voted Liberal provincially were protectionists and hence supporters of the federal Conservatives.[7]

Strangely, Fielding still hoped to "step back into the ranks" himself if he could do it without embarrassment to his associates.[8] But that was clearly wishful thinking. To Nova Scotia's Liberals the election had provided further proof that he was their greatest asset and one not to be parted with lightly. Actually he was in the process of beginning the Nova Scotia phenomenon, which enabled a premier of moderate views and common sense, who was content to make progress by small, patient steps, and who created the general impression that he had the province's best interests at heart, to hold on to the office as long as he wished once he had won his first election. He, like some of his successors, had the assistance of the Conservatives, who were generally negative in stance and who, according to him, "sought to make up in noise and violence what they lack in argument." So he remained premier even though he continued to be hard up. To one family with large claims on the Liberal party he expressed regret at his inability to provide assistance: "instead of being able to lend money just at present I have to be a borrower myself." But he did manage to install a hot water heating apparatus in his home: "It is particularly necessary in a house the shape of ours. We found that one hall stove could not heat the house; consequently we had to use two which causes dust, dirt, confusion and labor."

Even before the assembly met again he was using his talents to promote harmony and lessen friction within the party. Facing numerous claimants for the speakership, he decided to follow the same course as in 1887 and let his members decide. "For the Govt . . . to force a man on caucus might make so much ill feeling as to begin the term unpleasantly. In the interest of the party we wish to avoid that." At the same time he was counselling his Richmond members, Joseph Matheson and Abraham LeBlanc, to decide amicably between themselves "a few really important roads" to be worked on in that county; otherwise, "you may be sure that our opponents would . . . stir up trouble among the French people."[9] Of even more importance, the Liberals took the final step in the organization of the provincial party. Ever since Laurier had become the federal leader in 1887 he had sought to erase the impression that the party generally followed the dictates of Ontario. He was in Halifax, along with Davies, Fisher, and Choquette, on December 18, 1890, during the setting up of the Nova Scotia Liberal Association to manage "such portions of the business of the party as concern the province at large rather than particular counties." Under its urging Richmond and Guysborough quickly established county organizations for the first time.[10]

The Liberals were perfecting their organization just as the opening shots of the 1891 federal election — not yet formally called — were being fired. On the one side Sir John Macdonald set the style during a speaking tour of the maritime provinces late in

September 1890. To a Halifax audience he declared bluntly that Canada could get no relief from the Americans' highly protectionist McKinley tariff without taking action that would defeat the purposes of N.P. and endanger the British connection. On the other side, every leading Liberal but Edward Blake had come out for u.r. By year's end no newspaper had become more British than the *Morning Herald*. For more than two months it pounced upon the utterances of every American which suited its purposes and embellished every conspiracy which the Ontario Conservatives supposedly brought to light. In its view u.r. inevitably meant commercial union, the adoption by Canada of the McKinley tariff against Britain and the levying of direct taxation to make up for the loss of tariff revenues. On February 4, 1891 it nailed the red ensign to its masthead and on the 9th it proclaimed that "the people of Canada are brought to the parting of the ways." Would they become vassals of the United States or prosper as part of the greatest empire the world had ever seen?

In its attempt to meet the *Herald* head on, the *Chronicle* sought to distinguish between u.r. and commercial union. "Commercial union is not the Liberal policy. Unrestricted reciprocity is." But it quickly concluded that it could not discuss the matter rationally with the *Herald*: "it can only call names and make false representation of the Liberal position." Its basic position was that u.r. would lead to such contentment that Canadians would be completely satisfied with the political *status quo*. Unable to cope with the demagoguery of the *Herald*, it sought to divert the campaign to the bread tax, the inadequacy of railway subsidies, and corruption at Ottawa, but with no noticeable success. For Fielding fighting his third election against John A. Macdonald it was also a time of frustration. By mid-February Sir Charles Tupper, recalled from the high commissionership in London, arrived with his son Charles Hibbert and John Thompson to take charge of the Conservative campaign. As usual, the Liberals treated him with scorn: "There is a crisis in the history of my country and I am to save it." But the election returns of March 5 indicated in no uncertain fashion that he was still the master of Nova Scotia in federal politics. The Conservatives increased their share of the popular vote from 49.7 to 53.1 per cent and won sixteen of the twenty-one seats.

It was fortunate for the Conservatives that they had done well in two of the maritime provinces. In Quebec and Ontario combined they were in a minority of five, and eleven of their over-all majority of thirty-two seats came from Nova Scotia and ten from New Brunswick. As Richard Cartwright put it, the "shreds and patches" of the Dominion had saved Sir John. Fred Landon said, no less correctly, that u.r. had "enabled the Conservatives to snatch another victory at the polls."[11] The *Chronicle* was probably right that a flood of money helped the Conservatives. But in Nova Scotia pro-British feeling did much more, especially since it worked in concert with the conservative nature of the political culture. As in 1867, the voters may have looked askance at a party proposing policies which allegedly threatened the political *status quo*.

The first session of the Twenty-Ninth General Assembly in 1891 witnessed one significant change. The new Conservative leader, C.H. Cahan, possessed in abundance the vigour, knowledgeability, and oratorical ability which Dr. MacKay lacked. He also had what the *Chronicle* called a "scrapbook of appalling dimensions" to counter Fielding and his book of clippings. Certainly the assembly was likely to get doses of statistics from its newspapermen leaders. Some debates during the session merely repeated those of earlier years. When Fielding proposed to clarify the franchise law, Cahan demanded universal male suffrage as a means of removing "the perplexing qualifications that met every elector who sought to procure registration." When G.W. Forrest of Cumberland sought to repeal the disfranchisement of Dominion officials, Fielding replied that "in Halifax there was an influence, unmistakable, though some time silent, which gave Dominion officials to understand that they were not free to vote as they pleased."

The opposition concentrated, however, on two other questions, the first an alleged attempt to "blackmail" the Dominion government in two railway matters. When Ottawa, in effect, forced Nova Scotia to hand over the Eastern Extension, it had returned all of the province's outlay except the $671,836 which it had granted in subsidies. Since, with this exception, the federal government had paid the entire cost of the ICR, Fielding argued that Nova Scotia was entitled to recover it. He also contended much more dubiously that Ottawa should assume Nova Scotia's input of $679,197 into the building of the WCR since, in order to complete the "missing link," it had declared the railway to be a work for the general advantage of Canada and hence obtained legislative control, although not actual ownership. Cahan took the position that it was the government's duty to present a statement of claim for the assembly's approval, rather than leave it to an assembly committee, and the Conservatives refused to sit on the committee. "Could partisan slavery go further than this?" asked the *Chronicle*.

The opposition's second line of attack — on financial matters — took a variety of forms. It might assail the deficit of $45,600, or the increase in ministerial salaries from $2,500 to $3,200, with $800 additional to the premier, or the charging to capital account of the expenditures made on the school of agriculture and the Victoria General Hospital. But the most concentrated assault was on Fielding's Bridge Bill, which authorized the borrowing of $300,000 for the larger bridges. The fourth of its kind, it was defended as the only means of meeting an undoubted need. Cahan and the *Herald* expressed alarm on two counts. Because of interest deductions to cover previous loans, the counties' annual road grants had already fallen from $130,000 to $88,500 and would now suffer another reduction. Accompanying this criticism was the cry of imminent doom as Fielding allegedly moved the province more and more towards bankruptcy. Although the *Chronicle* called it a "complete farrago of misrepresentation" from beginning to end, even it might have agreed that under Cahan the Conservatives had resuscitated themselves in the assembly.

In 1892, circumstances caused both sides to take new ground. Despite its general careful handling of the finances and despite modest, although erratic increases in revenue from coal royalties, the government found itself with a deficit of $19,000 and a tightening financial strait-jacket. So instead of introducing contentious borrowing legislation, it followed the example of Ontario and New Brunswick and initiated succession duties on large estates at a low rate, the provincial government's first use of direct taxation. While Fielding considered it a highly appropriate way of paying for the increasing cost of public charities, the *Herald* held that the imposition of the tax and a second method of adding to the revenues — a modest increase per ton in coal royalties — were "both due to the scandalous waste . . . in recent years, and the end is not yet." Later in the year, as a means of getting out of his difficulties, Fielding suggested to the provincial treasurer of Quebec that the provinces should press for the implementation of the financial resolutions of the Quebec Conference of 1887. All the provinces except Ontario, he pointed out, were hard pressed and the Fathers of Confederation had not intended that they should have to resort to direct taxation to maintain provincial services. Accordingly, as provincial responsibilities expanded and as customs and excise duties increased, the provinces should receive more of these revenues.[12] But it would not be until 1907, when Fielding himself was federal minister of finance, that the demands of 1887 would be met.

The session of 1892 also saw the first tentative step towards divesting the rural municipalities of the responsibility for maintaining their roads which they had been exercising since 1879. Not only had they tended to divide the moneys into excessively small amounts but they had often let parochial politics dictate the location of the expenditures. Typical of the man, Fielding made sure that the Road Bill of 1892 was political caution itself; it would go into effect only in those municipalities which approved it at the next municipal elections. There the road moneys, together with statute labour, would come under the control of a board of five members, three appointed by the government and two by the municipal councils. The government's appointees would include the chairman and the inspector, who was the crucial officer. He would recommend expenditures to the board and direct the foremen whom it appointed. Hopefully the councils would provide amounts equal to the county school fund — not less than thirty cents nor more than sixty cents a head. Cahan called the bill "a mighty blow" against the system set up in 1879, establishing as it did a board almost free of the municipal councils and "practically and politically under the control of the government." The *Herald* dismissed it by saying that no municipality would bring the bill into effect when it knew what it meant.

In 1892, too, the assembly dealt with a significant case involving its privileges. In petitioning for the repeal of legislation affecting the town of Truro, Mayor David Thomas attached the complaint of the town council that assemblyman F.A. Laurence had promoted and caused laws to be passed which operated to Laurence's personal benefit and deprived the town of $475 annually. Although *prima facie* evidence supported the complaint, the Liberal majority coalesced to defend a Liberal representative against a Tory mayor. Without investigating the charges it found Thomas guilty of publishing a libel against an assemblyman and when he refused to accept a reprimand, it ordered him imprisoned for forty-eight hours. He sought his revenge by instituting a suit for damages of $50,000 against the assemblymen who had ordered his arrest. The courts had therefore to determine the validity of the statute of 1876 upon which the assembly relied to justify itself. Not until 1896 in *Fielding* v. *Thomas* did the Judicial Committee of the Privy Council decide that legislation to protect a provincial legislature from outside interference or its members from insult was valid, either under section 5 of the Colonial Laws Validity Act of 1865, which gave colonial assemblies the right to make laws relating to their constitutions, powers, and procedures, or under section 92 of the British North America Act, which empowered the provincial legislatures to amend their constitutions. Thus a Nova Scotian case became a sort of charter of rights for Canadian legislative assemblies and assemblymen.[13]

Causing the stormiest debates in 1892 were the charges relating to the expenditure of road moneys under the Road Acts of 1889 and 1890. Because Fielding had been wont to label his opponents as the party of corruption, the *Herald* clearly enjoyed the opportunity to produce evidence of scandal in his administration. In particular, it accused the premier of seeking to "burk enquiry and investigation," and the evidence suggests that Fielding and Longley used every legitimate means at their disposal to render difficult the full exposure of the facts. Eventually Cahan singled out the Liberal members for Cape Breton County, Angus John MacDonald and Joseph McPherson, as having usurped the functions of supervisor and paymaster under the road acts; as having allowed their political supporters to make expenditures without the prescribed warrants; as having permitted the submission of pay sheets showing larger expenditures than were actually made; and as having personally received and paid out much of the road money contrary to law. Cahan followed with similar charges against John A. Fraser of Victoria, but was frustrated when Fielding referred the entire matter to the assembly's committee of privileges, an action that severely limited the scope of the inquiry.

Nevertheless, the investigation demonstrated that the safeguards written into the road acts had been honoured more in the breach than in the observance. The majority of the committee reported, however, that not a tittle of evidence reflected on the honour of the Cape Breton members. It admitted to more serious irregularities in Victoria County, but except in the case of R.E. Burke it discovered no evidence of misappropriation and even there it believed that the money might have been honestly spent. In his turn the Conservative member of the committee found not only "an extraordinary looseness in the method of expenditure" but also, in the Burke case, "a clear instance of forgery committed by someone." More forcefully, the *Herald* declared that road moneys had been "expended in a corrupt and scandalous manner" to assist the Liberals at the last provincial elections.

Throughout these months Fielding was doing his best to help his party in eight federal by elections following wholesale unseatings in controverted elections. Running through his writing was still an exaggerated view of the Liberals as the party of purity and the Conservatives as corruptionists. In Halifax the election delighted him. "We did not even hire a cab," but so frightened the Conservatives that it was "the purest election that has been run in Halifax for many years." Overall each party won four seats in Nova Scotia, but elsewhere the results were disappointing to Fielding. Because of the Mercier scandals, he expected the Liberals to do badly in Quebec, but what, he wondered, was the matter with Ontario? The outcome was that the Conservatives would be more secure than before in Parliament. Yet he remained optimistic: "I still entertain the idea, perhaps without being able to give any good reason for it, that the end of [the Conservatives'] time is not far off."[14]

For Fielding the year 1892 had two other concerns, one of fear and one of hope. With the death of William Annand, the disposition of the *Morning Chronicle*, long the major organ of the Liberals, became for them a question of absorbing interest. Fielding intimated that, had he the needed capital, he would have liked to buy the paper, step out of politics, and devote himself to his old work for the rest of his life. The Liberals' fears were groundless, however, since the *Chronicle* remained their party's paper until its demise in 1948. Much more significant for the province and for continued Liberal dominance were the confidential talks beginning in the spring of 1892 between Fielding and Henry M. Whitney on the use of Nova Scotian coal in the latter's industrial establishments in New England. After the two had reached an understanding in Boston, Whitney's officials came to Halifax where new provisions were added to make the scheme more attractive to capitalists "without doing us harm."

Four days after the legislature opened in mid-January 1893 Fielding introduced a bill[15] which, he hoped, would allow "the treasures of the east which we possess" to promote provincial development. Between 1875 and 1890, he pointed out, the province's annual coal production had increased from 706,000 to 1,786,000 tons, most of it resulting from shipments up the St. Lawrence which, he admitted, were made possible by the protective duties that he disliked. Now, assisted by American financing, Nova Scotia had the opportunity to supply the New England market. "I do not believe in this foolish cry . . . against American capital . . . I am prepared to hold out both hands to any capital seeking investment in our province." Could there be any better prospect than Henry M. Whitney, a man of shrewd judgment and business integrity, whose street car system in Boston, the West End Street Railway, was an increasingly large consumer of coal, as was his Metropolitan Steamship Company, which had ships plying between New York and Boston?

Anticipating criticism, Fielding emphasized that Whitney was not being given, nor did he want, a monopoly. Although he would have a lease of all the coal mines in Cape Breton County, it was producing only half the coal and he would face stiff competition from the mines in Cumberland, Pictou, and Inverness. Because Whitney had agreed to pay a royalty of 12 1/2 cents per ton rather than the normal 10 cents, the province would have more money for its roads and bridges. He would also want to increase the output of Cape Breton coal which, mined at tide water, could be landed more cheaply in Boston and New York than coal from Pennsylvania.

Time would prove the *Chronicle* right that the agreement was one of the great events of Nova Scotian history, one concluded — so it said — by "the ablest and best government the province ever had." In its opinion the outcome would be the death knell of N.P. If protection was a fraud as it applied to coal, might it not be a fraud as it applied to everything else? It had no doubt that the development of the coal industry would prepare the way for a similar development in the iron industry. In contrast, Cahan and the *Herald* adopted an entirely negative stance and sought to frighten the public with the spectre of a dangerous monopoly for the unconscionably long period of ninety-nine years. Using its existing powers the Whitney syndicate would first take over the entire mining industry and then railways and telegraphs: "nothing will put a stop to their absorption but a rebellion or insurrection." The Conservatives also declared the lease to be invalid since the province's title only extended to eighteen years after the death of Queen Victoria. A furious *Chronicle* declared that "the contention was so preposterous that no lawyer of responsibility could give it credence." Throughout the debate the *Herald* appeared embarrassed because it could find scarcely any Conservative businessmen who agreed with it.

Compared with the syndicate bill, other issues appeared picayune in 1893. As usual, the Conservatives and the *Herald* bewailed the mounting debt and the continuing diminution of the municipal road funds; the *Chronicle* replied that the province's net debt was only $3.62 per head compared with the federal government's $49.10. Between sessions Attorney General Longley had personally investigated the Victoria County irregularities and especially the case of R.E. Burke. When he reported that one Norman McLeod had done the road work in question and signed Burke's name with the latter's consent, but that there was no evidence of misappropriation, the Conservatives declared that he was condoning crimes and frustrating the cause of justice. But not even this *ex parte* investigation, by which the government, in effect, declared itself not guilty, would damage Fielding's reputation as "Mr. Clean." He had some trouble, however, in forestalling his backbencher A.M. Hemeon, who having failed earlier to get limited voting rights for women, now tried to give them full voting equality with men. Supporting him strongly was the Women's Christian Temperance Union, which was hopeful that the success of his measure would further its ends. Although both Fielding and Cahan opposed the bill, it passed second reading by nineteen to seventeen. But because of procedural complexities, time ran out on the measure.

Confederation had brought a majority of Catholics back into the Liberal fold, but behind the scenes disagreements between Fielding and Archbishop Cornelius O'Brien of Halifax came to a head in 1893.[16] For a long time the government had given a grant to the non-sectarian Halifax Infants' Home, but when the Catholics set up their Home of the Guardian Angel, both institutions became, in effect, sectarian and, in accordance with government policy, neither received a grant. Preaching at St. Mary's Cathedral in December 1891, the archbishop called on Catholics to remember that fact at the next election. That led to correspondence in which he charged that Fielding determined government policy by himself and that for years he had been subsidizing the Infants' Home, knowing it to be "essentially a Protestant institution." Fielding denied it and insisted that the government did not act at the will or the whim of the premier. "The free air of Nova Scotia does not permit the growth of dictatorship in regard to public affairs. Such dictatorship would not be tolerated, whether attempted by a Premier or an Archbishop." Then he read O'Brien a lesson, pointing out that the Halifax Catholics among whom he had spent his whole life had given him as much political support as "any other public man in my day."

In mid-1893, when a controversy broke out on a new question, Fielding let the *Chronicle* present his case in public. By an unwritten compact arrived at in 1865-6 Halifax Catholics, in effect, received separate schools by accommodation rather than legislation. Their children followed the public school curriculum, but attended so-called Catholic schools staffed by Catholic teachers, who provided religious instruction before or after normal school hours. In 1893 the Catholic Archepiscopal Corporation offered to build new schools on Russell and Gottingen Streets, and rent them to the school board, but a board with a Protestant majority decided to build the schools itself. The result was another sermon from the archbishop alleging a violation of the compact of 1865-6. The *Chronicle* was correct, however, that the ownership of school buildings was not an essential part of the earlier bargain. To make his position clear, Fielding forwarded the details of both incidents to Laurier, who told him that he was "absolutely in the right," but almost begged him, short of doing something inconsistent with honour and principle, to avoid a serious collision. Having had so much trouble with the school question in Manitoba, "I would be disposed to go a long way, to prevent their recurrence in any part of the country."

In effect, the session of 1894 was part of the general election of that year. By having the legislature meet early in January, Fielding could schedule it for March 15. To him it appeared as if he needed no eye-catching legislation and he wanted to get it over with as quickly as possible. Pursuing his earlier efforts, Hemeon sought to give the vote to widows and unmarried females. Again he had to meet the formidable opposition of Attorney General Longley, who argued that the association of women with politics would "injure the attributes which naturally belonged to the higher and nobler sex." By one vote Hemeon failed to get second reading for his bill. Although not convinced that it needed anything more for electoral success, the government put forward two old proposals which could do it no harm and possibly some good. Since thirteen of the twenty-one legislative councillors had given written pledges to support abolition, it proceeded to test them. To avoid the charge that the introduction of an abolition bill in the assembly would violate the council's privileges, it had the bill introduced in the upper house by the government leader, George H. Murray. But the council had provided itself with protective insurance in advance, an opinion by distinguished counsel, Robert Borden and Benjamin Russell, that although the government had the right to appoint councillors who agreed with it on abolition anything further was unconstitutional and subversive of the general purpose for which the council existed.[17] Accordingly the upper house, by twenty-one to five, accepted the report of its committee of privileges that unless the pledges were withdrawn it was not in a position to deal with abolition. Without ado it then declined to extinguish itself.

The *Herald* put the primary blame on Fielding, whom it accused of not applying sufficient pressure to the councillors whom he had appointed. But he had protected himself against charges that he was not serious by agreeing to insert a provision in the bill that abolition would be dependent upon a favourable vote of the electorate at a plebiscite. Also, apparently hoping to shame some councillors, he made public all the pledges he had exacted. These devices having failed, he resorted to a third, an address to the Queen requesting an amendment to the BNA Act which would provide for the abolition of the council on the vote of two thirds of the assembly. Cahan, taking the position that the councillors held office during pleasure, proposed another course: the dismissal of councillors who had broken their pledges. Although the Liberals treated the proposal with scorn, it would be the means used to effect abolition thirty-four years later. Eventually the reply came from Britain that "resort to Imperial legislation would be inexpedient except in circumstances of urgent necessity," but Fielding had at least made sure that he would not be vulnerable during the election to charges of inactivity. The Nova Scotia legislative council had also demonstrated that it was unequalled anywhere in conjuring up devices to ensure its own preservation.

In a second action Fielding did not harm himself and hoped that Cahan would. Ottawa having refused the province's railway claims and Fielding having moved that they be referred to a select committee, Cahan rose to the bait and declared them to be neither legal, moral, nor equitable. So vigorous did he become that Fielding declared his closing passages as "worthy of a street brawl." Although Cahan was probably right on the WCR claim, the province's demands relating to the Eastern Extension had a much stronger basis. Preparing the way for the election, the *Chronicle* declared the Conservatives to be "so blinded . . . by partisan prejudice, so afraid . . . of doing anything to embarrass their political friends at Ottawa, that they scout Nova Scotia's equitable claims as bogus."[18]

Fortune favoured the government in other railway matters. Although its subsidies had been unattractive for many years, it could finally announce the signing of two contracts, one for a line from Orangedale to Broad Cove, especially intended to open up the coal deposits of Inverness County, and the second from New Germany to Sand Point near Shelburne with a branch line from Indian Gardens to Liverpool, the completion of which would give Shelburne and Queens Counties the railway which they had long been demanding. The opposition's continued criticism of the coal syndicate legislation also helped the government. While Cahan attempted to show that the proportional increase in production on the mines owned by the syndicate's company, the Dominion Coal Company, was less than that in other mines, Fielding boasted that larger royalty revenue was permitting him to deal with provincial services more liberally than ever before. Embarrassed when Fielding pointed out that "the best thought and mind of the Conservative party," including businessmen Adam Burns, J.A. Chipman, David McKeen, N.A. Rhodes, J.E. Shatford, James E. Graham, and James T. Burchell, supported the syndicate, Cahan lamely replied that they were "thirty against thirty thousand."[19]

As usual, the opposition sought to paint a gloomy picture of the province's finances, arguing that since 1884 Fielding had performed the "financial feat" of changing a surplus of $1,093,000 into a net debt of $1,763,000 and that by "cooking the books" he had managed to show a surplus where surplus there was not. But the *Chronicle* was more nearly right that the province's finances were healthier than at any time since 1867 and that it could look forward to "an era of development that has had no parallel in the past." Fielding, now the financial master of the province as well as its political master, estimated revenues at $821,000, the highest since Confederation and including an unprecedented $250,000 from coal royalties. As a result, he was able to do such things as provide an additional $12,000 for the road service and $15,000 for common schools. Clearly he had used the session to put himself in an impregnable position for the election to come. If anything else was needed, he also decided to hold a plebiscite on prohibition on the day of the election. That would ensure that the Liberals would not lose votes on the temperance question then being agitated vigorously throughout the province.

Never was there a campaign with so little new about it. Nova Scotians had read all of the opposition case in the *Herald*, some of it extending back a dozen years. Again the emphasis was on the government's financial record. "A new financier needed," proclaimed the *Herald*. Associated with it was a plea not to let the Liberals destroy the municipal system. Cahan's criticism on non-financial points also had much of a sameness about it: the refusal to dismiss legislative councillors who had broken their pledges; the "burking" of meaningful investigation into the Victoria road scandal; the outrageous treatment of Mayor Thomas of Truro; the raising of the standard of repeal; the support of the commercial union movement; the formation of an alliance with Count Mercier of Quebec; and the attempts to destroy N.P. The last four were enough in themselves for the *Herald* once again to place the red ensign at its masthead.

If ever there was an assured party, it was the Liberals. Why, wondered the *Chronicle*, should Fielding be opposed in Halifax? Could Nova Scotia put "so reckless and vindictive a man" as Cahan in power? Was the *Herald* "constitutionally incapable" of accurate reporting; otherwise why did it shoot continually "with a rusty gun and mighty poor ammunition"? Confident of their situation, the Liberals were content to rely on their record with a promise of the same for the future. Everywhere Fielding made one major point: "the province must go ahead" and be willing to incur moderate borrowing to "assist the enterprises which are required for the opening of the province."

Throughout the election Liberal workers were enjoined not to be overconfident, but perhaps they were, for it was surprising under the circumstances that the Conservatives won thirteen seats, a gain of three. Remarkably, seats changed to another party in eleven of eighteen counties even though the popular vote remained much the same. Guysborough, not surprisingly, returned to its former allegiance now that Otto Weeks was no longer in a position to divide the Liberal vote. Cahan, who four years earlier had won by nine votes over a Liberal who was *persona non grata* in his own party, lost this time by sixty votes. Supposedly the intervention of a Prohibitionist permitted a Conservative to win in Yarmouth. Not unexpectedly, Kings returned to its old Liberal allegiance and the Conservatives gained single seats in usually closely contested Pictou and Colchester. What was surprising, almost astounding, was the outcome in Halifax, Cumberland, and Cape Breton Island.

In Halifax, where each party had been nominating two Protestants and a Catholic since Confederation, the Catholics failed to win a seat for the first time. Some of it was due to general respect for Conservative W.A. Black; probably more was due to Protestant dislike of Archbishop O'Brien's intervention in the Russell Street school affair. Almost as striking was the reduction in Fielding's majority from 819 to 225; "how utterly unreliable *vox populi* is in Halifax," lamented one of his admirers. Cumberland, which was benefiting greatly from N.P., shocked the Conservatives no less by returning two Liberals.

But most amazing of all were the results on Cape Breton Island, where the Conservatives increased their seats from one to five, gaining one seat in Richmond, two in Inverness, and , most incredibly of all, two in Cape Breton County. Premier Blair suggested to Fielding that "the operators and managers of the Whitney syndicate ought to have been able, if apprised that there was any danger, to keep their men in line for you."[20] Actually, at the instance of Liberal George H. Murray, the manager of the Dominion Coal Company, Conservative David McKeen, had told Cape Bretoners what they wanted to hear: that his company would be hiring an increasing number of labourers and that the cries of monopoly were absurd. It would not be the last time that Cape Bretoners appeared to bite the hand that fed them.

The government's attempt to avoid dealing with the contentious temperance issue succeeded although not in the way that it had intended. When the plebiscite which it held on the same day as the general election indicated "a very strong public sentiment in favor of prohibition," it made use of a fuzzy decision of the Supreme Court of Canada to declare that the subject was beyond provincial authority.

Following the funeral of Sir John Thompson in January, the federal political situation dominated Nova Scotian politics in the early months of 1895. After years in opposition the *Chronicle* could almost taste federal victory. Naturally it was disappointed when "the Bowell-Tupper-Haggart combination" decided to have a session, not an election. As usual, the *Herald's* discussion of federal politics was related to protection, N.P., reciprocity, and traffic through the port of Halifax. Its main target was Richard Cartwright, whom it accused of a fiscal policy which would expose Canadian industry to ruin. The lack of interest in Nova Scotia politics stemmed partly from the Conservative leadership. Forced because of the defeat of Cahan to play a game of musical chairs, the party called again on Dr. MacKay, who had neither the drive nor the fire of his predecessor. Indeed the major interest during the 1895 session was in non-government measures. Hemeon sought to give the right to vote to spinsters and widows with the requisite property only to have the same determined opposition from Attorney General Longley. The lower house of the Thirtieth General Assembly turned out to be much less liberal than its predecessor. While the earlier one had been almost evenly divided on women's suffrage, the new one rejected it by twenty-one to twelve. The Conservatives also failed when they tried again to remove the disfranchisement of Dominion officials in provincial elections. This time Fielding used the argument that some of these officials believed that they would suffer harm if enfranchised since those who voted Liberal were likely to be deprived of an increase in salary.

The Liberals congratulated themselves on two announcements during the session: an increase in the revenue from royalties to $242,053, the largest amount on record, and the signing of contracts for the subsidization of three additional railways: the Dominion Coal Company line from Bridgeport to Louisburg, the Cape Breton Railway Extension Company line from Port Hawkesbury to St. Peter's, and the narrow-gauge Coast Railway from Yarmouth to Lockeport. But when the government claimed a surplus of $25,370 for the previous year, the *Herald* replied that it was actually a deficit of $55,651. The completion of the "missing link" having so improved the position of the WCR that it was able to repay its loan of $131,021, the government treated $81,021 of that amount as ordinary revenue. Although the *Herald* was probably right that all of it should have been entered into capital account, the *Chronicle* compared it to small boys who "sometimes fancy that they can reach the desired result in their 'sums' by simply adding, multiplying or subtracting any figures that happen to occur to them." Yet even it admitted that, contrasted with the Cahan years, the session had been "harmonious and businesslike."

If provincial politics had taken a back seat in 1895, they receded still further in 1896. In the early weeks the *Herald* gave so much attention to the hectic events in Ottawa — the Nest of Traitors incident and its aftermath — that it scarcely noted the opening of the legislature. On January 6 the *Chronicle* announced that Mackenzie Bowell's government had "gone to smash" and that Laurier was likely to be premier within twenty-four hours. When Charles Tupper became prime minister, it professed horror at the return to politics of a "most miserable specimen of a man" who had done "more to degrade public life than all other politicians combined." Tupper, having decided to run a by election in Cape Breton County, the *Herald* delighted in baiting Fielding to oppose him; otherwise, it said, "he might as well renounce all pretension to be grit leader within this province." But it was George H. Murray who again sacrificed himself for his party and established for himself the credentials which would give him a much higher political status in the near future. He faced difficulties galore. Having to meet the contention that N.P. had increased Cape Breton's coal sales to Quebec tenfold since 1878, he conceded the necessity for a duty on coal until the United States admitted it free of duty. The *Chronicle* pictured all sorts of people working against him: Bishop Cameron and the Roman Catholic clergy, the officials of the Dominion Coal Company, and the whole apparatus of the federal government. Whatever the cause, Tupper increased the Conservative majority from 728 to 781 and, according to an elated *Herald*, received "one long-continued ovation" as he moved from Sydney to Halifax.

Never did the legislature get so little attention as in 1896. Most of it was due to the unprecedented interest in federal politics, some to the lack of substance in the government's legislative programme. Basically it consisted of bills to consolidate the probate courts and to encourage the municipal councils to make a greater use of road-making machinery. The two bills which produced the most interest and the most controversy emanated from private members. Pictou County Conservative Charles Tanner sought to make Dominion Day a holiday in the public schools. Because of Anti-Confederation sentiment not yet dissipated, it still had no recognition by provincial statute and Liberal William Roche wanted it kept that way to "honor the men who stood up in the hour of the country's need." The assembly agreed with him in a straight party vote. A.M. Hemeon, unsuccessful with his women's franchise bills, took on the role of temperance reformer. Basically he contended that the act of 1886, designed to regulate the sale of liquor in Halifax, had been so "shingled, shangled, and shungled" session after session that it was doing little to promote temperance. But Fielding told him bluntly that "until the moral sense of the masses of the people in a community approved of a law it could not be carried out."

Economically and financially the previous year had been a difficult one. On subsidized railways the only substantial progress had occurred east of Yarmouth on the Coast Railway, now changed to standard gauge. Coal royalties, forecast at $290,000, amounted to only $251,000, and the surplus of $4,225 was made possible only because of unexpectedly high returns from succession duties, or, as Dr. MacKay put it, by "invading the abode of the dead." No one seemed to care since all eyes were on the drama of the federal Parliament. Both major newspapers adopted the basic stand of their parties when Tupper finally introduced his remedial bill to force separate schools upon Manitoba. The *Chronicle* objected to any attempt to run roughshod over that province and favoured the more conciliatory course proposed by Laurier. The *Herald* agreed with Tupper that the decision of the Judicial Committee on the matter required him to pass remedial legislation and was indignant at the obstruction which forced him to have Parliament prorogued, his bill unpassed, just before its life was to expire.

But neither paper was particularly satisfied with its position on the Manitoba school question and in the election which followed it quickly became a secondary issue. Once again the *Herald* brought out "the battered old flag" and campaigned almost exclusively on the denunciation of "grit" financial and trade policies and the extolling of N.P. More than ever before it bolstered its case for protection with all sorts of statistics. For the *Chronicle* and the Liberals the campaign amounted to a denunciation of Tory corruption and N.P. The Conservatives, they argued, used public works as "engines" to promote their followers' personal interests: witness the Langevin-McGreevy scandal. To them the tariff was a "tax" which, although useful to "a little handful of protected monopolists, imposes excessive burdens on the toiling masses." Periodically the *Chronicle* published the platform adopted by its party's national convention of 1893 with its advocacy of moderate trade policies.[21]

Although Quebec made the Liberal national victory possible, it was also a victory for Nova Scotia Liberals even though the provincial results could hardly have been closer — each party elected ten members and the Conservatives polled 50.4 per cent of the popular vote to the Liberals' 48.8 per cent. In effect, Sir

Charles Tupper, long the federal master of Nova Scotia, had been dethroned. Although doubts about the wisdom of his policy on Manitoba schools played some part, other factors appear to have been more important: going to the well once too often with N.P. as the main battle cry; inability to use the loyalty cry successfully because of the Liberals' more moderate trade policies; and a powerful Liberal provincial party organization.

Victory brought Nova Scotia Liberals something which they had been without for eighteen years: federal patronage. But it also led to the loss of their provincial leader. Through extensive correspondence since 1887 a feeling of mutual trust had developed between Laurier and Fielding along with the realization that they espoused much the same kind of liberalism. Fielding's performance during the national Liberal convention of 1893 was such that Laurier decided to leave no stone unturned to induce him to be a leading member of his team at Ottawa. In the eighteen months before the election of 1896, by himself or through others, he exerted continued pressure until in November 1895 Fielding agreed conditionally. A month before the election he actually proposed to run in Annapolis, but backed out when a temperance pledge, not part of the Liberal platform, was demanded of him. He might then have had the nomination in Queens-Shelburne, but decided that the time was too short to make a change without endangering Liberal chances. From the correspondence emerged the prudent Fielding who insisted on examining every possible ramification before making up his mind.[22] But as a non-candidate he probably made a greater contribution through his assistance to Liberals throughout the province and Laurier was no less insistent than before that he enter his cabinet.

Fielding could not have left his party in better shape. For a decade the unchallenged master of provincial politics, he had built up an organization which would be equally effective in federal politics. The policies which he had initiated would shortly launch Nova Scotia on its most prosperous years in the post-Confederation period. No one could have put his successor in a better position with the Nova Scotia electorate. The province was set to continue a long period of Liberal rule.

CHAPTER 11

186 Years of Politics

Fielding left for Ottawa 186 years after Nova Scotia fell permanently into British hands. By that time politics as it is generally understood had been played for 147 years, that is, since the founding of Halifax. Until the coming of the Loyalists in the 1780s New Englanders were a major participant in the game. New England merchants in Halifax applied the pressure which contributed to the calling of an elective assembly in 1758. For several decades New England pre-Loyalists were in a position to exercise a great deal of influence through their membership in the lower house. But for two basic reasons they could make very limited constitutional gains: forced to eke out a living from farms in the process of development they could not afford to remain in Halifax for lengthy legislative sessions without remuneration and whenever they did threaten to introduce more of the British practice, the merchant-official oligarchy in the council usually had the means to circumvent them. Even the New England town meeting failed to establish roots of any consequence in Nova Scotia, partly because one governor banned all assemblies of the people during the American Revolution as tending to "promote . . . the highest contempt of Government."

So it was still an immature assembly when the first Loyalist members took their seats in the mid 1780s. Some of their leaders had had considerable experience in governance in the more mature representative bodies of the Middle Atlantic colonies and although the Loyalists at no time constituted a majority of the lower house, they had a marked influence upon its proceedings. Any suggestions, however, that they tended generally to bolster the position of the governor and the prerogatives of the Crown appear to be lacking in substance. In the closing days of Parr's governorship it was they who provoked his wrath for seeking to introduce something like the practice of the British Commons in the assembly's handling of money bills. They were among those who over a period of years, without anyone noting what was happening, guided the assembly as it assumed some prerogatives of the Crown, especially in the voting of road moneys. When in the early days of the nineteenth century Governor Wentworth sought to turn the clock back, he failed abysmally. Although non-Loyalist William Cottnam Tonge was his most militant opponent, Loyalists like Simon Bradstreet Robie and Lewis Morris Wilkins fought the constitutional battle no less strongly than he and the assembly divisions indicate that Loyalists and non-Loyalists combined to thwart the governor.

The outcome was a *modus vivendi* which appeared to satisfy everyone but non-Loyalist councillor Richard John Uniacke and which pleased the majority of the assemblymen and particularly the rural assemblymen, because it permitted them a significant role in the all-important allocation and disposition of road moneys. Four military governors, Prevost, Sherbrooke, Dalhousie, and Kempt, all acquiesced in substantial deviations from British practice in the initiation of money votes and the appointment of road commissioners, and politically Nova Scotia remained quiet until the 1830s. Probably it is not too much to say that a genuine reform party appeared later in Nova Scotia than in the Canadas because most assemblymen were satisfied with a *status quo* which met their primary demand. Although the later 1820s witnessed highly articulate assemblymen distinguished for their oratorical prowess on specific issues, none of them came close to challenging the political system at its roots. That was left to Jotham Blanchard and the "Pictou Scribblers," who starting in late 1827 used the *Colonial Patriot* to introduce a radical element hitherto foreign to the province's politics.

The precise influence of Blanchard cannot be determined, but he undoubtedly induced Joseph Howe to peer more deeply into the intricacies of Nova Scotia politics and government with the result that Howe found many of the same ills that he did. Starting out as a supporter of the status quo, Howe, the son of a Loyalist, eventually became a conservative reformer and since he played the leading role in the movement for responsible government, it had little of the precipitate or highly radical about it. But the nature of the reform movement and the willingness to proceed step by step without resort to violence were also a reflection of the province's conservative political culture which had evidenced itself in other directions as well. As stated earlier, the pre-Loyalists' use of town meetings, suffocated by an authoritarian governor in the 1770's, did not survive in the Nova Scotia political environment. By statute, meetings of ratepayers might assemble to make provision for the support of the poor and the maintenance of schools, but generally they were little used because of the abhorrence of direct taxation which developed early and became a primary ingredient of the political culture. Ordinary Nova Scotians were content to have governmental services, especially road maintenance and construction, financed through impost and excise duties, the incidence of which they did not feel. In the 1850s, when the legislature provided for the establishment of local self-government on a voluntary basis, only Yarmouth Township, originally established by pre-Loyalists, incorporated itself and it quickly reverted to the undemocratic system of local government by sessions and grand juries when the threat of heavier taxes loomed.

Some have suggested that by the 1850s the Nova Scotia political culture had congealed and they have substantial evidence to back their claim. For one thing, the two parties which appeared as a necessary adjunct of the movement for responsible government continued to exist after there was little grist to grind. By the mid-1850s, when at times party squabbling came close to turning the assembly into a bear-garden, some onlookers could find no reason for the existence of two parties regularly organized to annihilate each other in the legislature. In a very real sense the province's conservative political culture had much to do with its attitude towards Confederation. It was too much to expect Nova Scotians to accept a violent rupture of the political order at a time when they were enjoying the best of times economically and to face extensive dislocation of which it was hazardous to forecast the outcome. They found union all the more unpalatable because they had no opportunity to express their opinion on its acceptability at the polls. So great was the trauma of the Confederation issue that it transmitted its bitterness to the generations which followed. It took many years for July 1 to be recognized in any way by the provincial legislature and sixty years later some Nova Scotians were still flying flags at half-mast on that day.

Confederation affected the province's politics in two major ways. Because many more people moved to than withdrew from the Liberal party, it destroyed the fairly even balance which had previously existed between the two parties and left the Liberals substantially the stronger. Since Confederation also meant the transfer to the Dominion government of the larger legislative responsibilities, it resulted in a marked diminution in the power of the provincial legislature. Hence, when the question of repeal was set at rest in the early 1870s, the provincial arena lacked matters of substance to occupy its attention and, as often happens in such circumstances, internecine party warfare replaced debate of substance. Philip Carteret Hill simply could not deal adequately with an assembly which often resembled a bear-pit rather than a deliberative body. Simon Holmes might have had similar difficulties if the Liberal opposition in the assembly had not been excessively weak. Obsessed with railways, he almost forgot that as premier he headed a team and he ended up losing the confidence of his fellow executive councillors, his rank-and-file followers, and the province at large.

Time would show that Fielding had none of the disabilities of Hill and Holmes. Above all, through his experience in the editorial offices of the *Chronicle*, he had gained broad insights into Nova Scotia's politics and especially into what was politically practicable and what not. He had witnessed the intense opposition to Tupper's bill imposing compulsory assessment for education and appreciated that if the Conservatives (Confederates) had not lost the 1867 election on the Confederation issue, they might well have lost it on the earlier question. He also realized that the County Incorporation Act of 1879, which forced the newly created municipal governments to levy direct taxes for the road service, contributed in part to the downfall of the Thompson government in 1882. Accordingly, he made certain that his measures for increasing revenue through new or increased taxation — his succession duty and coal royalty bills — were of a kind that would not cost him the support of the ordinary voter. He also understood, and perhaps taught some of his successors, that government borrowing would not be unpalatable or, at least not as unpalatable, if he linked it directly to some service, in his case road and bridge construction, from which the electorate derived immediate benefits such as employment, better communications, and the like. Always the careful financier, he made borrowing a charge against the counties' road moneys, thus avoiding an increase in the province's net debt and ensuring that the moneys were spent to better advantage than if left to the municipal councils.

Within the orbit of the limited provincial legislative sphere he was generally content to initiate useful, non-radical legislation and create the image of one who knew the province's needs and was meeting them successfully. He had implemented his one-eye catching measure — the Whitney Syndicate bill — with consummate care. He realized that Nova Scotians would strongly support provincial development provided that it did not leave undesirable consequences in its wake. Accordingly he made certain that no one could charge that accelerated coal-mining production in Cape Breton County would require an outlay of provincial funds. He also put himself into a position to answer charges that he was creating a dangerous monopoly or granting long-term leases without compensatory advantages. As a result, he found it easy to convince the public that his opponents were adopting a negative stance and engaging in criticism for criticism's sake.

Fielding's approach to government and politics meant much more than success for himself. In two important ways it would leave its mark on Nova Scotian politics of the twentieth century. An all-out effort to secure repeal had convinced him of the futility of movements of this kind. By entering the Laurier cabinet, he had irrevocably committed himself to securing the betterment of Nova Scotia's position through policies adopted within the Canadian federation. At times in the twentieth century great discontent has arisen supposedly because of the deficiency or lack of federal policies, but to this day no movement for repeal has again commanded substantial support.

The techniques and style of Fielding's governance fitted in admirably with the province's political culture and their adoption by his successor permitted him to carry on the government of the province for more than a quarter of a century. Consciously or not, he and the two other most successful premiers in the twentieth century have also employed Fielding's general aproach to politics. The evidence is that it is a major key to long-term political success in Nova Scotia.

CHAPTER 1

Endnotes

1. J.B. Brebner, *New England's Outpost* (New York: Columbia University Press, 1927), chapters III, IV.
2. *Ibid.*, p.67.
3. C.B. Fergusson, "Thomas Caulfeild," *Dictionary of Canadian Biography* (hereafter *DCB*), vol.II, pp.122-3.
4. Brebner, *New England's Outpost*, chapter VI.
5. *Ibid.*, p.148.
6. Maxwell Sutherland, "Lawrence Armstrong," *DCB*, vol.II, p.22.
7. *Ibid.*, p.23.
8. Maxwell Sutherland, "Richard Philipps," *DCB*, vol.III, p.517.
9. Sutherland, "Armstrong," pp.23-4.
10. Maxwell Sutherland, "Paul Mascarene," *DCB*, vol.III, p.439.
11. Brebner, *New England's Outpost*, p.114.
12. *Ibid.*, p.133.
13. Sutherland, "Mascarene," p.439.
14. Brebner, *New England's Outpost*, p.180.
15. *Ibid.*, p.212.
16. Dominick Graham, "Charles Lawrence," *DCB*, vol.III, p.364.
17. *Ibid.*, p.362.
18. *Ibid.*, p.364.
19. Brebner, *New England's Outpost*, p.233.

CHAPTER 2

Endnotes

1. J. Bartlet Brebner, *New England's Outpost* (New York: Columbia University Press, 1927), p.237.
2. J. Murray Beck, "Edward Cornwallis," *DCB*, vol.IV, p.170.
3. S. Buggey, "Jonathan Belcher," *ibid.*, p.53.
4. Dominick Graham, "Charles Lawrence," *ibid.*, vol.III, p.362.
5. C. Bruce Fergusson, *The Origin of Representative Government in Canada* (Halifax, 1958), p.25.
6. This opinion was later confirmed in *Campbell v. Hall*, [1774] 1 Cowper 204.
7. J. Murray Beck, *The Evolution of Municipal Government in Nova Scotia 1749-1973* (Halifax: Queen's Printer, 1973), p.7.
8. J. Bartlet Brebner, *The Neutral Yankees of Nova Scotia* (Toronto: Carleton Library Edition, 1969), pp.4-5.
9. *Ibid.*, pp.23, 40.
10. *Ibid.*, p.65.
11. For details of Belcher's difficulties see Buggey, "Belcher," pp.51-3.
12. See Donald F. Chard, "Joshua Mauger," *DCB*, vol.IV, p.528.
13. Buggey, "Belcher," p.53.
14. See Phyllis Blakeley, "Montagu Wilmot," *DCB*, vol.III, pp. 663-4.
15. Brebner, *Neutral Yankees*, pp.194, 198-9, 199n.
16. *Journals of the Nova Scotia House of Assembly* (hereafter JHA), June 14, 1766, p.99.
17. L.R. Fischer, "Michael Francklin," *DCB*, vol.IV, p.275.
18. Brebner, *Neutral Yankees*, pp.201-2.
19. *Ibid.*, p.196.
20. Francis A. Coghlan, "Lord William Campbell," *DCB*, vol.IV, p.131.
21. Brebner, *Neutral Yankees*, pp.208-9.
22. J. Murray Beck, *The Government of Nova Scotia* (Toronto: University of Toronto Press, 1957), pp.26-7.
23. Brebner, *Neutral Yankees*, p.212.
24. J.M. Bumsted, "Francis Legge," *DCB*, vol.IV, p.450.
25. Brebner, *Neutral Yankees*, pp.214-5.
26. Wendy L. Thorpe, "John Day," *DCB*, vol.IV, p.199.
27. For the unfolding of events leading to Legge's downfall, see Brebner, *Neutral Yankees*, pp.222-40.

28. Bumsted, "Legge," p.452.
29. Brebner, *Neutral Yankees*, pp.161, 256-7.
30. *Ibid.*, p.261.
31. For their thesis see Gordon Stewart and George Rawlyk, *A People Highly Favoured of God: The Nova Scotia Yankees and the American Revolution* (Toronto: Macmillan of Canada, 1972), pp. XIX-XXII, 186-9.
32. Donald F. Chard, "Mariot Arbuthnot," *DCB*, vol.IV, p.29.
33. Beck, *Government of Nova Scotia*, pp.28-9.

CHAPTER 3

Endnotes

1. Quoted in J. Murray Beck, *The Government of Nova Scotia* (Toronto: University of Toronto Press, 1957), p.14.
2. James S. Macdonald, "Memoir of Governor John Parr," *Collections of the Nova Scotia Historical Society*, vol.14 (1910), pp.45-6.
3. Beamish Murdoch, *A History of Nova Scotia or Acadie* (Halifax: James Barnes, 1867), vol.III, p.39.
4. Beck, *Government of Nova Scotia*, pp.9-10.
5. My *Government of Nova Scotia* (p. 56) wrongly sets the number at thirty-eight.
6. *Supra*, chapter 2.
7. JHA, June 23, 1786, pp.16-7.
8. Beck, *Government of Nova Scotia*, p.57.
9. Murdoch, *History*, vol.III, pp.59-60. Non-Loyalist Morris won by 415 to 274.
10. JHA, Mar. 14, 1789, p.11.
11. Murdoch, vol.III, pp.66-72.
12. Parr to Sydney, Sept. 26, 1788, PANS, RG1, vol.47, no.90.
13. *Ibid.* to Grenville, Apr. 24, 1790, *ibid.*, vol.48, no.15.
14. *Ibid.* to Nepean (private), Mar. 18, 1790, *ibid.*, no.9.
15. Address to Parr, JHA, Apr. 3, 1790, pp.60-2.
16. Council to Grenville, May 4, 1790, N.S. A 114, 113.
17. Parr to Grenville, Apr. 24, 1790, vol.49, no.12; Parr to Nepean (private), May 8, 1790, *ibid.*, no.20.
18. Peter Burroughs, "John Parr," *DCB*, vol. IV, p. 605.
19. For a full account of Wentworth see Brian Cuthbertson's biography, *The Loyalist Governor* (Halifax: Petheric Press, 1983).
20. Judith Fingard, "Sir John Wentworth," *DCB*, vol.V, p.849.
21. Cuthbertson, *Loyalist Governor*, p.59.
22. *Ibid.*, p.89.
23. Sir Adams Archibald, "Life of Sir John Wentworth," *Collections of the Nova Scotia Historical Society*, vol.XX (1921), pp.71ff.
24. Brian Cuthbertson, *The Old Attorney General* (Halifax: Nimbus Publishing Co., 1980), pp.26, 34-6.
25. JHA, July 4, 1799, pp.346-7.

26. *Ibid.*, Apr. 26, 1800, p.92.
27. For details of the contention in this period see Beck, *Government of Nova Scotia*, pp.30-2, 58-61.
28. *Ibid.*, Mar. 29, 1802, p.65.
29. Wentworth to Hobart, Apr. 21, 1802, PANS, vol.53, pp.341-4.
30. JHA, July 4, 5, 11, 1804, pp.20, 22, 35.
31. Wentworth to Castlereagh, Feb. 3, 1806, PANS, vol.54, pp.78-83; to Windham, Nov.14, 1806, *ibid.*, pp.341-4.
32. Assembly Papers, Jan. 13, 1807, vol.13.
33. See Cuthbertson, *Loyalist Governor*, pp.129-30.
34. Beck, *Government of Nova Scotia*, pp.53-4.
35. Wentworth to Castlereagh, Mar. 28, 1808, PANS, vol.58, doc.7.
36. Fingard, "Wentworth," p.851.

CHAPTER 4

Endnotes

1. Prevost to Cooke, July 30, 1808, PANS, RG1, vol.58, doc.28.
2. Brian Cuthbertson, *The Old Attorney General* (Halifax: Nimbus Publishing Co., 1980), p.49.
3. JHA, Jan. 17, 1809, p.99.
4. Murdoch, *History*, vol.III, p.288.
5. Croke to Castlereagh (private and confidential), Feb. 11, 1809, PANS, RG1, vol.58, doc.66.
6. *Ibid.*, (private), Apr. 3, 1809, doc.69.
7. Council *Journals*, Apr. 3, 1811, n.p.
8. Prevost to Liverpool, May 12, 1811, PANS, RG1, vol.59, doc.4.
9. JHA, Apr. 1, 1812, p.117.
10. *Ibid.*, Aug. 13, 14, 1812, pp.25-6.
11. *Ibid.*, Feb. 11, 1813, p.5.
12. *Ibid.*, Feb. 9, 1815, p.4.
13. *Ibid.*, Apr. 1, 1815, p.107.
14. See William B. Hamilton, "Education, Politics and Reform in Nova Scotia, 1800-1848" (unpublished Ph.D. thesis, University of Western Ontario, 1970), pp.96-104.
15. V.P. Kelleher, "George Ramsay, Lord Dalhousie," *Dalhousie Review*, vol.18 (July, 1938), p.198.
16. Marjorie Whitelaw, ed., *The Dalhousie Journals* (Ottawa: Oberon Press, 1978), pp.28-31.
17. *Ibid.*, p.78.
18. JHA, Mar.13, 1818, p.63.
19. *Ibid.*, Apr. 17, 1819, p.131.
20. Whitelaw, *Dalhousie Journals*, pp.110-1; Dalhousie to Bathurst, May 24, 1819, PANS, RG1, vol.112, pp.70-4.
21. Joseph Howe, "Notes on Several Governors and Their Influence," *Collections of the N.S. Historical Society*, vol.XVII (1913), p.197.
22. Whitelaw, *Dalhousie Journals*, pp.175-6.
23. Dalhousie to Bathurst, May 20, 1818, reproduced in K.E. Killam, "Lord Dalhousie's administration in Nova Scotia" (unpublished M.A. thesis, University of Toronto, 1931), p.64.
24. Whitelaw, *Dalhousie Journals*, p.183.

25. JHA, Apr. 3, 1820, p.245.
26. *Ibid.*, Mar. 25, 1820, p.223.
27. Whitelaw, *Dalhousie Journals*, pp.188-9.
28. Thomas Roach to Robie, May 5, 1820, Robie Papers, PANS, MG1, 793:1:50.
29. Whitelaw, *Dalhousie Journals*, p.194.
30. J. Murray Beck, *Joseph Howe vol.I: Conservative Reformer 1804-48* (Kingston and Montreal: McGill-Queen's University Press, 1982), p.20.
31. Kavanagh took his seat in the assembly on April 3, 1823.
32. Murdoch, *History*, vol.III, p.517. For details of the debate see *ibid.*, pp.506-13.
33. Kempt to Bathurst, June 28, 1824, PANS, RG1, vol.113 1/2, pp.45-6.
34. Murdoch, *History*, vol.III, pp.534-5.
35. *Ibid.*, p.527.
36. *Ibid.*, p.535.
37. Council *Journals*, Mar. 22, 1826, n.p.
38. Blowers to Peleg Wiswall, Feb. 27, 1826, Wiswall Papers, PANS, MG1, 979:3:12; Stewart to Wiswall, Feb. 27, 1826, *ibid.*, 980:11:106.
39. Murdoch, *History*, vol.III, p.567.
40. *Ibid.*, pp.576-7.
41. *Novascotian*, supplement, Mar. 29, 1827.
42. JHA, Apr. 3, 1828, p.352.

CHAPTER 5

Endnotes

1. D.C. Harvey, "The Intellectual Awakening of Nova Scotia," *Dalhousie Review*, vol.13 (April 1933), pp.1-22; Beck, *Howe*, I, p.39.
2. Peter Lynch, "Early Reminiscences of Halifax," *Collections of the Nova Scotia Historical Society*, vol.16 (1912), p.186.
3. See Beck, *Howe*, I, pp.58-62.
4. *Ibid.*, pp.48-52, 63-7.
5. For the details of the Brandy Dispute and the election see *ibid.*, pp.67-80.
6. See W.B. Hamilton, "Education, Politics and Reform," pp. 220ff.
7. *Novascotian*, July 6, 20, 1831.
8. Beck, *Howe*, I, p.121.
9. For details of the trial see *ibid.*, chapter 9.
10. For an account of the election see *ibid.*, pp.149-57.
11. *Novascotian*, May 25, 1837.
12. For details of the events of 1839 see Beck, *Howe*, I, chapter 13.
13. Howe to Huntington, n.d., Howe Papers, vol.10, pp.39-41.
14. For details of the election see Beck, *Howe*, I, pp.217-9.
15. For an account of the testing and breakdown of the coalition see *ibid.*, chapters 15 and 16.
16. Chester Martin, *Empire and Commonwealth* (Oxford: Clarendon Press, 1929), p.217.
17. For the letters see Joseph A. Chisholm, ed., *The Speeches and Public Letters of Joseph Howe* (Halifax: Chronicle Publishing Company, 1909), vol.I, p.631.
18. Grey to Harvey, Nov 3, 1846 (private and confidential), CO 217/193, 241, 243.
19. For details of the election see Beck, *Howe*, I, pp.304-11.

CHAPTER 6

Endnotes

1. Patterson to Young, May 12, 1849, George Young Papers, PANS, MG2, 722:2:671; Howe to Buller, Feb. 12, 1848, CHR, vol.6 (Dec. 1925), p.326.
2. *Novascotian*, Apr. 10, 1848.
3. Address of Executive Council, July 21, 1848, *JHA*, 1849, App. 6, pp.111-14.
4. Howe to Henry Troop, July 9, 1849, Joseph Howe Papers (hereafter JHP), vol.35, n.p.
5. *Ibid.*
6. Debate of Feb. 7, *British Colonist*, Feb. 9, 1854.
7. See, for example, speech of Mar. 25, *Sun* (Halifax), Apr. 29 and May 1, 1850.
8. Chisholm, vol.II, p.181.
9. Speech of Feb. 5, *Morning Chronicle*, Feb. 7, 1852.
10. Speech of Feb. 1 and 2, *ibid.*, Feb. 3 and 5, 1853.
11. Howe to unknown, Apr. 19, 1854, "Howe Letters" collected by J.A. Chisholm (PANS), pp.117-8.
12. C.J. Townshend, "History of the Court of Chancery in Nova Scotia," *Canadian Law Times*, vol.XX, p.115.
13. *Acadian Recorder*, Jan. 20, 1855.
14. *Eastern Chronicle*, Mar. 19, 1852.
15. John McKinnon to Howe, July 4, 1856, *JHP*, vol.2, p.757.
16. *Morning Chronicle*, Dec. 27, 1856.
17. J. Murray Beck, *Joseph Howe volume II: The Briton Becomes Canadian 1848-1873* (Kingston and Montreal: McGill-Queen's University Press, 1983), p. 121.
18. Binney to Howe, Mar. 3, 1857, *JHP*, vol.2, pp.851-4.
19. Beck, *Government of Nova Scotia*, p.110.
20. *Acadian Recorder*, Apr. 3 and May 15, 1858.
21. J. Murray Beck, "The Nova Sccotian 'Disputed Election' of 1859 and its Aftermath," *CHR*, vol.36 (Dec. 1955), p.295.
22. Assembly *Debates*, Feb. 4, 1859, pp.11-13.
23. *Morning Chronicle*, May 14, 1859.
24. *Novascotian*, Mar. 12, 1860.
25. Beck, *Howe*, vol.II, p.142.
26. Beck, "Disputed Election," p.306.
27. Mulgrave to Newcastle, Jan. 8, 1861, *JHA*, 1861, App.2: Constitutional Issues, pp.39-40.
28. *Morning Chronicle*, Apr. 17, 1862.
29. Beck, *Howe*, vol. II, pp.169-70.
30. *Ibid.*, p. 173.

CHAPTER 7

Endnotes

1. Assembly *Debates,* 1864, pp.23, 25, 51, 70.
2. *Ibid.,* p.183.
3. *Ibid.,* p.232.
4. Supplement to *Morning Chronicle,* Apr. 30, 1864.
5. Assembly *Debates,* 1865, p.247.
6. *Ibid.,* 1866, pp.240-1.
7. For an account of the debate see Beck, *Howe,* II, pp.214-7.
8. *Ibid.,* p.217.
9. *Ibid.,* p.222.
10. Delphin A. Muise, "The General Election of 1867 in Nova Scotia: An Economic Interpretation," *Collections of the N.S. Historical Society,* vol.36 (1968), p.347.
11. Doyle to Macdonald, Dec. 31, 1867, PAC, Macdonald Papers, vol.114, 46183-6.
12. Macdonald to Howe (private), Oct. 6, 1868, *JHP,* vol.4, pp.481-9.
13. Howe to Ross, Dec. 7, 1868, *ibid.,* vol.38, n.p.
14. Beck, *Howe,* II, p.252.
15. Assembly *Debates,* 1869, pp.77, 96.
16. *Ibid.,* 1870, p.239.
17. *Ibid.,* pp.155-6.
18. Beck, *Government of Nova Scotia,* p.265.
19. Assembly *Debates,* 1871, p.93.
20. Doyle to Macdonald, Apr. 6, 1871, PAC, Macdonald Papers, vol.114, 46577-84.
21. Beck, *Howe,* II, p.266.
22. Doyle to Macdonald, Apr. 6, 1871, PAC, Macdonald Papers, vol.114, 46577-84.
23. Chisholm, II, pp.599-619.
24. *Morning Chronicle,* July 8, Aug. 17, 1872; *British Colonist,* Aug. 17, 1872.
25. The opinion of legislative reporter Benjamin Russell in "Reminiscences of a Legislature," *Dalhousie Review,* vol.3 (Apr. 1923), p.9.
26. *Morning Chronicle,* Feb. 5, 1874; *British Colonist,* Feb. 5, 1874.
27. J. Murray Beck, "Thomas Fletcher Morrison," *DCB,* vol.XI, p.619.
28. *Presbyterian Witness,* May 16, 1874.
29. *Acadian Recorder,* Nov. 26, 1874.

CHAPTER 8

Endnotes

1. *Morning Chronicle*, Oct. 31, 1870.
2. Assembly *Debates*, 1875, p.4; *Morning Herald*, Mar. 13, 1875.
3. *Acadian Recorder*, May 5, 1875; *Morning Herald*, May 4, 1875.
4. *Morning Herald*, Mar. 11, 1876.
5. *Morning Chronicle*, Feb. 27, 1877; Assembly *Debates*, 1879, p.29.
6. Assembly *Debates*, 1877, p.99.
7. *Ibid.*, p.121.
8. *Ibid.*, p.177.
9. *Morning Herald*, Feb. 22, 1878.
10. Assembly *Debates*, 1878, p.18.
11. *Morning Herald*, Feb. 21, 1878.
12. Dale C. Thomson, *Alexander Mackenzie: Clear Grit* (Toronto: Macmillan of Canada, 1960), p.329.
13. See, for example, *Acadian Recorder*, July 13, 27, 29; Aug. 3, Sept. 12, 1878.
14. *Morning Herald*, Sept. 19, 1878.
15. Cameron to Thompson, Dec. 28, 1877, PAC, Thompson Papers, C-9234, Vol. 1, item 70; to Holmes (private), Feb. 10, 1879, PANS, Holmes Papers, MG2, 554:3:51.
16. Holmes to Macdonald, Jan.2, 1879, JHA, 1879, App. 11, pp.1-14.
17. Holmes to Tupper, Dec. 31, 1878, *ibid.*, App. 13, pp.2-21.
18. *Morning Herald*, Apr. 11, 1879.
19. Townshend to Holmes, Feb. 13, 1879, Holmes Papers, MG2, 554:3:61.
20. See memo of Courtney, Jan. 7, 1880, JHA, 1882, App. 14, pp.5-8; Costley to Holmes, Feb. 26, 1880, *ibid.*, pp.12-16.
21. Assembly *Debates*, 1880, p.31; *Morning Chronicle*, Mar. 18, 1880
22. Holmes to McDonald (private), Mar. 5, 1880, Holmes Papers, 561:226; McDonald to Holmes (telegram), Mar. 6, 1880, *ibid.*, 555:6:64.
23. Holmes to Tupper, Apr. 30, 1880, *ibid.*, 561:245-50; memo of Courtney, Oct. 29, 1880, JHA, 1882, App. 14, pp.32-5; Costley to Courtney, Apr. 4, 1881, *ibid.*, pp.42-7.
24. Holmes to Tupper, June 3, 1880, Holmes Papers, 561:269-70.
25. Smith to Holmes, May 6, 1880, *ibid.*, 555:7:10.
26. MacDonald to Thompson (private), Dec. 10, 1880, and Jan. 14, 1881, Thompson Papers, C-9236, vol.18, item 1661, and vol.19, item 1769; Townshend to Thompson (private), Jan. 18, 1881, *ibid.*, vol.19, item 1751.

27. *Morning Herald*, Apr. 15, 1881.
28. Holmes to Macdonald (private), Mar. 2, 1881, Holmes Papers, 561:437-41; to Plunkett, Dec. 3, 1881, 561:585-6.
29. Assembly *Debates*, 1882, pp.60-73.
30. Cameron to Thompson, Mar. 21, 1884, Thompson Papers, C-9237, vol.25, item 2541; MacDonald to Thompson (private), Apr. 17, 1884, *ibid.*, item 2628.
31. Holmes to G.J. Parker, May 20, 1882, Holmes Papers, 561:643.
32. Cameron to Thompson, April (?), 1882, Thompson Papers, C-9237, vol.25, item 2572.
33. See Gayton to Thompson, July 1, 1882, *ibid.*, vol.28, item 2871.
34. *Morning Herald*, June 26, 1882.

CHAPTER 9

Endnotes

1. Fraser to D.W. Crockett, Feb. 21, 1883, PANS, Fielding Papers, MG 2, 503:1:10.
2. *Morning Herald,* Apr.18, 1883.
3. For the various positions on the railway question see Assembly *Debates,* 1884, pp.131-40, 143-54, 156-213.
4. *Ibid.,* 1884, pp.41, 43.
5. Richey to Macdonald (confidential), Aug. 2, 1884, PAC, Macdonald Papers, vol.117, 47747-58
6. *Morning Herald,* July 19, 21, 23, 1884.
7. Richey to Macdonald (confidential), Aug. 2, 1884, PAC, Macdonald Papers, vol.117, 47747-59.
8. Fielding to Blake, Aug. 30, 1884, Fielding Papers, 489:87.
9. Fraser to Fielding, July 29, 1884, *ibid.,* 503:1:26; Pipes to Fielding, July 31, 1884, *ibid.,* 503:1:28.
10. Fielding to McKinnon and Macdonnell, Jan. 15, 1885, *ibid.,* 489:417-20.
11. Assembly *Debates.* 1885, p.180.
12. *Ibid.,* pp.344-72.
13. *Ibid.,* p.252.
14. Fielding to Blake (confidential), May 6, 1885, Fielding Papers, 489:543-9.
15. *Ibid.* (confidential), Jan. 8, 1886, 490:1:150-61.
16. Fielding to C.F. McIsaac (private and confidential), Oct. 30, 1885, *ibid.,* 490:1:49-50.
17. Assembly *Debates,* pp.255, 176.
18. For debate on the resolutions, see *ibid.,* pp.468-502; for editorial comment see *Morning Chronicle,* May 10, 1886.
19. An independent Conservative, Dr. J.L. Bethune (Victoria), won the remaining seat. The Liberal popular vote increased from 51.8 to 54.7 per cent; the Conservative dropped from 46.9 to 43.6 per cent.
20. Colin D. Howell, "W.S. Fielding and the Repeal Elections of 1886 and 1887 in Nova Scotia," *Acadiensis,* vol.VIII (Spring 1979), pp.28-46.
21. Fielding to Mowat, July 7, 1886, Fielding Papers, 490:1:405-8; Blake to Fielding, Aug. 1886, *ibid.,* 503:1:51; Fielding to Blake (confidential), Oct. 5, 1886, *ibid.,* 490:1:582-8.

22. J. Murray Beck, *A History of Maritime Union* (Maritime Union Study, 1969), p.30.
23. Fielding to Fraser, Aug 25, (private and confidential) and 30 (private), 1886, Fielding Papers, 490:1:501-7 and 521-4.
24. Howell, "Fielding and Repeal Elections," p.43.
25. Fielding to C.F. McIsaac (private and confidential), Feb. 25, 1887, Fielding Papers, 490:2:184-7.
26. For Fielding's correspondence on the 1887 federal election see *ibid.*, box 490.
27. For the letters on party and patronage in this period see *ibid.*, boxes 489, 490, 491.
28. Fielding to Pipes (strictly confidential), unknown (confidential), and Lovitt (private and confidential), Nov. 22, 1887, n.d., and Jan. 7, 1888, *ibid.*, 490:2:590-1, 675-6, and 677-81.

CHAPTER 10

Endnotes

1. Assembly *Debates*, 1887, p.109.
2. See, for example, *Morning Herald*, Mar. 10, 14, 16, 1888.
3. *Morning Chronicle*, Feb. 25, Apr. 16, 18, 1889.
4. *Ibid.*, Mar. 19, 21, 1889.
5. *Morning Herald*, Mar. 20, 1890.
6. Fielding to Ellis, May 20, 1890, Fielding Papers, 491:2:897-8.
7. Fielding to Hardy (private), June 17, 1890, *ibid.*, 1086-90.
8. Fielding to Burrill (private), June 3, 1890, *ibid.*, 975-7.
9. Fielding to A.M. Hemeon (private), June 11, 1890; to Matheson (private), June 27, 1890, *ibid.*, 1091-3 and 1146-7.
10. J. Murray Beck, "The Nomination of Candidates in Nova Scotia," *Dalhousie Review*, vol. 36 (winter 1957), p.367.
11. J. Murray Beck, *Pendulum of Power: Canada's Federal Elections* (Scarborough: Prentice-Hall of Canada, 1968), p.68.
12. Fielding to John Hall (private and confidential), June 20, 1892, Fielding Papers, 492:1:670-2.
13. J. Murray Beck, "Privileges and Powers of the Nova Scotia House of Assembly," *Dalhousie Review*, vol. 35 (Winter 1956), pp.357-9.
14. Fielding to L.H. Davies (private), Feb. 23, 1892; to unknown in Surbiton, Feb. 28, 1892, Fielding Papers, 492:1:378-83 and 402-4.
15. For Fielding's speech see Assembly *Debates*, 1893, pp.13-28.
16. For the correspondence on the religious controversy see Fielding Papers, 503:3:163ff.
17. Beck, *Government of Nova Scotia*, pp.246-7.
18. Assembly *Debates*, 1894, p.112; *Morning Chronicle*, Jan. 24, Feb. 13, 14, 1894.
19. Assembly *Debates*, 1894, p.17; *Morning Chronicle*, Jan. 9, 1894.
20. Blair to Fielding, Mar. 17, 1894, Fielding Papers, 503:5:250.
21. See *Morning Chronicle*, May 22, 27, 29; June 1, 3, 1896.
22. For the details see D.C. Harvey, "Fielding's Call to Ottawa," *Dalhousie Review*, vol.28 (January 1949), pp.369-85.

Appendix

A

Governors, Lieutenant-Governors, and Administrators
of Nova Scotia
(1710-1749)

Governors	Lieutenant-Governors of the fort at Annapolis Royal	Lieutenant-Governor	Administrator	Date
			Samuel Vetch	1710-11
				1711
	Charles Hobby			1711-17
	Thomas Caulfeild			1712-1714/5
Francis Nicholson				1714/5-17
Samuel Vetch				1717-49
Richard Philipps				1717-26
	John Doucett			1717-20
				and
				1722-26
		John Doucett		1724/5-39
		Lawrence Armstrong		1740-49
			Paul Mascarene	

B

Governors, Lieutenant-Governors, and Administrators of Nova Scotia (1749-86)

(The dates indicate their actual time in office)

Governor	Lieutenant-Governor	Administrator	Time in office	
			From	To
Edward Cornwallis			July 13, 1749	Aug. 2, 1752
Peregrine Thomas Hopson	Charles Lawrence		Aug. 3, 1752	Oct. 31, 1753
		Charles Lawrence	Nov. 1, 1753	Oct. 20, 1754
	Charles Lawrence		Oct. 14, 1754	July 22, 1756
Charles Lawrence		Jonathan Belcher	July 23, 1756	Oct. 19, 1760
	Jonathan Belcher		Oct. 19, 1760	Nov. 20, 1761
	Montague Wilmot		Nov. 21, 1761	Sept. 26, 1763
			Sept. 26, 1763	May 30, 1764
Montague Wilmot			May 31, 1764	May 23, 1766
		Benjamin Green	May 23, 1766	Aug. 23, 1766
	Michael Francklin		Aug. 23, 1766	Nov. 26, 1766
Lord William Campbell			Nov. 27, 1766	Oct. 7, 1773
	Michael Francklin		Oct. 1, 1767	Sept. 10, 1768
	Michael Francklin		Nov. 4, 1768	Dec. 4, 1768
			Oct. 17, 1771	June 1, 1772
	Michael Francklin	Benjamin Green	June 2, 1772	July 10, 1772
Francis Legge			Oct. 8, 1773	May 12, 1776
	Mariot Arbuthnot		May 13, 1776	Aug. 16, 1778
	Richard Hughes		Aug. 17, 1778	July 30, 1781
	Andrew Snape Hamond		July 31, 1781	Oct. 18, 1782
John Parr			Oct. 19, 1782	April 24, 1786

C

Lieutenant-Governors and Administrators (1786-1867)
(The dates indicate their actual time in office)

Lieutenant-Governor	Administrator	Time in office	
		From	To
John Parr		April 24, 1786	Nov. 25, 1791
	Richard Bulkeley	Nov. 25, 1791	May 13, 1792
John Wentworth		May 14, 1792	April 12, 1808
Sir George Prevost		April 13, 1808	Aug. 25, 1811
	Alexander Croke	Dec. 7, 1808	April 14, 1809
	Alexander Croke	Aug. 26, 1811	Oct. 15, 1811
Sir John Sherbrooke		Oct. 16, 1811	June 27, 1816
	Duncan Darroch	Aug. 26, 1814	Sept. 20, 1814
	George Stracey Smyth	June 27, 1816	Oct. 24, 1816
Earl of Dalhousie		Oct. 24, 1816	June 1, 1820
	Michael Wallace	Mar. 29, 1818	April 25, 1818
Sir James Kempt		June 2, 1820	Aug. 23, 1828
	Michael Wallace	May 1, 1824	Aug. 18, 1825
	Michael Wallace	May 26, 1828	July 17, 1828
	Michael Wallace	Aug. 23, 1828	Nov. 27, 1828
Sir Peregrine Maitland		Nov. 28, 1828	Oct. 8, 1832
	Michael Wallace	Oct. 14, 1829	May 30, 1830
	T. N. Jeffery	Oct. 9, 1832	July 1, 1834
Sir Colin Campbell		July 2, 1834	Sept. 30, 1840
Viscount Falkland		Sept. 30, 1840	Aug. 2, 1846
	Sir Jeremiah Dickson	Aug. 3, 1846	Aug. 28, 1846
Sir John Harvey		Aug. 29, 1846	Mar. 22, 1852
	John Bazalgette	May 30, 1851	Sept. 29, 1851
	John Bazalgette	Mar. 22, 1852	Aug. 5, 1852
Sir Gaspard le Marchant		Aug. 5, 1852	Feb. 15, 1858
Earl of Mulgrave		Feb. 15, 1858	Sept. 17, 1863
	Hastings Doyle	Sept. 18, 1863	June 21, 1864
Sir Richard Graves MacDonnell		June 22, 1864	Sept. 28, 1865
	Hastings Doyle	Sept. 29, 1865	Nov. 7, 1865
Sir W. Fenwick Williams		Nov. 8, 1865	June 30, 1867

D

Lieutenant-Governors (1867-1900)

Sir William Fenwick Williams	July	1, 1867
Sir C. Hastings Doyle	Oct.	28, 1867
Joseph Howe	May	10, 1873
Sir Adams G. Archibald	July	23, 1873
M. H. Richey	July	4, 1883
A. W. McLelan	July	10, 1888
Sir Malachy B. Daly	July	14, 1890

E
Ministries in Nova Scotia (1840-1896)

Years	Ministry	Party
1840 - 43	Coalition	
1843 - 48	J.W. Johnston	Tory (Conservative)
1848 - 54	J.B. Uniacke	Reform (Liberal)
1854 - 57	William Young	Liberal
1857 - 60	J.W. Johnston	Conservative
1860	William Young	Liberal
1860 - 63	Joseph Howe	Liberal
1863 - 64	J.W. Johnston	Conservative
1864 - 67	Charles Tupper	Conservative
1867	Hiram Blanchard and P.C. Hill	Confederate
1867 - 75	William Annand	Anti-Confederate (Liberal)
1875 - 78	P.C. Hill	Liberal
1878 - 82	Simon H. Holmes	Conservative
1882	J.S.D. Thompson	Conservative
1882 - 84	W.T. Pipes	Liberal
1884 - 96	W.S. Fielding	Liberal

F

Federal Elections in Nova Scotia
1867-1896

Year	Elected				Popular Vote					
	C	%	L	%	C	%	L	%	Other	%
1867	1	5.3	18	94.7	14,862	40.9	21,139	58.1	362	1.0
1872	10	47.6	11	52.4	19,939	49.96	19,974	50.04		
1874	3	14.3	18	85.7	16,466	42.4	22,377	57.6		
1878	14	66.7	7	33.3	33,226	51.8	28,880	45.0	2,054	3.2
1882	14	66.7	7	33.3	28,967	51.4	25,345	45.0	2,058	3.7
1887	14	66.7	7	33.3	41,411	49.7	39,255	47.2	2,584	3.1
1891	16	76.2	5	23.8	46,934	53.1	40,155	45.5	1,223	1.4
1896	10	50.0	10	50.0	50,772	50.4	49,176	48.8	737	0.7

G

Nova Scotia Provincial Elections
1836-1894

Year	Elected						Popular Vote					
	Tory or Conservative	%	Reformer or Liberal	%	Other	%	Conservative	%	Reformer or Liberal	%	Other	%
1836	20	40.8	28	57.2	1	2.0						
1840	20	39.2	30	58.8	1	2.0						
1843	26	51.0	25	49.0								
1847	22	43.1	29	56.9								
1851	22	41.5	31	58.5								
1855	20	37.7	33	62.3								
1859	26	47.3	29	52.7								
1863	40	72.7	14	25.5	1	1.8						
1867	2	5.3	36	94.7			29,095	38.5	44,339	58.6	2,182	2.9
1871	14	36.8	24	63.2			33,878	45.1	38,938	51.8	2,332	3.1
1874	14	36.8	24	63.2			29,492	43.6	37,169	55.0	921	1.4
1878	30	78.9	8	21.1			52,311	51.7	45,672	45.1	3,268	3.2
1882	14	36.8	24	63.2			45,247	46.9	49,945	51.8	1,205	1.3
1886	8	21.1	29	76.3	1	2.6	49,216	43.6	61,822	54.7	1,943	1.7
1890	10	26.3	28	73.7			63,720	46.7	71,202	52.2	1,407	1.1
1894	13	34.2	25	65.8			68,455	47.3	75,121	51.9	1,073	0.8

INDEX